Out of Romania

Out of Romania

DAN ANTAL

faber and faber
LONDON · BOSTON

First published in 1994
by Faber and Faber Limited
3 Queen Square London WC1N 3AU

Photoset by Datix International Limited, Bungay, Suffolk
Printed in England by Clays Ltd, St Ives plc

© Dan Antal, 1994

Dan Antal is hereby identified as author of this work in accordance with
Section 77 of the Copyright, Designs and Patents Act 1988

A CIP record for this book is available from the British Library
ISBN 0–571–17220–2

Contents

To my parents. This book is also dedicated to all the young people who gave their lives for freedom and a true democracy in Romania.

A veteran fighter in the Romanian anti-communist uprising two years ago has hanged himself out of disillusionment with the new government. Dumitru Vlaic, aged 31, left a recorded suicide message to his family, saying: 'Forgive me. I can no longer bear the mockery or the injustice.'

Guardian, 11 January 1992

Romania 1989

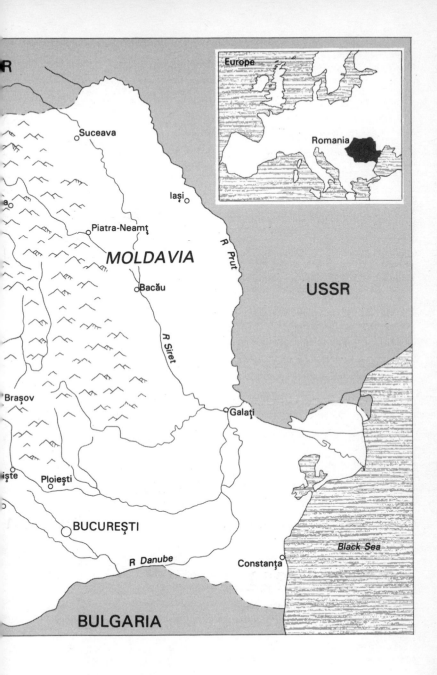

Acknowledgements

Many thanks to my wife, Sue, who helped me with a Chinese patience at every stage of this book.

I am also grateful to my friend Robert Lipscombe who worked hard on my manuscript and lifted my spirits whenever I felt down.

Special thanks to Robert McCrum at Faber & Faber who encouraged me to write this book and to Julian Loose for his time spent in editing it. Dr Dennis Deletant was also of great help with his advice and verification of certain historical facts.

I hope my parents, George Stănică and Constantin Rotaru (Dudu), will forgive me for the intrusion into their private lives. I thank them for allowing me to use their names so that I could tell the true story of my life.

I

Romania, December 1989

The time of preparation was over. Swimming in icy mountain rivers, running five miles a day and the rigorous diet were all behind me. A small plastic rucksack with bars of chocolate and a jar of grease lay waiting in the wardrobe as I studied the stolen Army map of Romania's south west. Not that there was much to see on the tattered yellow paper. I pictured the place where the forest cleared, a sandy plain with straggly pines and two rocky grey outcrops. After whirling and boiling among high Carpathian cliffs, the River Danube then widens again a few hundred metres lower down, lazy and sure as always. And on the other bank, Yugoslavia.

This was the place from which I would swim for freedom, at midnight on New Year's Eve, while the frontier guards with their bulldog faces would knock together Army-issue mugs of plum brandy, then kiss and embrace. Inside their concrete posts, they would neglect their patrolling of the border for half an hour or so. A moment of happiness – what the hell, let the dogs bark, we have three hundred and sixty-four other days and nights to catch the traitors – '*Noroc!*' (Cheers!) they would shout, while I slipped into the river.

This time I could not afford to fail. Everything was carefully planned and yet ill omens were making me anxious.

Living for thirty-five years in a country built on fear, any small cloud over the sun was enough to leave you frightened for the rest of the day. But I had good reason to be uneasy.

At the beginning of December 1989 a strange seething had overtaken Romania. Standing in a queue for food, crushed against people on a bus or just walking in the streets, you could feel an uncertainty, a foreboding that something terrible was about to happen.

[1]

Monks living high in the mountains foresaw a bloody time to come and their apocalyptic visions were swiftly conveyed by word of mouth. Rumours and speculation came to my ears from all around. The night itself seemed to embody the imminence of danger.

This was not the first time that fears about the end of the world had spread across the country. After the Chernobyl disaster of 1986, people in my city of Bacău started washing fences, gardens, windows and walls, even though they were fully convinced of the futility of what they did. Sooner or later, they believed, everyone would be affected by the radiation fall-out and before long, there were stories of newly-born monsters. And yet, strange as it seemed, the general sadness was covered by a calm acceptance of a fate that all would have to share. After all, what can you do? 'Your destiny is written on your forehead,' Romanians often say. Not only is our fate in the hands of God, but there are wars, earthquakes, floods and dictators as well, too powerful for us to rebel against.

But this was different. Even nature seemed to confirm the dark whispers. It was unusually warm. Small tremors shook the earth, and snowdrops blossomed in the gardens three months earlier than usual. Rats were seen coming out of their hidden places. In trees, small owls sang as never before, a bad sign for Romanians. If you hear one singing, it means that someone close to you is going to die.

Politically, there was no hint of any change. Earlier in the year, six former high-ranking officials had signed a timid letter to the father of all fathers, dear President Ceaușescu, about the true situation in Romania. They pointed to the abuse of basic human rights by the secret police, the disastrous economic policies, the bulldozing of the heart of Bucharest; Romania is no longer part of Europe, they complained. These were the first intimations of rebellion inside the Party. Yet they seemed a too coy token in a year which shook the Communist world.

In Hungary, the Communist leadership had already accepted a multi-party system. Free elections had led to Solidarity's victory in Poland. In November, the Berlin Wall had tumbled down, and the Czech Václav Havel was leading a non-Communist government in Prague a month later. Not that we knew much about these events through the official media. But tall antennae installed on our roofs brought us bits and pieces of news about what was happening in the outside world.

The hundreds of thin spikes piercing the sky from the top of each block of flats didn't seem to disturb the secret police. After all, Romania was surrounded only by Socialist countries. But now, Romanians living in the south of the country could watch the news from Bulgaria, where the dictator Todor Zhivkhov had been deposed. In the east and north, Russia's *glasnost* and *perestroika* gave good reason to learn Russian, while to the west you might even see a Hungarian broadcast with László Tökés, a young Romanian pastor who was attacking the President's policy of *sistematizare* ('systematization').

Officially, *sistematizare* aimed to transform the rural environment into 'agro-industrial complexes'. In the perfect new Socialist society, the difference between villages and cities had to disappear completely. By the end of the century, half of all villages were to be wiped from the maps – no more family houses, signs of the old and undeveloped past, only new blocks of flats along the highways.

In reality, the plan meant erasing thousands of communities for the sake of better surveillance, especially of those awkward Hungarian minorities from Transylvania.

Tökés spoke out courageously against this *sistematizare*. So did Doinea Cornea, one of the few dissidents whose recorded voice we could still hear on the banned Radio Free Europe. And so did western diplomats and politicians, causing the United Nations to condemn Romania for serious violations of human rights. So what? For the presidential couple it was water off a duck's back. In the very year the Berlin Wall came down, Ceauşescu had raised a barbed-wire fence along the border with Hungary.

The six former officials who had signed the letter of protest were placed under house arrest, and Doina Cornea was kept under strict surveillance. As for Tökés, a national court evicted him from his parish, and in November masked patriots gave the 'foreign spy' a hard beating. Meanwhile, it was business as usual at the XIVth Romanian Communist Party Congress. The Great Leader was enthusiastically re-elected and spoke of the exceptional achievements of the new era.

[3]

It was true that Ceauşescu was no more liked by Gorbachev than Bush, but could that be grounds for hope? When did the great powers ever care about a small, forgotten country in the centre of Europe? And yet, you could hear the whispers:

'It will happen soon!'

What would happen soon? Nobody knew.

Throughout the country, patriotic guards marched through the streets in the dead of night. Securitate people made their presence felt more than usual, checking for unauthorized meetings of more than five people or the use of more than one 40-watt light bulb to a room. One evening that December two men in light blue shirts, navy ties and dark blue suits burst into my apartment.

Three years earlier I had applied for emigration, just one more reason to increase the interest of the secret police in my personal welfare. Now they were checking to see whether I was at home and who I was with. They asked me some stupid questions and left. But what if they had searched the flat and discovered the rucksack hidden in the wardrobe?

Little things always endanger great plans. So, the very next day I took the train and went straight to my uncle, who was one of the Communist *nomenklatura*. He lived in Bucharest.

I came straight out with it and promised my uncle I'd give up my idea of emigration. I'd become a good patriot. I told him everything I knew he'd like to hear from the black sheep of the family. If only he'd help me get into hospital – a good one preferably, as I was unbearably ill. This wasn't entirely a lie. Sharp pains were slicing at my guts; at times I felt I couldn't breathe. My throbbing temples kept me from sleep, and to cap it all, I was losing weight. At ten stone nothing on my six-foot frame, surely something was wrong with my body.

If only to do his bit by our relatives, my uncle picked up the phone. That was all it took. In the twinkling of an eye they'd arranged a bed for me in Elias Hospital. Ten days of blood tests, X-rays, body scans, electro-therapies, pills, drugs – whatever was needed to make the best of me.

Hidden behind tall trees and a strong iron fence, in the corner of a little street near the centre of Bucharest, Elias was the place where

Communist leaders, Securitate and Army chiefs were treated. For me, it seemed more like a luxury hotel. Every room, for just two, three or four patients, had a colour TV, a video, radios with leather headphones, magazines, newspapers, books and flowers, push buttons above each bed which brought nurses running to you. And then there were the saunas, the swimming-pool, the dining-rooms with crisp clean table-cloths, Siemens and Philips equipment in the treatment rooms alongside shining arrays of medical instruments.

This was all quite different from what I had previously met with in hospital: wards with six beds and twelve patients, two to a bed, dirt and traces of blood on floors and walls, mouldering cupboards, bugs scuttling in the dining-rooms, the night-long screams of patients ignored.

There was no paleness, there were no drawn, suffering faces, no dark rings around the eyes of the men in Elias. Full of contentment and full of themselves, as though the whole universe belonged to them alone, they strode along the corridors with eyes empty but presumptuous.

Lying on our beds, listening to their fatuous conversation, I found it easy to visualize them in their lavish offices, protected from those who begged for help.

Perhaps I should have been more sympathetic to my fellow patients. Maybe some of them were much closer to death than me. But how could I be when I saw them pinching the nurses' bottoms and laughing shamelessly, swimming or playing table tennis in rooms brightly lit day and night while, for the sake of the economy, the rest of the country was in darkness? Their visiting relatives wore fur coats and gold rings, and carried crocodile leather bags. Meanwhile, the rest of the country remained in misery and poverty.

Securitate chiefs, Communist activists, mayors, high-ranking officers; weren't these the ones who were really to blame, the ones most responsible for the collapse of the country? Where would Ceauşescu have been without these sycophants? Theirs was always the most frenzied applause for every new speech of the President, approving the latest insane aberrations of his wife. These men, representatives and leaders of an ideology in which no one believed, chose to trample on souls and bodies in their scramble to the best positions. For lack of medicine and broken instruments, hundreds of babies lay dying in hospitals while they were treated like kings. Children were locked away in abominable orphanages.

People shivered with cold, haunted by the spectre of hunger and horror, while those in power revelled in all the creature comforts. Innocent people were killed at the border, or tortured for the 'crime' of seeking to live in another country, while they spent long lazy holidays on the sunny beaches of France and Italy. People were imprisoned indefinitely for telling jokes that these men now told loudly and confidently. An entire population lived in terror because these bastards knew how to take advantage of the simple failings of everyday human beings: weakness, cowardice and fear.

Far from being ashamed, they were proud, so very proud that nothing in the world could shake their self-confidence. Despite myself, they made me feel small.

But then, late at night on Saturday 16 December, sprawling in comfortable chairs, they listened in disbelief to the incredible news being broadcast by Radio Free Europe about Timişoara, the City of Flowers. Wasn't it forbidden to listen in groups or repeat what you heard from Free Europe? Who cared! In their world you could listen to, and comment on, anything.

The decision to evict Pastor László Tökés had outraged his parishioners, who had gathered on Friday outside the church, shouting words of encouragement. 'We won't let you down!' They were bent on protecting him whatever the cost. The pastor pleaded with them to go home, rather than incur the wrath of the regime. The people would not listen but stayed through the night, singing psalms and reading prayers by the light of hand-held candles. Next morning and throughout the whole of the next day parents brought along their children and children brought their parents. The crowd grew to thousands. By nightfall, while hundreds linked arms in a long chain of human shields around the church, others rallied in the streets, shouting and chanting: 'Romanians awake!', 'Down with the ration cards!' and 'Down with the dictatorship!'

Bystanders joined in, and by late evening the crowd had broken into the local Communist Party headquarters. Bookshop windows were smashed; the books and portraits of the hated dictator were carried off and slung into the Bega river, or burned in the Opera Square, right in the heart of the city.

The Elias patients turned off their radios and prepared for bed, some mumbling their indignation at this bunch of hooligans.

On the next day, Sunday 17 December, Ceauşescu left the country for a short visit to his friend, the President of Iran. Romanian radio, TV and daily newspapers made no mention of any disturbances of course, though Radio Free Europe brought us different news.

That morning, the demonstrators of Timişoara had returned to Opera Square. It was then that the Militia and Securitate troops turned aggressive. Panicky crowds dissipated but soon regrouped again, shouting 'No violence!'

In the afternoon, they started arresting people from the back of the crowd. Children, women and old people were beaten up, pushed topsy-turvy into vans and taken away. Tear gas and water cannons were used. Then, at six o'clock, the guns opened fire.

'Schoolchildren and students, fleeing from Opera Square, are being hunted down by helicopter gunships . . . Tanks and armoured cars are firing indiscriminately on shops, on entrances to the blocks of flats, at balconies . . . The square is strewn with corpses.'

I couldn't believe my ears.

This was not the first time that there had been an uprising in Romania against the dictatorial system. In 1977 the miners of Tîrgu Jiu Valley went on strike and even dared to throw stones at the presidential helicopter. Ten years later, the workers at the Red Flag tractor factory in Braşov marched into the city and attacked the Communist Party headquarters, looting its food warehouse. Both uprisings were quickly put down; all their leaders later disappeared or had mysterious car accidents. But still there had never before been such a massacre in the streets.

For the following three days I was like a ping-pong ball, bounced between the news of the day on the one side and the news of the night on the other.

During the day, we watched the two hours of Romanian television; there were only two because that was the maximum viewing time Ceauşescu allowed himself each day. Even so, this was enough to keep the censors on their toes. Imagine a country with over twenty million people, having nothing to watch on the TV but a daily two-hour broadcast which always started with the clock, the map of Romania and the national anthem, always drearily followed by shots of Ceauşescu's busy working day. This, and documentaries on the latest economic achievements, and children singing for the Party, and nice women dancing in garish costumes to folkloric music, and poets and actors reciting from the books of our great Socialist country, and finally the news, which for years had not brought us any news at all.

During the night, Radio Free Europe reported, the dead were taken from Opera Square. Their bodies were cremated, or thrown into unknown mass graves.

During the day, hymns of praise were sung as usual on the radio. Enthusiastic men and women read aloud the passionate letters of thanks sent to their beloved leader, and the papers were full of other great achievements of our Golden Age.

During the night, we were told that the Army had opened fire again on people returning to the streets to ask for their dead, whose numbers had risen to four thousand, then ten thousand, then four times more.

Only after Ceauşescu's return from Iran on 20 December was the name of Timişoara mentioned in the official media. He made a televised speech about some 'hooligans', 'small gangs of terrorists' and 'fascists', egged on by foreign agents bent on destroying our beloved country. Peace and order had been established in the area and 'clear evidence' had been discovered of Hungarian *agents provocateurs* initiating 'small incidents' in Timişoara.

The night brought other rumours to my ears.

Army units around the country were being supplied with ammunition. A state of emergency was decreed to prevent a *coup d'état*. No foreigner was allowed into the country. The Army was patrolling the streets with strict orders to shoot at the first sign of any unrest. That was what I heard the patients of Elias whispering to each other.

The nurses, doctors and cleaners looked more and more anxious. Agitated gestures accompanied their startled looks, although they said little. Muttering in small groups here and there, they shut up when I approached, thinking I was not on their side. But no one could hide the tension in the air.

The morning of 21 December was filled with gloom. At noon we all gathered in front of the TV to watch Ceauşescu address a major rally from the Palace Square in Bucharest. I guessed what we were going to see. The dictator would speak from the balcony of the Central Committee building, he would give the usual speech on the great achievements of our economy, full of stammers and badly pronounced words which were meant to be interrupted by applause, while he waved to the crowd in complete self-satisfaction.

Only this time, the first view of the square shows us a silent crowd. From the balcony, Ceauşescu looks down, waves his hands and begins to speak. But not for long. Shouts come from the back of the crowd. 'Killer!' . . . 'Timişoara!' Then the clear sound of boos, while the cameras are still filming from the side of the square. There are scuffles at the back of the crowd, and we see the smoke of a tear-gas grenade. 'Ti-mi-şoa-ra!' . . . 'Murderer!'

There is confusion on the balcony. Ceauşescu looks puzzled. A bodyguard approaches and whispers something in his ear before leaving the balcony. The President smiles and waves uncertainly in the direction of the din. Then he falls silent, looking at the crowd with his hand in the air. The transmission is cut.

We sit petrified in front of the blank screen. We almost forget to breathe in those moments. Within minutes the picture returns to show a rigid Ceauşescu speaking into the microphone. He doesn't know whether the people are cheering him in a new, modern way or what. Elena Ceauşescu is quicker to guess at what is happening down there. We hear her telling her husband: 'Promise them something, Nicu . . . Talk to them!'

The President starts again, stuttering and confused. Now he's making promises to increase pensions and family allowances. But the catcalls and boos and shouts grow louder and louder. 'Ti-mi-şoa-ra!' . . . 'Romanians awake!' Bewilderment changes in a second to a look of terror; his bodyguards step forward. The presidential couple scuttle behind them. The TV screens go blank for a final time.

A deep silence reigns in the rooms of Elias.

We had never imagined that we would ever see such scenes on Romanian TV. Presidential addresses were always so tightly controlled. There were loudspeakers hidden in trees, behind pillars or on the balconies around the square, ready to blast forth cheers and applause, masking any possible lack of enthusiasm from the bussed-in workers. But inexplicably, that day, the loudspeakers were silent. The square was filled with the boos and taunts of the crowd. Where thousands in their ranks would have stood like puppets in a sea of staged applause, today they were real with hate.

How could it be that for several long minutes we were permitted to see the panicking face of Ceauşescu? How was it that we could clearly hear the not-so-clever voice of his wife? Every previous broadcast of the presidential couple's appearance had been so carefully stage-managed that any less than perfect view or unexpected event was cut in a matter of seconds by scores of censors and Securitate officers. Each controlled each other in such a complicated web that no one knew who was watching whom and who was the final censor. Where were all those censors and Securitate officers that day?

I didn't know what to think or believe.

Like the silence before a storm, the hospital was hushed throughout that afternoon. For a while, I remember, most of us continued to watch the static on the blank screen. The early night of winter fell over the city, and hours passed as if nothing else would ever happen. At seven o'clock in the evening the TV began broadcasting again. The same clock, Romanian map and national anthem, then the news, just like any other day.

But then came a call to guard the revolutionary achievements and the independence of our country, followed by patriotic songs and scenes from our glorious history. Then the same call was repeated. Something was definitely happening in Bucharest.

Suddenly, a heavy noise was heard in the distance and the earth itself started to tremble, like during an earthquake. Booms were heard in the distance, and the sounds of tank chains rolling down the streets. A helicopter buzzed in the sky. Within minutes, the hospital was in turmoil.

The phones started ringing madly, patients rushed from one room to another, nurses hurried down the corridors spreading terrifying rumours. No one was whispering any more, or listening to the radio. There was no need for that. Relatives, friends, doctors and other staff came in with news of what was happening in the city outside, speaking in voices so loud that I no longer needed to bend my ears.

Bucharest was in uproar.

During the afternoon, helmeted troops with shields and rubber truncheons had dispersed the crowds in the Palace Square. But thousands of people, mostly teenagers and students, flocked into the nearby University Square, in the heart of the city.

'Timişoara's bleeding, Bucharest is weeping! We can't go home! Our dead comrades from Timişoara won't let us go back! . . . Down with the assassins!'

The morning shift from two factories marched empty-handed into the centre to join with the demonstrators. The troops attacked them with rifles and tear-gas grenades. People scattered and regrouped again in the same place – between the Intercontinental Hotel and the university – while the square filled with suffocating gas. Armoured cars came up against hastily erected barricades: thin ones, made of tables, chairs, bags, garbage bins, beds, banners, clothes, strengthened only by the anger and the determination of the young people there. Two fire engines with water cannons broke through, dousing everyone. Boys and girls clambered on to the engines and deactivated the guns; the engines disappeared to the sound of boos. Soon the boos were drowned by shrieks and shouts of horror.

There was talk of a massacre. Tanks, armoured cars, helicopters, all opened fire on the crowd. A girl rushed into the hospital, and everyone gathered round.

'Snipers on the rooftops are firing on the students. The spotlights pick them out and then they are shot. There's blood all over the pavements.'

Some patients of Elias shrug their shoulders. They seem not to like what they hear and anyway, it's none of their business. Others go into their rooms and hide.

I feel like running away. I want to do nothing but run. But where to? Into the streets? I'm too scared for that. I return to my room and open the window. The sky is red, an infernal noise assaults my ears; shells burst and crack, machine guns clatter in the distance, helicopters are whirring overhead.

There is another patient in the room, an old man, groaning on the bed next to mine.

'Close the window, young man . . . It's cold in here!' he whines.

'Just shut up!' I tell him. I cannot control myself any more. The old man goes quiet, covering his head with the blanket, not saying a word. For a second I feel pity for that old man. Maybe he is in real pain. But so what? Others are dying that very minute, younger and more innocent than him. Because of men like him. Why should I feel pity?

I close the window, leave the room and stride along the corridor. It's way past midnight, there's nobody around. I sit on a window ledge and peer out into the darkness. Do I hear sharp cries and the groans of women, or is it only in my mind? What is really going on outside?

I feel like I am going mad. This is what happens when you cannot hide, when you cannot lie to yourself any more.

Who was I trying to fool? There was a war out there and I was filled with fear and shame. People were giving their lives for freedom and justice, while I was doing nothing. I was only scared that my plan to flee Romania was going to be swept away like a sandcastle. That was the truth: I was hiding, pacing from one end of the corridor to the other, like a rat caught in the trap of its own fear.

Gripped by a strong desire to speak to my parents, I rushed to a phone fixed on the wall and dialled their number. The line was busy. I tried to reach Dudu, an architect, my best friend. It rang and rang at the other end of the line. Finally Dudu answered with a flat, drowsy voice.

'What is going on there?' I shouted down the receiver.

'How should I know what is going on anywhere at this time of night?' he answered.

I hung up. I called other people. In my city, no one knew anything. They slept on while the guns were rattling in Bucharest.

But not my parents. I heard my mother's voice falter.

'Daniel, don't do anything foolish! Don't leave the hospital, I beg you! Please stay there, where it's safe.'

My poor mother! Always thinking of me. I had been a nasty child, then a turbulent adolescent, and then a rebel. My mother knew more than anyone how much my rebellion could hurt those who really loved me. Useless pain for her, for me, for anybody else.

And now I felt like a coward.

Why else was I there, sitting again on the ledge of that window? Timişoara was about sixty miles north of the place from where I had planned to flee the country. To go to that area, now packed with Securitate troops, was utterly stupid. But then, what alternative was open to me? To finish the hospital tests, go home, wait for another year to pass? No way! Well then, why not join the people in the streets, a mile away from Elias? They were the real rebels. Maybe they were starting a revolution . . .

No, I am making this bit up while writing. No thought of a revolution crossed my mind at that moment. All I could think was that my own personal hopes had been dashed.

The guns stopped firing in the distance. Everything went silent again. I returned to my room and hid under the blanket, like the patient in the bed next to mine.

Next morning, 22 December, the hospital awoke to shocking news. On a stretcher wheeled towards the operating theatre lay General Milea, the Romanian Defence Minister.

I dashed out of my room and caught the convoy of people following his stretcher, still not fully aware of what was going on. Milea had refused to carry out Ceauşescu's order to fire on civilians in front of the Central Committee building that morning.

'I didn't shoot myself', he muttered to the doctors and nurses in white round the stretcher. His words spread from one patient to another until they reached me.

The General died shortly afterwards in the operating theatre. All those huddled outside its door were sent back to their rooms. I shuffled back along the corridor, still dazed by the sleeping pills I'd taken the previous night. Turning a corner, I walked passed a tall, thin man with dirt on his face. He was talking to one of the doctors.

'I saw the kids in front of the tanks, Radu. They were even younger than mine. I can't stay home any more. I'm meeting the others in Romana Square. Ring Maria and tell her I'm here with you.'

Half asleep, back in my room, I sat on the edge of my bed, listening to the morning news. A state of emergency is announced. General

Vasile Milea had betrayed the people and committed suicide, the newsreader reported. Order must be restored in the country, he continued. Then, patriotic songs started up as the old man who was my roommate came and sat by me.

'I hope it's all over ... I hope they cleared the garbage from the streets,' he whispered. At first I did not understand what he meant.

'What garbage?'

'The hooligans ... The fascists of last night!' he explained, and suddenly, his words woke me up. They triggered my soul and my body. No trace of dizziness, no thought, no fear. No mind control, just my body. In that instant I felt for the first time the taste of freedom.

I dashed to the wall where the portrait of Ceauşescu hung, with his familiar smile. I snatched it from its hook and smashed it to the floor. I pushed the old man away, and then I started to run. Out of the room, down the corridors, down the stairs, through the garden, towards the entrance gate which was guarded by militia troops. Guarding who against whom? No time for answers. I turned back, across the garden, towards the iron railings at the back. Climbing up and jumping over, I thought: from now on I'm free, in the world of action.

Hundreds of people are hurrying along the pavements, in front of me, behind me, in the middle of the street. I follow the wave. There's a look of fierce determination on every face, though here and there I also notice some strange glances in my direction. Rumours reach my ears – of a crowd storming the Party headquarters. University Square is packed with demonstrators. In Romana Square people are clambering over the tanks, shoving branches of a Christmas tree down the gun barrels.

'The army is with us!' I hear men shouting.

'Down with Ceauşescu,' cries someone close at hand. I get a rush of confidence and power.

'Down with the dictator,' I yell in my turn, my face to the sky. I notice more odd looks directed towards me.

Soon I find myself in the middle of a large square facing the Television Tower. The crowds are streaming towards its gates. I push, bump and squeeze my way to get closer to the front when, suddenly, euphoria erupts around me as from a volcano.

'*LIBERTATE!* ... *LIBERTATE!*' A giant roar springs from the crowd, and everyone seems to be embracing. There are people falling to their knees, crying like children. For a second I am totally confused, standing like an idiot, understanding nothing. Then the bush telegraph starts humming again.

Ceauşescu has fled Bucharest. Despite the firing from within, the crowds in Palace Square broke into the Central Committee Building, captured the head of Securitate and fought their way up to the roof just as the white presidential helicopter took off with Ceauşescu and his wife on board. Romania is free.

At the Television Tower everyone goes mad. We jump up and down, wave hands, throw ourselves into each other's arms. I laugh and cry at the same time.

The staff at the television studios are hanging out from their windows, cheering, applauding, throwing down flowers, red books, posters of Ceauşescu. It is snowing with Communist papers.

In the streets, cars are dementedly honking, the people inside giving two-finger victory salutes. From the backs of open-topped lorries teenagers are waving Romanian flags with a hole cut in the middle – the Communist escutcheon removed – men and women are parading up and down, singing and kissing in the middle of the streets, on the balconies, their eyes sparkling with happiness. There is so much euphoria it is almost unbearable. It is undoubtedly the happiest moment of my life.

And only then, while kissing scores of unknown people, did I realize at last what was wrong with me.

I was still in the hospital dressing gown, now open over my new red-and-white striped pyjamas.

I went back to the hospital, to collect my clothes and identity papers. At the entrance gate I was stopped by iron-faced policemen, guns pointed towards me. Who were they guarding so fiercely? Didn't they know that the men they guarded were no longer the leaders?

'Don't worry,' I thought while waiting for my clothes. 'Your turn will come. Soon enough!'

Dressed at last, I ran back towards the Television Tower.

Dusk was falling over the city. Groups of people were walking to and fro, talking loudly, everyone desperate to tell their story. Cars and lorries continued to hoot, but when I reached the Tower I saw Army tanks blocking the mouths of the narrow streets which opened on to the square; and there were lines of troops in front of the television building. I made the two-finger sign of victory, and walked past the soldiers as if coming home.

Nobody stopped me, and I joined the crowds in the yard watching the TVs which had been positioned at the first- and second-floor windows. They were broadcasting images from inside the Television Tower itself.

It seemed like everyone wanted to speak into the microphones. Agitated men read bewildering messages, poets recited poems, journalists mumbled interminable excuses for the lies they had told throughout their careers, women yelled about troops opening fire at the airport. Army officers declared there was no reason for panic, former dissidents warned us to be vigilant and not to trust anyone, Securitate and militia men called for trust and brotherhood – in short, it was chaos. I went back into the street to mingle with the people gathered around the tanks and armoured cars.

Soldiers and civilians sat on the pavement, passing between them bottles of home-made wine and eating from parcels brought by women and children. I listened in, eager to catch as many stories as I could. Then children arrived, handing out newspapers. We clustered round, almost fighting to grab a copy. Small as they were, with their big black *Libertatea* mastheads, they were the first free newspapers of Romania and they were hot off the press. My heart almost burst with pride thinking that I could show this paper to my friends back home. I started to read.

'Isn't it strange?' I heard the voice of a middle-aged man near me. 'Romania was declared free shortly before two o'clock. Now it's just seven,' he continued. 'How could this paper be written, edited and delivered within five hours? Not five! Four! . . . I mean, it would surely take an hour just to get it here from the printing house.'

It was strange indeed, but at the time I gave it little thought. Eager to tell someone of his experiences, the man grabbed my arm and began telling me what had happened on Magheru Avenue during the night when I was watching from the hospital window.

'After the shooting stopped, the troops went round sticking their bayonets in the wounded. Then trucks came and loaded up the bodies – the corpses in front of Dalles Hall, on the steps of the Intercontinental, at the School of Architecture. There were lots of them, all young kids, students I suppose, with big holes in their heads. They used explosive bullets, murdering bastards. The place reeked of blood. We were scared shitless. We ran away and hid. But we came back in the morning. Around eight, fire engines and street-cleaning machines raged into us. We threw iron bars, stones, planks and Ceauşescu's books at them.'

He was trembling, reliving the emotions of that moment with such an intensity that I felt scared.

'We were all of us heroes. I don't know . . . You should go to the Square and see for yourself.'

So that's what I did. I went downtown, turning left, right, along streets unknown to me, until I eventually reached Romana Square, a large intersection at one end of Magheru Avenue.

In the middle of the Square stood a round concrete support, about a metre high, the unfinished base of yet another monument to our 'Great Thinker'. At first I didn't notice anything other than the plinth, encircled by flowers and candles, with a few women and men kneeling in front of the grey wall. Then I saw the words, written on it in black and red:

LOOK, MAMA, WHAT THEY HAVE DONE TO US!

I asked around and pieced together what had happened there the previous night. When the Army came into the square, with tanks and armoured cars, the men had linked hands in front of the crowds, pushing the women and children into the middle, towards the concrete plinth. No one had really believed that they would open fire as they had in Timişoara. Some children were lifted on to the plinth and a few of them managed to climb up it, so that the troops could see them. Not hooligans, fascists or foreign agency stooges as the radio had reported. Not irresponsible rioters, but children.

The machine guns opened up and people scattered in terror, leaving the children stranded on the unfinished monument. The tanks rolled towards the middle of the square, trapping the young against the concrete block. They stretched out their hands, begging for mercy.

[17]

But there was no mercy. The tanks opened fire and the children fell. Now the plinth was their shrine.

THIS CHRISTMAS WE GOT OUR RATION OF FREEDOM!

was written on the other side of the wall, and I shuddered to see it. My knees started shaking. A feeling of shame and guilt arose in me. It was deep in my bones, a horror at the human race, much stronger than sorrow or grief.

Walking down Magheru Avenue, surrounded by hundreds of people, I craned my neck to see where the bullets had pockmarked the walls of the buildings. Broken windows gaped upon a darkness which seemed to accuse me as I looked. My feelings grew stronger and stronger.

Near the Scala cinema, 'TIMIŞOARA!' was written on a wall, the red paint dripping from each letter. A Russian movie poster proclaiming 'It was Thursday!' hung in the cinema window, like a grim irony. It was Thursday indeed, when they started shooting the people in Bucharest.

Sticks, table legs, car wheels, broken glass, cardboard placards, shoes, banners – 'KILL US, WE DON'T GO AWAY!' – burned scraps, purses, stones, umbrellas, torn clothes and brown stains of dried blood littered the pavements. The only lighting in the streets was from flickering candles surrounding bunches of flowers, propped up on window-sills or where walls met the pavement. Some of the trees lining the pavement had little wooden crosses against the trunks. Pinned to the crosses were scraps of paper bearing hastily written words:

Passer-by
Here is where Raluca, aged 12, and Ion, 14, brother and sister, died for freedom.

Think on this!
When we left the house there were four of us.

And on the walls, chalked up by shaking hands: 'SOLDIERS! AREN'T WE ALL BROTHERS?' On the pavement, among wreaths, little cakes, fresh flowers and candles: 'Mum, I'm sorry. I had to be here.'

As I came into University Square, its walls chipped with bullet holes at body height, I saw lighted candles everywhere. People were stepping carefully among the flowers and wreaths, now shrines to fallen students.

I walked on slowly, my last drop of curiosity gone. Yes! For a while it was curiosity that had led me down Magheru Avenue. Now feelings of shame and guilt overwhelmed me. Not the shame and guilt of being me, a coward without the guts to go out into the streets when I heard cries and shouts for help from the window. But shame and guilt that I belonged to the human race. What kind of human beings are we when we shoot, or let others shoot, at young innocent people?

I felt shame, guilt and hate. Hate against myself, and against those people who were picking up cartridges and putting them in their pockets to show later, as souvenirs. I felt hate against life, against everything.

I crossed the avenue towards the Intercontinental Hotel. Near a pillar, a little old woman was bent in front of a wreath. With shaking hands she arranged flowers, candles and small cakes in front of her. She was taking infinite pains. I knelt down beside her, feeling I had no strength left to walk any further. Yet, within moments I was running as never before.

Suddenly the sound of gunfire bursts from the top of a building to my left. For a fraction of a second I am paralyzed. The old woman is like a statue, her head bent in silent communion. Maybe I'm just imagining it – no, the gunfire breaks out again, filling the square.

There are no booms or bangs, as you hear in movies. Up there a gun spits sharp noises like the crack of whips. The bullets whistle overhead, they strike the street behind me, snap, snap, snap, they ricochet off the asphalt, people cry out and run in all directions. 'Oh, my God! It's not over! . . . Oh, my God!'

I leap to my feet. No more philosophy, no hate, no fraternity, no grief, no guilt, just running. Rammed and pushing in panic, I fall, get up and run again till I am safe inside the entrance to a block of flats. I look back down the street. It is empty – there is no sign of the old woman. And the shots have stopped just as suddenly as they started.

Nobody hit, or so it seemed. Some encourage others to come out of their hiding places. They look up and point towards the roof where the shooting appeared to come from. We all follow. In a matter of seconds the street is filled again.

'Let's go and get them!' Get whom? With what?

Then the shooting starts again. Everybody runs, trying to hide behind trees, pillars, parked cars and dodging into buildings. And once again, silence. Nobody is lying injured in the street. It is as if someone is playing with us.

I feel anger. We gather again. I am near the middle of the street when again the shots start up. This time the rattling is heavier, longer, apocalyptic. Tracer bullets spray across the street, pinging closer, so close that I can see little sparks right by my feet. I hear the hiccups of people hit, I hear cries, shouts and the sound of bodies slamming on to the tarmac. I run towards a flower shop opposite. I trip on a body lying in the street. He is face down, his hair full of blood. I could smell that blood as I could smell the sulphur-iron odour of the bullets coming nearer and nearer. I swear they are chasing *me*, not the others. I get up, sprint and throw myself into a dark, empty space. It is not as empty as I thought. There is a window; its glass falls over me and I feel a warm fluid covering my face and my hands. The bullets are incredibly loud, they explode like grenades in shards around me. I don't want to move any further. A strange tiredness fills my body. Hair soaked in blood – I can't get the image out of my mind.

Is it the arm of death encircling my waist and lifting me up? No, of course not. A man built like a mountain has his strong arm around me. I feel light as a fly while he carries me along the pavement. Shards of glass and bullet cases crackle under his feet, the bullets still whistling around us. He drops me behind a burned-out van, out of harm's way. I fall in a heap, still not really aware of what is happening. I lift my head to look at him. All I can see is the back of the man as he runs away, vanishing round a corner.

Am I shot? No! But something has happened to me. Something deep. In that moment, behind the van, I felt unchained. I remember it clearly. Resurrected. No fear of death any more. Death suddenly became ridiculous to me. No more selfishness, no more need to save my skin, just a strong desire to melt with the others, to be part of the crowd. It was like a miracle. What am I saying? It *was* a miracle – a miracle had hold of me.

I stood up and went back up the street towards the shooting. The spirit of self-preservation had disappeared completely. I rushed towards the place where I guessed the face-down body lay. He was not there any more. I wanted to do something. I did not know what. Deaf to the sounds around, I took the small folded *Libertatea* newspaper out of my coat pocket, crumpled it and lit it with my lighter, dead calm, right in the middle of the street. Keeping the burning paper in my hand, I approached the buildings in front of me.

'Shoot, bastards! Assassins! Shoot here!' I yell. I cannot do anything else but shout and walk in the street. Hundreds of others are doing the same thing. They emerge from their hiding places, carrying candles and burning papers which flicker in their fearless eyes. I am in the middle of this miracle; it is as if an invisible hand has taken away our fear. No one runs away any more. Everyone seems to want only one thing – to be shot there, to be washed of guilt and shame for ever.

From that moment, for the following hours, and for the next two days, while the shooting continued in Bucharest, I was no longer a spectator. Melting with the crowds, I did what all the others did. I ran in the streets wherever shots were heard. Shots were followed by boos; the boos were followed by more shots. I saw ordinary people place their bodies in the firing line as though they had barricades built into their blood and lions in their souls. Carrying white carnations and loaves of bread to the soldiers, I saw gun barrels pointed towards us from rooftops, balconies and windows of the blocks of flats. Tanks and armoured cars returned with heavy gunfire chasing the snipers, though sometimes it seemed to me that the Army was shooting at random. But the buildings blazed, and the explosions were followed by sudden flames licking at windows. The convulsion of those days went deep into my bones. I only have to recall that time and I am overwhelmed with emotion.

And yet . . . I did nothing.

I mean, I had no gun in my hand, I did not kill any enemy, I did not save anyone from death, I did not even throw a single stone against . . .

Against what, against who?

That was the question that tormented me days later and still stays with me now, as I write this account. Who were those people who shot at us? Who was the enemy?

At first, the Army shot at people, until the afternoon of 22 December. Then, the Army 'was with us'. At first, the blue-coated militia troops massacred people with their bayonets. Then the blue-coated men were shooting at those who were shooting at the people. Who were they? Securitate forces, apparently. Yet from the evening of 22 December Securitate was declared officially dissolved and put under the control of the Army to 'defend the innocent people'. Who were the terrorists they claimed to be shooting at? These terrorists were rumoured to be Ceauşescu's secret guards, who were trained to fight to the death. But what did they look like? I saw men with guns and pistols and men with nothing in their hands. Here and there, the men with guns directed us, while they were shooting. Shooting at whom? At other civilians who were shooting at them. How did they recognize each other? How did we know who was on which side? We did not. We took things at face value; if someone was shooting in our direction, that was our enemy.

Two days before Christmas there were no carols, only the rattle of machine guns as we huddled behind an armoured car. Me, a girl and four others, who carried water and a box of ammunition for the soldiers.

An hour later, the shooting stopped. Then we discovered who was on the other side of the Square, shooting at us from behind the corners of streets and from barricades. They were Army infantry men. That was what was happening. The Army was shooting at the Army and nobody understood anything – least of all the little boy I saw leaning against an iron railing who, in a moment of lull, was caressing the face of an injured soldier.

In a revolution, you do not think. You are in the middle of it and that's it. We were in a battlefield and yet not in a war, for in a war you are sent to defend or conquer and everyone knows the name of the enemy you face. We were neither defending nor conquering. The enemy was invisible and, in the confusion of those days, the killers were taken as heroes and heroes were arrested as terrorists.

During the afternoon of Christmas Eve I decided to go home, eager to know what was happening back in Bacău. The Ceauşescus had been captured and life in Bucharest seemed ready to return to normal. Well, as normal as it could be in those days.

The air still smelled of gunpowder; the bullet holes were still fresh on the walls of buildings; the pavements bore witness to the grief of the events of the last few days. Everywhere there were shrines, wooden crosses, plaited loaves with money and lighted candles. You could still hear the sporadic pistol shots from the top or from behind a nearby building, but people were moving beyond the traumatic events. Men were replacing the broken windows of their flats, women were cleaning and sweeping up around the front of their houses.

As I walked down the street towards the metro station, patrols of young civilians with tricolour banderoles on their arms were checking passers-by for identity cards and searching every car for concealed weapons. Even in the chaos of no one knowing exactly who was checking whom, no one seemed impatient, no one nervous. Those to be checked waited patiently for their turn; those who were checking were smiling politely and confidently. Unbelievably, there was a sense of discipline everywhere.

In the underground, I looked at the people around me. Some were full of joy, talking passionately; others silent, with a deep unspoken grief in their eyes. Some looked straight into the eyes of their fellow travellers, as if trying to understand the expression they saw there, as if needing to prove without words that they were part of a world in which there was no reason any more to hide the expression in your eyes. Others looked relaxed, or just sunk deep in their own thoughts.

And yet, no matter what people looked like, there was a common understanding that linked us somehow together. We were the same community, the same family. It was a feeling that I had never experienced before; I doubt whether I ever will again.

I had felt this feeling already that morning, while walking down the street on my way to the metro station. It was something strong, a determination that sprang from deep inside, a powerful desire to start something new; it felt as if everyone was ready to wipe out the past, replacing it with a new life. We would have a completely new life, with no roots in the past. You could feel an invisible thread linking us all together, and linking every one of us to the future.

I was experiencing the great magic of solidarity: a solidarity that grows inside, from somewhere even deeper than your heart or mind. This solidarity had banished the fear from my soul during the night of 22 December and the following days. That wonderful feeling of love felt like magic, the magic spread by the shared desire of thousands of souls.

There had been times in my past when I was so down and disgusted by what I saw that I had had to ask for hate to keep me alive. But now, there was no longer a trace of hate in my soul. Ready to forget and forgive, I could hardly wait to get back home, to start a new life, a life in which selfishness, envy and resentment would have no place. I was ready to forgive even the Securitate people who had tormented my youth. Life would never be as it was before, for people would never forget the martyrdom of their children.

Such thoughts and feelings filled my mind as I stood on the escalator, waiting to reach the underground exit. Then suddenly, my peace and calm were completely snatched away. It all happened in a moment, half a minute or even less. Someone started shooting from the exit of the underground station, down towards us on the escalator. We did not see faces, we did not see guns. All we heard was a terrible noise, like thunder. At first I thought bombs were exploding above my head, but then I quickly realized there were bullets whizzing around, ricocheting from walls, their deafening noise reverberating in the tunnels.

Instinctively we threw ourselves down, hands over heads, faces to the floor. Then silence. Then the clear moaning of a child just behind me. I looked around.

A girl of about six lay bleeding, almost touching my foot. I moved to cover her somehow with my body, though I knew it was useless. The shooting had stopped just as quickly as it had started, replaced now by the sharp screams of men and women thrown into panic. A bullet had passed clean through the child's leg. Her limbs were tiny, the hole so big and dark that her whole body looked like an open bleeding wound.

Someone bandaged her with a strip from his shirt, took her in his arms and started running towards the exit.

Two men – Securitate? – had fired several volleys of shots into the entrance of the underground before climbing back into their car and speeding away, witnesses told us.

A strong premonition arose in me as I sat on the train, travelling back to my city, looking at the people in the carriage and listening to their words in the corridor. Dark thoughts started to blacken the feelings of joy and love I had experienced earlier. The solidarity between people would not last long; adults would quickly forget who the real martyrs were and what they had really died for. As I was returning to my home town, I did not yet know how right my premonition would turn out to be.

The train reached my home town early that evening. I left the railway station as I was, dirty, the smell of gunpowder in my nostrils, cuts on my face and hands, a tricolour banderole round my arm, my blood still pumped by vivid memories of the events I had witnessed.

Bacău was completely dark. The lamps were unlit and the shop windows were empty. Only a few people walked quietly towards the bus station, their footsteps echoing on the broken pavements. There were no shootings, no cars, no tanks or lorries in the streets. It was as if I had stepped into another world.

Tension, excitement, fervour, turmoil, fever; you name it! I was feeling them all. I couldn't go home to my bachelor flat with nobody there to share my feelings. So I made my way to the city centre. In front of the Town Hall, a small crowd was listening to a group of men clustered on a balcony. A long-bearded priest proclaimed the Holy Revolution; a teacher lectured on education for the young. An actor started reciting, the loudspeakers crackling with the courage of our national heroes. Nice, well-constructed phrases, but empty for me. For I knew that priest, and I knew he was utterly without faith. And that very teacher had forced me to learn by rote dozens of poems in praise of Ceauşescu. The actor too I knew.

I pushed forward towards the side door of the building, which was guarded by soldiers and civilians.

'Just back from the streets of Bucharest,' I told them. 'I want to talk to the people.'

'To say what?' a voice mocked.

At first I could not place the man who spoke, but he seemed somehow familiar. Then I recognized him. He was one of the Securitate officers who had once interrogated me.

When the lamp is shining in your face you remember everything. Every detail of your past flashes in front of you. But when it is all over, the voices, the eyes, the faces of those behind the lamp also remain embedded in your memory for ever.

I thrust my way past the soldiers and entered the hall like a bull charges into the ring with toreadors waiting. Running through the long corridors, up the interior stone steps, I had almost reached the room with the balcony, when they caught hold of me. As I struggled, the actor finished his speech and came towards us.

'It's OK, I know him,' he told the others. He then made a sign for me to follow him through a dark brown leather-upholstered door.

'A coffee? A small vodka? You seem exhausted . . . What's going on? Please sit down.'

A girl with a short tight skirt and big red lips brought us two coffees and some Kent cigarettes. She winked at me as she winked an eye at everybody.

'I want to tell the citizens of Bacău what I saw in the streets of Bucharest,' I started, 'about a revolution against Communism . . . not only against Ceauşescu . . .'

'Don't you think we know all about it, Dan?' The actor cut me short. 'There was a revolution here too, my dear Dracula.'

He used my nickname. So much familiarity confused me. I knew this man from the town theatre, where he would show off his good-looking body by carrying a tray or broom from one corner of the stage to another. But I could not remember us ever exchanging more than a passing 'Hello'.

While we talked, other men came into the room. I recognized most of them. Communist Party members, Securitate officers, black marketeers and informers. How could I tell who was an informer? After all, an informer looks like everybody else, his work hasn't made his ears any larger. But after years of being watched by Big Brother, you develop a sixth sense. I could just smell an informer or a Securitate officer a hundred metres off.

The men sipped from the glasses the girl brought. Laughter and giggles came from the room opposite as she closed the door behind her. I felt the world crumbling around me. It must have shown on my face.

'You definitely don't look well. I quite understand. Why don't you go home and rest? Here's my card! Look for me tomorrow so we can have a longer talk. We need people like you around us in these crucial times. People we can trust.'

He got up and went with me to the stairs. I had no strength left to react. So that was it! A revolution in Bucharest, but in my city, just the same old faces. In Bacău, the revolution was seen as just a good opportunity for charlatans to squeeze their way up in the vacuum left by the confusion.

A group of young students stopped me outside.

'Our brothers died in Bucharest. We want people to know that we'll never forget them. They won't let us in, won't let us speak,' one of them told me, tears in his eyes. These students believed that I could help them. What could I answer? Dejected, I walked away, towards my parents' house. There, at least, I was welcomed as if returning from war.

We hugged, kissed each other, cried together, and talked long after midnight. I told my parents about the children in Bucharest; they told me the news about the dictator from two days before, 22 December.

The presidential helicopter had risen from the roof of the Central Committee building, above the mob. It then flew sixty kilometres north-east, landing on the lawn of Ceauşescu's palace at Snagov. Then it quickly took off again, landing later in a field near the highway going north-west. Nicolae, Elena and a bodyguard then got out and flagged down a red Dacia car, forcing the driver to take them to a nearby village. Here, they changed the red car for a black one, and continued their flight to the city of Tîrgovişte, convinced that the local Securitate headquarters would be loyal to them. They were not. One by one, the Securitate officers tiptoed out of the building by the back door.

The presidential couple were alone in the building when the Army arrived; Securitate hadn't had the courage to arrest them or the loyalty to assist them. Not a single shot was fired.

The next day, 25 December, the radio announced that the dictators had been tried and executed.

At first none of us believed it. It was too quick. Only four days before, Ceaușescu had still been part of us. Whenever he appeared we just closed our minds, as you close the shutters in heavy rain: avoiding the storm, but hearing its beating against the window, feeling it in your bones. That's what Ceaușescu was for us. You could turn the TV and radio off, you could throw the newspapers in the dustbin and you could close your eyes whenever you passed a shop window full of his portraits. But still Ceaușescu was there, deep in our minds. You could not avoid him. Step by step, he became part of nature and part of ourselves. So how could he have disappeared so quickly?

Yet, late the following night, on 26 December, a recording of the trial was broadcast by Romanian television, heavily censored 'for security reasons'.

The Ceaușescus were accused of murdering more than 60,000 people, ruining the national economy, illegally holding millions of dollars in Swiss banks, and of attempting to flee the country. A hasty, botched job, the trial quickly turned into a ridiculous mockery. It was obvious that the court had decided the sentence in advance.

We do not see the Prosecution on screen. We only see the old couple who sit on a tiny school bench in a corner of a room, behind a small wooden table. The image shocks us. Elena is in her overcoat with a scarf round her head; Nicolae is pale and unshaven but still scornful and disdainful.

'I don't recognize any court. I recognize only the Grand National Assembly. This is a *coup d'état*,' we hear Ceaușescu saying. Charged with hate as we are, we give little thought to what he really says.

The couple are blamed for bringing the Romanian people to a state of humiliation, of giving orders to kill in Timișoara and Bucharest, of starving their own people, of lack of medicine and heat in the hospitals, of the horrors of the systematization plan.

'Nobody was killed out there . . . There has never been such a level of economic development as there is today,' Nicolae answers. 'I do not recognize you . . . I will not answer your questions,' Nicolae Ceaușescu repeats, nervously looking at his watch, as if perplexed that his men are not coming to rescue him. Elena is wrinkling her nose and shouts back at the interrogators. 'Lies!' . . . 'How dare you!' . . . 'Proof! Show us proof!' . . . Nicolae pats her hand to calm her down. The couple bicker like big children refusing to entertain the smaller kiddies' make-believe courtroom.

Not that the court seems to mind. They are in a hurry to get rid of the couple; they are not very interested in what the accused are saying.

'What do you know about the Securitate?' the prosecutor asks.

'They are just across from us, there,' Elena says, looking towards the court. Again, we give little thought to this answer.

Only now, while writing, can I see how right she was. Off camera stood the general who only a week before had flown to Timişoara to carry out Ceauşescu's order to shoot. Alongside him was a former colonel of Securitate, Virgil Măgureanu, who later was to become the head of Romania's new secret police. They all needed to get rid of the Ceauşescus quickly. On Christmas Day the newly-formed government announced that 'the Antichrist is dead'. What better day for such a *coup de théâtre*? Those in the new government were to be our saviours from evil.

Finally, the judge read the death sentence and asked the Ceauşescus whether they wanted to appeal. Nicolae refused to reply. The announcer went on to say that the couple had subsequently been shot by firing squad. A photograph of the dead dictator's face was shown, accompanied by Beethoven's 'Ode to Joy'.

'Hm!', my father mused disbelievingly. Why was there no footage of the shooting? Later, when more of the trial was broadcast and the apparent execution of the Ceauşescus was indeed shown, my father added other questions to his 'Hm!' Why so late? Why were the pictures so unclear? We certainly got to hear the firing squad, but the gunsmoke was so dense that we actually could not see anything. When the smoke cleared, the wall behind was filled with holes, and at its bottom lay two corpses. A thick stream of blood flowed from Elena, and someone lifted Nicolae's head towards the camera to convince us that he was really dead, dispelling the rumours that he could not die.

But what happened to the corpses? Apparently, they were buried in the middle of a stadium playing field in a suburb of Bucharest. But rumours soon appeared, claiming that the corpses had vanished. Then apparently the bodies were found again, buried a few metres away, the newspapers wrote . . . Hm!

Later, my father would tell me of other strange events which happened after the Ceauşescu trial. The defence lawyer had been ambushed on his drive back to Bucharest. A bullet just missed him. But they didn't miss his son, a few days later. Two months after the trial, Gică Popa – the president of the court who pronounced the death sentence – went on to commit suicide. 'Stress and depression,' they said. Hm! That's my father, distrustful of everything. But, for the time being, the dictatorship was over, there were reasons to celebrate.

In the city centre people paraded up and down in the winter sunshine. Many were tipsy. There was much hugging and kissing. Men reeled about with women on their arms, shouting 'Ceauşescu is dead! We are free!', raising their fur caps to salute passers-by. Teenagers carried the red, yellow and blue flags with the hole cut in the middle, the tricolour banderole on their arms. They walked slowly, filled with pride, the hero's look in their eyes. I did not like it. Too much heroism when nothing heroic had happened there made a mockery of young people's bravery elsewhere.

The church bells tolled, the old were first to come, then others followed. In fact, the whole country erupted into some kind of religious hysteria at that time. Priest after priest appeared on TV, kissing crosses, chanting psalms. In between, they would ask for seats in the new provisional government. Even Theoxit, Patriarch of the Romanian Orthodox Church, talked about the role of Our Lord in the new order. He conveniently forgot that just days before, his congratulations were sent to the dictator for putting down the 'hooligans' in Timisoara.

What would young children make of this? They were taught in school that Jesus Christ was an invention of the powerful to rule the poor, yet they found little crosses and icons on the walls in their homes. Keep your mouths shut, parents warned. Going to church was bad for your future; a belief in the Communist Party, not God, was what you needed to get a good job.

A week earlier only the insane had talked about God in public. A week later, everyone discovered within themselves a strong religious conviction. The parents who once taught silence now rushed into the streets proclaiming their faith.

New Year's Eve came. Confused or not, children knocked on neighbours' doors singing the traditional songs of New Year, while I retreated to my friend Dudu's flat with strangely low spirits. The architect was in his usual cynical mood. We sat on the sofa, a bottle of wine between us, in no hurry to finish it. 'Who are we kidding?' Dudu asked. Whether he was asking me or himself was not clear.

'Do you really think it was *our* revolution? Less than two weeks ago even a whisper of a rebellion against the system was enough to make you disappear. Then a few thousand people stand in front of the Central Committee building, start booing the leader and, abracadabra, twenty-four hours later we are free. Hip-hip-hooray!'

'Let's be serious!' Dudu went on. 'On 21 December, people gather in Palace Square. The next day, Ceauşescu flees by helicopter. Two hours later he is caught, three days later he is executed. On 24 December, the anti-Communist revolution is officially declared victorious. Therefore, in just four days, over forty years of Communism, twenty-four years of Ceauşescu's dictatorship, a former Communist Party of four million members, a Securitate with its special force of a hundred thousand people, all are finished . . . Gone! . . . In just four days! My, my! How powerful we, the people, are!

'Come on,' he continued relentlessly. 'No organized opposition to the Communist Party, no Walesa or Havel, everyone watched everywhere, phones bugged, letters opened, informers straining their ears at work, in the restaurants, on trains, buses, in queues . . . And overnight, empty-handed people topple a leader backed by one of the fiercest and most sophisticated security systems in the world. You think all that can disappear into the void? Just like that?'

Indeed. For forty years, Securitate had developed a perfect system of oppression, both psychological and physical. Philosophers, teachers, soldiers, officers, Communist Party activists, informers and professional killers were all part of a system which had spread its tentacles throughout the country.

[31]

'But Dudu, I was there in the streets . . . I saw it with my own eyes! I witnessed the miracle by which fear vanished from the hearts and souls of thousands of people. How could so many people have been manipulated? What I saw was real!'

'I believe you, I believe you . . . But just think for a moment about the leaders of this new National Salvation Front of ours, Ion Iliescu and Petre Roman. Surrounded by Militia colonels, former Securitate officers and Army generals, all assure us that they'll guard the revolution, punish the terrorists, build a brilliant future . . . Who are they fooling! Ion Iliescu, a former Communist Party activist and friend of Ceauşescu until he fell from grace, was a colleague of Gorbachev in his youth. And wasn't he in Moscow just before the events of Timişoara started? Look at the link with *perestroika* and the other things happening in Eastern Europe! Don't you smell a rat? I heard Ceauşescu complained to Elena after their arrest that his fate was decided at the Malta Summit earlier this month when Gorbachev met Bush. For the first time in his life he was right, I tell you!

'And take our charming Petre Roman. Isn't he the son of Walter Roman, the founder of Securitate? Didn't he once go out with Ceauşescu's daughter? And what about the rest of them? Haven't we seen them somewhere before? Who really chose them? With all the turmoil and confusion, couldn't we find anyone else to push inside the Central Committee building to take the reins of power?

'Look at them! Don't we just love their smiling, clever faces on our new TV? They know what to say in three foreign languages, so different from the hateful couple. I bet in six months' time our dazed compatriots will make them into gods to replace that pair of devils. You mark my words. And what is worse, they'll have forgotten their past as they'll have forgotten the dead in the streets of Timişoara or Bucharest. Cheers! It's midnight. A happy new year to us all!'

As we knocked our wine glasses together, I thought for a second of the frontier guards with their army ration of plum brandy. Were it not for the uprising, I would be swimming the Danube at that moment.

But what chance would I have had? Somehow I was sure that I would have drowned, or been caught and sent to prison, if not shot dead. At the last moment, fate made a sacrifice of the young and innocent. The events, revolution or not, completely changed my life, and the dead gave me a second chance to live.

And before I talk about what happened next, it's time to tell you about my life, the country which I still love – and how it was that I so desperately needed to leave.

II

Descendant of Dracula

One Thursday evening, in September 1954, my mother was lying in a horse-drawn cart with a woollen rug over her body when sharp cries pierced the night. And . . . there I was! Born on a stony track between two villages in the Carpathian mountains, with half-Hungarian and half-Romanian blood in my veins.

That's putting it simply. The ancestry of people born at the crossroads of Europe is never so straightforward.

Two thousand years ago, the Romans conquered Dacia, then roughly the area covered by modern Romania. One hundred and sixty-five years later they withdrew south of the Danube, leaving behind the roots of a Latin language and the nuisance of fighting nomadic hordes. Over the centuries, Goths, Huns, Gepids, Tatars, Mongols, Slavs, Bulgars and so on and so forth invaded 'that land of honey' from all points of the compass. To squeeze over a thousand years of history into a line, three independent principalities were founded, and endless battles against Turkish rule followed. The principalities united, fell out, united again, weakened or strengthened by the flow of Magyars, Saxons, Greeks, Russians, Jews, Gypsies – with such a mill of ancestors, how many would dare to draw their family tree, I wonder?

If you look at the map of Romania, the Carpathian mountains divide the country in half. To the west lies Transylvania, where many people are, or think they are, Hungarian rather than Romanian. To the east and south lie Moldavia and Muntenia, where most people are, or think they are, more Romanian than anything else. But again, things are not as simple as they appear. Take my family for instance. My father, born in Moldavia, believes he is pure Romanian, but has a typically Hungarian surname. My mother, born in Transylvania, is proud of being

Hungarian, yet has a notoriously Romanian maiden name – Ţepeş, meaning 'the impaler'. So now you have an idea of the whole confusing mess.

As for the cart which carried the new family that chilly autumn evening, it still exists, covered in chicken droppings in the barn at Hagota, the most remote Transylvanian village I know.

Just forty households live in a valley surrounded by densely wooded mountains, almost completely isolated from the rest of the world. There are no electric lights, no TV sets, no supermarkets, no cars, no tourists, no entertainment. Just tall pine forests, a stream running alongside the road, houses in blue and light green painted over with woodland scenes, alpine flowers in the gardens and neat vegetable rows, horses, cows, hens, pigs, chained dogs and half-wild vagabond cats. There is a tiny school with two classrooms, a small shop which opens three days a week when it also becomes the village tavern, and a church with its graveyard nearby.

In winter, when men test the air by spitting, life is hard. If the spit cracks sharply on the snow, you can go out with a fur cap over your ears. If it freezes on your lips, you had better stay inside, watching the bear walking peacefully on the white road, catching a glimpse of the wolves and foxes sneaking into the gardens. But that's another fish soup, as we Romanians say.

At other times of the year, men leave the village at dawn each day to work the land, to fish, or to tend the sheep and docile cows. They return in the early evening to sit on wooden benches at their ornamented gates, lighting their pipes, drinking strong *palinka* and talking passionately while the women are inside cooking with children huddled round the wood-burning stoves. When supper is ready, children exuding the smell of goulash run out and call the men, who pretend not to hear. Women emerge to drag their husbands away, sometimes with a quarrel, how else? The whole world would collapse without the men's dissection of the day's events. The women cannot understand this.

Bound by the same rules for hundreds of years, life has its past and future inside the village. What is beyond the mountains counts for little. Is the rest of the country prospering or in turmoil? Who cares? Now and then, amid rumours about the authorities imposing laws to improve agricultural production or increasing the state levy, the men would take up hunting rifles, axes and knives, women would grab pitchforks and shovels and they would all gather at the end of the road, waiting. Fortunately, the capital did not bother much with a bunch of people in the middle of nowhere. So the Hagotans were left alone, to take care of their children and animals.

I spent my childhood in a large wooden house with red tiles on the roof, its front windows opening towards the village. My parents left for the city where they could make a better future for their son, while I stayed with my grandmother and dozens of little cousins, happy to grow up in the fresh and healthy air.

We had no fears at that time. We would run all day long, mindful only of the sleepy serpents in the garden, which were harmless, but cold enough to make us scream if we touched one with a bare foot. When it rained we played in the barn, me and my little blonde cousin, in the warm dry hay, copying what our parents did when they thought we were not looking. As dusk fell, we hid behind the fir trees to scare each other with all sorts of monster noises, so well done that one of us would always turn tail and run down the mountain shouting for grandma. She always saved us. She was a strong character, my grandma.

At sixteen, my grandma had married the richest man in the village. Listen to this: Ion the Little Grasshopper of Dumitru the Impaler, that was my grandfather's name. He had once owned two mountains: I could see their rocky peaks in the distance from the window of my room. But there was little talk of my grandfather in the house. Not much was said about his father either, Dumitru the Impaler, who had come to the village years before, descending from the mountains with his hundreds of sheep and his seventy years of age. The family story goes that when he was young he drank wine from silver and golden cups. But why Dumitru took to the wide world, leaving behind his land, a huge house near the ruins of an old castle and the fame of being descended from a famous prince, nobody knows.

It was in Hagota that Dumitru my great-grandfather got married for the fourth time, to a woman thirty years younger than himself. Late in the evenings, on the way back from his shepherd's hut, he would pass through the village, whistling like a grasshopper, his tremolos louder than the thousands of croaking frogs and other night forest noises. Nothing could stop him being happy and healthy, no illness, no amount of years. At ninety, he married again, to a woman forty years younger than himself, and I am sure he would have continued this rhythm had not the villagers one day found him at rest, smiling in a field full of grasshoppers, on the day when he was a hundred and five.

Ion the Little Grasshopper of Dumitru the Impaler inherited his father's nickname, his father's riches, his father's love for women, and something else besides. More than women he liked good wine; more than good wine he liked to gamble, so much that he often went far to the cities to play poker, his favourite game. A bad player and a stubborn man, the more he played the more he lost, till one night, with four aces in his hand, he bet all he owned, the mountains, his house and his wife. But the devil poked his tail into the game, and another player laid a royal flush on the table. Next morning my grandfather put the gun barrel in his mouth and pulled the trigger. A stupid thing to do in any case since a few years later, following King Michael's forced abdication in 1947, nationalization stripped everyone of their private land.

My grandmother, his wife, never forgave him, though the winner allowed her to keep the house. There she stayed to raise her children, then her children's children, over the years. In my memory I always see her surrounded by children.

In the long winter nights, when Hector, on his chain in the yard, started barking fiercely, Grandma went out with a lamp, shouting '*Hustinee! Hustinee!* . . .' She shooed away the wild boars which came into the garden to root out our potatoes. '*Hustinee!* . . .' But her '*hustinee*' had more reproach in it than hate, and the boars could feel it. They ran away trampling everything in their path, only to come back later, as if playing with her.

When Hector barked fearfully, she went out with a heavy iron triangle and a bar. Talanga-talanga . . . Talanga-talanga . . . She hit the triangle with the iron bar and drove the stags away. At night towards the end of autumn, the deer would fight right behind our house. I loved the sound of their clashing antlers, but in the morning all the cabbages were crushed and my grandma was angry.

If Hector was yelping, Grandma would take the long gun and shoot into the night air, driving away the bear, always the same one, Martin, as we named him. Martin was in love with our biggest cow, Ileana, who wore long scratches on her back from his claws. We all loved Ileana, with her mild, soft eyes. It was hard to guard her from the big bear's lust.

'*Hustinee!* . . .' Talanga-talanga . . . Grandma was in the garden at midnight, alone, with her lamp which shone on the beasts of the forests. I was ashamed to let her see my fear.

'Don't be afraid of wild animals,' she used to say. 'They are not as wild as we think. They only attack people to protect themselves. As for men . . .' And then she would tell us a story about something that had happened a long time ago, with good animals and bad people.

In time, I learned to understand the forest. I went deeper and deeper into it, listening carefully to the rustle of fir trees, the splashing of streams, the animal sounds. I began to identify the tracks on the damp soil and to find my way by the stars. I would lie on the ground and watch the trails of ants, the dance of butterflies or the smooth floating of the eagles in the sky. Hours passed. Then, late in the evening, pricking up my ears to hear the beating of bats' wings, I would come home at last, no longer afraid of the distant howling of wolves.

Those mountains taught me that deer are born to be free, that captivity kills the sparkle in their eyes, that the fir trees never complain but thrust straight up towards the sun and only worms pass their lives hiding in the gloom. Later I would learn the language of pain and pleasure, of body and soul – how to love a woman, how to be cunning and survive. Securitate would teach me to keep my head down and my mouth shut, but they could never kill in me that spirit of freedom and light that I took from the trees of Hagota.

I was so much in love with the place that when my parents brought me to the city, a place with no animals, no fir trees, the sun scratched by grey concrete blocks of flats, I did not want to eat. I cried all the time and bit everyone in the kindergarten.

'Where the hell has this boy been living? He's like a wild animal. He doesn't like toys, he doesn't like the other children, he doesn't like me. Did he live in the forest or what?', the kindergarten mistress complained to my parents.

She was not too far from the truth, they had to admit. It was time to civilize me. I would have to learn the rules of the city. Look right and left when you cross the street and wait for the green light. Play only inside the courtyards, don't touch the street cats because they spread diseases, be polite and say 'good morning' even to the neighbour who poisoned our little dog for messing up his doorstep. Don't climb our neighbour's walnut tree, don't jump over the fences, don't swear, don't get your trousers dirty, don't clean your teeth with salt on your finger, don't dash about so much, breathe slowly when the chemical factory is filling the sky with its choking black smog, be home early. Soon enough, I had become a sickly child. My first city memories are of being ill.

Scarlet fever, measles, mumps, whooping cough . . . I had them all. And tonsillitis, which took my temperature to 40°C and more. And as if that wasn't enough, when I was six I caught hepatitis from an unsterilized needle. My metabolism changed overnight. From being a 'charming little piglet' I became 'as thin as a rake', a quality I have kept to this day.

I left the isolation hospital with my buttocks turned into sieves from all the injections. Neither the pills nor the yoghurt and carrot soup could take the sallow tinge from my jaundiced face. I was still very weak. The doctors shrugged their shoulders – 'we did our best'. My mother was crying and pulling her hair out, while my father looked for other ways to save his little treasure.

At that time an old woman lived alone on top of a hill just outside the town. The blind, the lame, hunchbacks, crippled women hobbling on crutches, people swathed in bandages, all went up the hill to her cottage. She was known for healing by ancient and mysterious techniques; her hands performed miracles, it was said. You wouldn't believe how weak I was. I was always asleep, waking up only to vomit. So I joined the queue up to her house.

'It's simple,' the old woman explained as soon as she saw my face. She would hit my forehead with a sharp instrument, in a particular spot known only to her, so the poison in my liver would flow out with the blood from the wound: as simple as that.

I didn't know what the others thought of the idea. But I preferred to die quietly at home rather than be hit on the forehead with a chisel, which was what the surgical lancet looked like to me. To encourage me, first my father then my mother then my uncle took turns at pretending to hit their heads with the lancet, laughing wildly in the old woman's courtyard as if there was no greater pleasure in the world than having someone strike your head with a chisel.

Did they take me for an idiot? I tried to run but they caught me, tied me to a chair, held my head still and . . . Trosc! The old woman hit the chisel with a wooden hammer, the chisel hit my forehead and left me to this day with a small mark between the eyebrows, right above my thin nose. A trickle of blood, black as coal, ran down my forehead. Within moments the black blood flowing from the wound turned a healthy red, and the old woman smiled.

'Give him red wine and steak! The bad blood is out and he'll be healthy from now on,' she said. 'When he dies, it will not be because of his liver.' Then she showed us the door.

Within days I was haring about again, wild and naughty as before. Me, dying? Death was too far off, what could it mean? One month later I was packed off to another village, this time in eastern Moldavia, to enjoy my last summer before school and to learn to temper my nature with my father's people.

There were no mountains and forests in Moldavia. But there were plains, hills and endless fields of corn, surrounding unadorned small houses with earthen walls and thatched roofs. One gust of wind seemed enough for them to tumble down on everyone inside. The people were not quick and hot-tempered like those in the mountain valley of Hagota. Calm, placid and silent as the wide river which crossed the plain near the village, they sat in the yards on tiny round chairs every noon, while the world fell silent under the burning sun. In the shadow of the chestnut trees, men smoked hand-rolled cigarettes, drank red home-made wine, and scratched all the time because of the fleas. It was a poor village where families had more children than spoons on the table and the little boys wore shoes only on Sundays for church. But what bothered me most was that the men were dirty; bad smells wafted from behind their black, rotten teeth. I did not like to sit on their laps.

Later, I read about the great pride of the Romanian peasant, his love of the land, his bravery in turning back the Turks and then the Germans, throwing aside the chains of the oppressor to achieve freedom at last.

Strange freedom he experienced.

Romania was never a poor country. When God shared out his gifts among the nations, one of our legends tells, He found that He had given all nature's riches to that land. High mountains covered in forests, fertile hills rich with gas, oil, minerals, with iron and gold beneath. Long rivers watered the verdant valleys on their way to the friendly sea, a temperate climate warmed the earth in spring and sent sunny days in summer, a generous rain in autumn and a thick snow for the months of hibernation. God felt envious. Paradise was for heaven, not earth, so, to strike a balance, he sent bad people to that land.

Bad rulers, my grandfather would insist.

Sovereigns appointed by Turks, Greek Phanariots, potentates and princes all sank their teeth deep into the land. The rulers demanded submission from the boyars; the boyars raised the taxes levied on the peasants, poor lads. By the end of the eighteenth century the peasants had to pay a head tax, a hearth tax, a tax on every cow or pig, a tax on vines, fields, household chimneys and cellars, a 'flag tax' for the ruling prince on goods sold in the market, a salt tax, a bridge tax, and even a tavern tax for those who could still afford to stick their heads out of their taxed houses. When the peasants revolted, their leaders were disembowelled alive, then roasted on a wheel in the town square. Pieces of their flesh were given to the onlookers to feed them better.

At the turn of the present century, landowners' vineyards were still being harvested by starving men, women and children forced to wear muzzles to keep them from the grapes. Empty stomachs belched forth, and for one week of 1907 Moldavia was on fire. History books called it the last European peasants' revolt, and it started a few miles north of my grandparents' village in Moldavia. With pitchforks, knives, clubs or just bare fists, the peasants attacked everything in their path. The earth trembled with their wrath. Then the repressions came: thousands were slaughtered, the earth soothed by their blood.

In the 'Liberation' of 1944, fate was finally on our peasants' side; or so we learned at school. But there was no word of the sad stories which my grandfather told me when I was a child.

For generations the laws of the village were decided by a council of twelve wise old men who met each Sunday under the leafy branches of the walnut tree in the village square. They were the ones who determined what was right and what was wrong. The man who stole, who was too lazy, who raped or killed, or hit his father or beat his wife, was first publicly judged by the twelve wise old men in front of the whole village. Only after he had suffered his shame would he be given over to the authorities.

Just before the Second World War broke out, two young men were caught stealing, my grandpa told me once, the flies buzzing round his moving hand. They didn't want to work and called themselves Nazis, fighting for a new world order. The Council, knowing only of the old order, called them hoodlums, and threw them and their philosophy out of the village. Soon after the 'Liberation' they were back, with pistols on their hips, this time calling themselves Communists and imposing collectivization by force. The twelve wise old men were put in a lorry and driven away, never to be seen again. Their bodies were never laid to rest in the village graveyard. As Grandpa finished his story his eyes were wet with tears.

I didn't understood too much of Grandpa's grief at the time, as I could barely understand his war stories. One day we were with the Germans and against the Russians; the next day we were with the Russians and against the Germans; 'bad' German prisoners giving chocolate to the village kids, 'good' Russian liberators stealing his watch and robbing the house – it was all confusing to me, though I liked to look at his eyes. They sparkled, lighting his face as his mouth opened, closed, opened again, lips working hard, telling the events of his life, sad, funny, with all the detail you liked. I could not believe how he managed to remember so many things from his past when he always forgot where he'd put his dentures just one hour before.

Under the gaze of his eyes, I had to sit still, which was exactly what the horseflies and squadrons of flying insects wanted from me. They buzzed round my head in such thick clouds that I often had to leave my grandpa talking to himself. I ran to the hills to be with the other kids, though I was never fond of their games. The kids stuck needles in the backs of cockchafers to make small buzzing handmills, pulled the wings off butterflies and let them crawl in the dust, threw jack-knives into the trunks of trees, then started to fight for no good reason and cheered the one who could spit furthest over the line drawn on the earth. Had I not known Gelu, a nine-year-old gypsy boy, I wouldn't give them a mention in this book.

When I first met Gelu, he carried the whole weight of his body on his arms, dragging his legs behind him like a cripple. In fact, there was nothing wrong with him. He was simply practising for a lifetime's career, begging in the city.

'He who knows how to crawl today will learn how to survive tomorrow,' his father taught him. And, in his turn, Gelu taught me other wise things, like dirty words and how to cheat the villagers, who could never catch us stealing their plums or the apples and pears from the orchards of the collective farm. Most of these tricks Gelu had learned from his father who, when not showing his fourteen children how to crawl, handle a stab knife or pick a pocket, was far from the village, especially on stormy nights in early autumn, the best time for rustling horses.

Only once in his life did Gelu's father have a job: working at the railway station near the village, I was told. He changed the points, which was boring but not heavy work and gave him plenty of time to dream up smart ideas. One day he diverted a freight train of chickens into a siding. He delayed it there for a day and a night while the chickens laid their eggs. There were thousands of eggs, which he loaded on to carts and took to the city to sell. He got caught and was imprisoned, and ever since he had refused to work for the state. Instead, when drunk, he played the violin. His audience would spit on banknotes and stick them on his forehead while he played the instrument on his left shoulder, on his right one, behind his back. With a bottle of wine in his hands he would hold the bow with his toes. He played like nobody else in the world.

Gelu obeyed the rules of his father without question, crawling all day long on the dusty earth. But when nobody could see us we ran up the hills to play the only patriotic game we both knew. We were the Romanians and the crows were the Nazi German invaders that we shot at with imaginary guns. They counter-attacked with their cawing, one time wounding me so that Gelu had to carry my injured body to the headquarters; another time it was my turn to carry him. When we captured a Hitler, Gelu always threw him to the ground. One day we decided to oust the enemy from its nest.

'Come and see how good the crows' eggs taste,' he said to me, then started climbing up a tall poplar tree, as agile as a monkey. I did not follow him. I was not scared by the height of the tree. Coming from Hagota how could I be? I just did not want to follow him. I waited below, watching him climb through the branches. Then, suddenly, without rhyme or reason, a huge wave of panic swept over me. A second later, Gelu was falling through the air. I saw him hit a branch, his legs on one side, his head and arms on the other; then he spun into the air again and hit the soft ground. I started to scream. Villagers ran up and took him away in a cart. No blood, no moans: only Gelu's pale face, eyes wide open, seeming to ask why so much fuss was being made of a simple fall. He died two days later. The whole village went to his funeral.

The little open coffin in the cart was followed by women in black, wailing and crying. The church bells were tolling, as always when someone dies in the village. I walked with the others, my head down, trying to look as sad as those around me, though I felt nothing. Death still had no meaning for me; I was seven, after all. In fact, I was more concerned about the feeling I'd had just before Gelu fell.

'I knew he was going to fall,' I told my grandpa when we got back from the funeral. He was sitting on the porch, his eyes fixed on the horizon.

'Mm?'

'I knew Gelu would fall,' I repeated, then tried to explain how I had felt.

'Oh yes.'

Obviously he was not listening to me. Or maybe he was in one of his strange trances. From time to time he came home silent, no word. He would not eat or sleep; he just sat on the porch like a stone. Either he had drunk too much or someone had given him the evil eye, my grandma believed. She would go to the earthen oven, take five embers out of the fire and put them in a mug of cold water. While the steam was rising she chanted strange words about little evil spirits dancing out the bad spell. Grandpa would take three swallows from the mug, no more. In ten minutes he was lively again; well, as lively as he could be.

Sometimes I hated him, as I still hate anyone who does not listen when I talk about things dreadfully important to me. He sat there scratching himself and yet he wasn't there. I had to hold on to that feeling inside me, a secret not to be shared with anyone else, so it seemed.

Returning to the city that autumn I was a changed child. The soft-hearted laziness of the Moldavians and the cunning of Gelu were added to the hot-tempered beast of Hagota.

'Daniel, you are not a bad scholar, but you are impossible. I just hope you become a teacher and one day understand what you are doing to me!' my headmaster told me once.

School! I did not like it, I have to admit.

Instead of chasing a ball in the freedom of the countryside, I had to cower on tiny, wooden benches, hidden behind the wide back of a schoolmate as stupid or even more stupid than me, confused by questions like 'what is an isosceles triangle?' I wanted to laugh but instead forced myself to cry to stop my parents punishing me for bad marks. How could I like school?

Not the least of my problems was my nickname and the teasing I got towards the end of primary school. All because of Vlad Dracula, known as 'Vlad the Impaler', whom it is now time to tell you about.

'He was a fearless voivode, the bravest and most cunning of the sons of Wallachia, then the principality between the Carpathians and the Danube. He came to power in 1448, with an oath to avenge his father, who had been buried alive by the boyars. At Christmas of that same year – I still know the dates, we had to learn them by heart – Vlad was betrayed and had to flee to Moldavia. From Moldavia he rode to Transylvania across the mountains through the Borgo Pass, the very location of Dracula's castle in Bram Stoker's book.

I only came across the story of Dracula many years later, while a student, and even then just bits and pieces, not the whole thing. Think of it! Dracula sucking blood from his fellow Romanians; how could such a tale find a home in our Socialist country? Funny, isn't it? The only Romanian legend known in the West was almost unknown in its country of origin!

But let's get back to Vlad Dracula, the real one, who came to reign a second time, the same day as what we now call Halley's Comet appeared in June 1456.

Vlad had great ambitions, indeed. He won glorious battles against the Turks, cleared the country of thieves and established order where before was chaos. He had to be ruthless. He decapitated people, he cut off arms, noses, ears, he strangled, hanged, burned, boiled, roasted, nailed, stabbed and buried alive. And mostly he impaled people, for which reason history named him 'the Impaler'. His name inspired such fear that he could leave a golden cup beside a wayside drinking fountain for years on end and no one dared to steal it. The Turks or his own boyars, all manner of hypocrites, criminals, all those who disobeyed, were shown no mercy.

When Vlad received a group of his enemy's peace emissaries, it is told, he enquired why they did not remove their high velvet turbans in his presence. 'Why should we? We don't recognize you as our sovereign,' they answered. 'Don't you?' he replied. 'Very well.' Then he ordered his guards to tie up the ambassadors and nail their turbans to their heads.

As for his own countrymen, he had no sympathy for the weak, the lazy or the sick. One time, Vlad invited the old, the ill, the lame, the blind and all the beggars of the city to a feast fit for a prince. They were eating and drinking their fill, amazed at their good fortune, when the *voivode* asked them if they wished to be rid of life's sufferings. 'Yes!' they all pleaded. 'Rid us of them!' So he locked the great doors, set fire to the banquet hall, and roasted them all alive.

Of course, our teachers taught us nothing of this, nor, indeed, of his strange lunch habits: for without a Turk impaled in front of his table Vlad took no pleasure in his food. He liked nothing more than to converse with men impaled before him while he ate. And God help that soldier who failed to impale the victim properly! The stake had to pass smoothly parallel to the backbone and touch no vital nerve so that the wretch would live for at least two days, time enough for the great hero to have a chat with him. If the victim died too soon, the soldier would be next in line.

How was it that Vlad could eat amid the stench of corpses? One foreign visitor who questioned this himself ended up impaled on the highest pole to be found, in order that he could more easily breathe fresh air.

Vlad's habits certainly made him not short of enemies. Betrayed by his cousin and imprisoned for twelve years, 'the son of the Dragon' escaped again to rule briefly for a third time before he was killed in Tîrgovişte. His head vanished and the headless corpse was buried in a monastery in Snagov, not so far from Ceauşescu's villa – as history likes to arrange it.

Coincidence? At Christmas time, Vlad the Impaler is betrayed by his closest friends and has to flee. Over five hundred years later, Ceauşescu is betrayed by his own inner circle and has to do the same. Vlad the Impaler met his end in Tîrgovişte, the same town in which Ceauşescu faced the firing squad. Then, both their corpses disappeared: Vlad's never to be found again, Ceauşescu's moved overnight to a new grave, though some say it's a fake. Rumours, of course. Like the rumours that Ceauşescu reinvigorated his blood once a year with the blood of children: healthy children declared missing, recruited by a whole secret army of Securitate officers and doctors. These rumours were never proved, but then history books don't deal with such details.

History deals only with battles, like the one in 1462, when Vlad the Impaler, with only 20,000 men, slaughtered the 200,000 troops of Sultan Mohammed II's great army. Thus the Turkish invasion of Europe was stopped in its tracks. How could we kids not be proud of such a hero? And who more than me, who bore the name 'Impaler' in his family?

One day my mother took me from Hagota to a village on the other side of the mountain where I found a lot of other cousins to play with, all with the name of Impaler.

'They are descendants of your great-grandfather Dumitru, whose ancestor was Vlad the Impaler. You are related to him by blood and should be proud,' my uncle told me. Soon the whole school knew who I was.

Was Vlad the Impaler merciless towards his enemies? Then so was I. If anybody disagreed with me I hit them right on the nose. I became famous. No one dared oppose me and I don't know how far my fame would have gone if Herghelegiu, I will never forget him, hadn't burst into the classroom during break one day and called me '*Dracula bozgor*'. *Bozgor* – a bastard without a homeland – is the insulting word used by Romanians to be rude about Hungarians.

We fought in the middle of the classroom, between, on and under the benches, the others watching, most of them girls. But Herghelegiu got the better of me. From that day on my nickname stuck to me as a sign of weakness.

Later, Herghelegiu and I became friends. He taught me to smoke a pipe, play dice and steal money from the church, things much more interesting than my mother's old folksy proverbs. My mother would always say things like 'he who steals an egg today will steal an ox tomorrow . . . and end up murdering his mum,' all this followed by torrents of tears. It was enough to stop you from ever living life to the full.

And it was Herghelegiu who took me to *our* Maracana, named after the world's largest stadium, a small grassy football pitch surrounded by a cornfield. It was so well-hidden that our parents could never find us there.

Every morning I would kiss my mother goodbye and lug my heavy school-bag up the road.

'I'll be late today, mum! We have to stay after class to learn another patriotic song,' was my usual lie. It always convinced her.

At that time she worked in a factory that sent frogs' legs to Italy. I visited it once.

Thousands and thousands of living frogs were kept in huge wooden barrels. You cannot imagine how much they croaked. It was the women's job to take the frogs out of the barrels and put them on a wide leather conveyor belt. The freed frogs were jumping madly, though not for long. Other women further down the slowly moving belt, with a knife in one hand and a plastic glove on the other, chopped the legs off the poor little beggars. The legs were left on the belt; the rest ended up in a metal bucket on the floor by the women's feet.

The bodies in the buckets continued to croak while their legs, still jumping, were carried along by the belt. It was quite a thing to see. In the next room other workers, including my mother, packed the legs into cans of olive oil. I remember how the legs went on jerking.

My mother worked ten hours a day if not more, leaving the house at five each morning, coming back late at night. At the end of most shifts she had to use her wonderful voice for the patriotic songs that the workers performed once a month. They prepared for this every night. It was the Stalinist era: if you didn't want to sing along, you lost your job.

My father, whose voice was not so good, also had to work long hours. So if the school kept me late, my parents had other things to worry about. This suited me just fine. I could spend as much time as I liked at Maracana.

Centre-forward, right-wing or goal-keeper, what a life! ... The cornfield stood in for the spectators and I just had to dribble the ball to imagine the roar of the fans. Whenever I scored, thousands leapt into the air, girls fainted, the stadium was alight! And so it went on until one sunny day of 1966, the year when my love for England started.

In those days Romanian television still broadcast international events and Western soccer was not considered subversive. So everyone was watching the World Cup.

Huddled on the floor between our parents' legs, we the kids were wild with excitement. The grown-ups were talking loudly, betting wildly and gulping their beers, their eyes glued to the black-and-white TV set while we were shouting, booing or cheering on the one team or the other. That is how Romanians are. They cannot just sit back, relaxed and calm. If there is no love or hate, there is nothing at all. My heart would beat like hell when Bobby Moore passed the ball to Bobby Charlton; I'd jump to my feet when Roger Hunt scored, I'd weep when the ball slipped in past Gordon Banks. I do not know why I was so crazy for the English team. My heart was with them and that is all I can say.

That autumn, I felt as if we were in the final. Our opponents, the rest of the world. I was Banks and had black shorts and a white T-shirt, with a small British flag glued on the back. The game was almost over when I bravely leapt to save the ball. All I saw was a big black boot kicking me smack in the eye. I put my hand to my face, blood started trickling between my fingers.

The next thing I saw was a man in white, sewing something on my left eyelid. I couldn't feel anything, but I clearly heard his voice. He was talking to my father.

'The eye was saved. But you should take care now. Don't forget that your boy has already had hepatitis. You should make sure he's more careful with his sport.'

What did he mean? At that time my life was filled with football. I was playing, talking, eating, sleeping, dreaming football. To stop football would be the end of the world for me.

'From now on football is out!' my father decreed.

Well, if you think I would have abandoned my first love so easily, you would be wrong. I took up table football instead. With counters and buttons on cardboard or baize, or directly on my bedroom table. I spent hours playing table football with the same passion I'd had for the real thing.

I kept my teams of buttons in small round plastic boxes and polished them by hand with the greatest care, each of them inscribed with the name of a real English player. They soon became famous abroad – in all the neighbours' houses that is, where the European championships were held.

My smoothest button, no scratches at all, was for Bobby Charlton, since he was bald. Every night before I put him in his box, I kissed him, and congratulated him on all the wonderful goals he had scored. Later the button was replaced in my affections by one with many scratches on it, showing the long-haired George Best. I became so obsessed with Best that my parents thought I was becoming deranged whenever they heard me talking to that button in the next room.

'You ought to go out more and not spend so much time bent over that tatty cardboard,' my mother urged. 'One of these days I'll throw out all those buttons!'

How could she understand? In her mind the big Old Trafford stadium was a piece of tatty cardboard. And more than once she really did throw my buttons in the dustbin.

When such a catastrophe occurred, it was commented on for weeks in our private newspaper, edited by my gang, a group of kids who shared the same hatred of school. It had news from home – I mean our neighbourhood gossip, sports events, our schoolmates' latest fads – and from abroad, the foreign football results. Our magazine was another thing my parents threw in the dustbin whenever they found it.

'You should study, Daniel, not waste your time with make-believe!'

Everything important for me was make-believe for them! And it was the same with my premonitions.

My first premonition had been that nameless wave of panic that seemed to come from another world a few seconds before Gelu fell. The next time, I felt a heaviness in my heart for a day or so before we got the news that Grandma had died in Hagota.

'Mum, I knew that Grandma had died,' I told my parents. 'I felt it,' I insisted. But they wouldn't listen. We went to Hagota for the funeral, then came back to the city. Maybe they would have completely forgotten about my strange feelings had it not been for my dream.

We were living then in a small house next to the city railway station. The trains made the windows tremble; the smut always settled on our washed clothes, hanging out to dry in the garden. The house had two rooms. One was not only the hall but also the kitchen where my mother cooked and we all ate, the living room when we had guests, and the bathroom where we washed, bent over a tin basin. The other one was my father's study and library on Sundays, my room the rest of the time and our common bedroom, in which we all slept in one big bed, our three heads all in a line.

I do not remember the dream, but of one thing I am sure. In the middle of the night I sat up in terror, leapt out of bed and ran screaming across the room to crouch in the doorway – the place where I was told to put myself in the event of an earthquake. My parents jumped out after me.

'What the . . .! What's going on?' A terrible crash was heard behind them as half the ceiling collapsed on the bed, covering the pillows in plaster, dust and concrete. A gaping hole had opened above us in the loft. My parents made the sign of the cross. Imaginary or not, my feeling had saved our lives this time.

[51]

After that they took a different view of something that had happened a couple of years before. My mother had come home from work to find me lying on the table, draped in a white sheet, my hands folded on my breast, lighted candles round my body and one flickering taper between my fingers. I was pretending to be dead and don't ask me why.

My mother passed out. Later, Father found her crying and gave me what for, as you can imagine. Whether it was the next day or the day after I don't remember, but what I do remember is that in the same week of March 1965, suddenly the whole country went into mourning. The death of Romania's head of state, General Secretary Gheorghiu-Dej, who had been in power for eighteen years, was announced. Artillery salutes were thundering on the TVs, factory sirens were howling and people were weeping as if they had just lost a close relative. Even my parents were in tears, quite forgetting how much they used to curse his name just days before.

I was eleven at that time and, of course, I had no idea that from that year a new era was starting in Romania. The Grand National Assembly then elected a forty-seven-year-old man as the General Secretary. His name was Nicolae Ceauşescu. Not that many people had heard of him.

Born in a village, the third child of ten and son of a farmer, Ceauşescu went to Bucharest as a teenager, where he joined the Communist Party, which numbered several hundred members at that time. It seems he got involved in the strikes of 1933, a year of unrest and turmoil for our workers, and his hot temper often saw him behind bars; some say for theft, some say for political reasons. It was in prison, where he spent the Second World War, that Ceauşescu met Gheorghiu-Dej. That's how they became friends.

In August 1944, Romania was 'liberated' with the help of the Russian Army. Ceauşescu was still one of the Communist Party members; there were now about a thousand in the country. Ceauşescu was now twenty-six, and things had started going well for him.

The rigged elections of 1946 established the power of the Party and led to him gaining a seat in the Grand National Assembly. The following year King Michael attended the wedding of Princess Elizabeth and Prince Philip in London. This would be his last great feast. The King had become the only obstacle to the Socialist Revolution and at Christmas he was deposed. Soon after, Dej was elected General Secretary of the country, which now had only one party, a puppet regime of Moscow. By then, the Communist Party had a million members. Can you believe it? In just four years.

Ceauşescu's political career developed fast. He was in charge of collectivization, where he exhibited great zeal and a merciless attitude. He took charge of the Army's political education, rising to Major-General. He became a member of the Party's disciplinary commission, where he enthusiastically helped rid the country of bourgeois elements, helping Dej to get rid of his rivals.

Then, suddenly, Dej changed his attitude towards Moscow. By 1958 the Russian troops were leaving the country. Four years later Dej had signed agreements with China, Moscow's old enemy. At that time, our man kept himself in the background; best to keep a low profile when the waters are murky. Maybe that's why Ceauşescu was hardly known at that time. He was just another of the shadowy figures round Dej.

Young, enthusiastic and a hard worker. That was how my parents described him once, I remember. Ceauşescu was the kind of person I should grow up to be.

III

Hell's Angels

Every Sunday we'd meet in the park. Bedecked with flags and scarves, we then went together to the football stadium ready to sing for our home team till our throats were hoarse. That's what the English fans did for their teams, we heard on the BBC. That's civilization, not like in our city stadium where men gathered only to shout, swear and boo.

I know it may sound strange that a bunch of kids in Romania were idealizing the atmosphere at English football matches. But that's how it was with us at the end of the 1960s.

We were so enthusiastic that our team gave us free tickets and bussed us to their away matches. Little things like that make you happy and proud at a certain age, though for me the thrill didn't last for long. Wherever we went, people jeered and booed at us. Even at home they started pointing fingers. We did not swear or spit at the pitch. We just dared to applaud both sides – we were different and that's what the others didn't like. One time I came home with my clothes in tatters. Another time I was hit by a stone wrapped in a piece of paper. Eventually I stopped going to the stadium, much to my father's delight.

'You've got to study, Dan. You won't get anywhere without the *Bacalaureat*.'

I wasn't convinced. My scorching passions were much stronger than his wise advice.

'Learn, learn and learn!' Lenin had said. His exhortation was our parents' watchword during our teenage years.

As our parents saw life, there were only three ways for their beloved children to survive in the tough world outside. One was simply to forget about education and prepare for hard, physical work. Alternatively, we could bone up on our ideology and start believing blindly in

Communism. Then, later on, we might become important pawns in Romanian society or, who knows, maybe even Party activists, which behind the Iron Curtain was like being a millionaire anywhere else.

But it seemed that we were too weak, too skinny, too lazy, too dreamy, too disobedient and naughty to be good for either of these options. By 'we' I mean George, Cesar and me, three boys who had started primary school together and were still together at the age of seventeen. Neighbours, schoolmates and each of us an only child, we became 'brothers in all our joys and sorrows', as George used to say.

So, all that was left for us was to learn, learn and learn and graduate from senior school, 'the *Liceu*, as it was called; 'the graveyard of our youth', we called it.

As my passion for football waned, music took over. From Manchester I jumped train to Liverpool and the Beatles entered my life. Soon I was John Lennon. Who else?

My guitar became all too familiar to the neighbours. We were living in a flat on the sixth floor and above and below us there were plenty of families to appreciate my virtuoso performances. Each night they'd bash their radiators with forks and spoons to shut me up as I twanged away in the bathroom. You wouldn't believe the racket you could make in those concrete and chipboard flats. The walls were so thin that I could always tell which of our upstairs neighbours was in the bathroom. Was the sound of the fluid going into the toilet bowl fluent and abundant? The fat boy with dark glasses was peeing confidently, as always. Was the sound a drip, drip, drip, then a more convincing flow, then again drop, drop? That was his father, who had prostate problems. Was the flow shy, delicate, careful not to splash too noisily in the middle of the bowl? That was Mother, as you may already have guessed.

Did I ever knock on the radiators because of the noise of their relievings? Of course not. I let them be. What did they know, anyway? I was going to be a singer, a famous one. Cesar and George were convinced I had the nerve for it.

Lunging to the left on the stage, throwing my head towards the floor, brown waves of hair dancing in the air. What a life I had ahead of me! Applause, screams, moans, the audience chanting my name, the girls reaching for me hysterically. They want to touch my skin, my moustache, the neck of my guitar; the boys have heart attacks in their ecstasy. Clustering round, the journalists shoot off their film at me; that's my best profile . . . See? Next day my face will be in all the newspapers and magazines, on T-shirts, posters, jackets, on knickers and shoes. Twang! my fingers go. Woaw! You love me? . . . Yeah, Yeahhh!

Well, I never got to be a singer but on my way I spent several years at least trying to look like a rocker. It was not easy, I tell you. For a start, I could not have my hair as long as I wanted. Yet I dared to let it grow just a bit over the ears at a time when long hair was considered a 'capitalist' deviation.

At school, two teachers would stand at the gates every morning, with rulers in their hands to check the length of boys' hair and girls' skirts. I had to enter the classroom by jumping the wall and climbing through a window. Only at night in front of the mirror could I let it flow.

During the day I pinned my hair back behind my ears with hairpins, as there were frequent police swoops with Militia men ready to drag any Western-looking teenager into their blue vans. In the streets, no shame at all, they ripped up the short skirts of girls who dared to let us see more of their fine long legs than a palm's breadth above the knee. Boys with beards were carted off to the police station for a quick shave and a haircut. To tell them about the hairdos of Marx and Engels was useless – we had to run when the Militia vans appeared.

And there was one other little problem which did not help my singing career. At that time Western pop music too was considered subversive. The radio and TV played only folk music, and at discotheques there was only Romanian light rock music to dance to. This had a kind of sickly rhythm, a bit like that sentimental Italian music; only the Romanian sort was censored here and there by the Ministry of Culture. Fortunately we could still listen in to foreign radio broadcasts. We were not going to let ourselves be brainwashed that easily.

We used to meet every night in George's house. First we drew the curtains and locked the doors. Then we tuned in to the banned Radio Free Europe. Ear-splitting rock music invaded the room as we lost ourselves in Led Zeppelin, Deep Purple and the Rolling Stones. I got so carried away by it all that one morning, during the break between Maths and English, I went so far as to write on the blackboard the three fateful words: 'John Lennon' and 'Freedom'. Then I drew the Ban the Bomb sign, very proud of my vast knowledge of the world.

A few days later the phone rang at home. I still remember my mother's white face as she put the receiver down. It was Securitate, inviting me to pay them a visit at their office next day. When my father came home, my parents bombarded me with questions. They were scared to death for me.

I could not remember doing anything wrong; nothing that could provoke the attention of the secret police, neither in school nor outside, except that one night, maybe, when my friends and I drank a bottle of vodka between us and got a bit drunk. We were sixteen and unused to alcohol, I have to admit. Cesar cut different letters out of the newspapers and I glued them on to blank A4 sheets to make some phrases which were music to our ears:

LET OUR HAIR GROW, IT CAN'T HURT ANYBODY!

We concluded, of course, with FREEDOM! in big black letters, covering half the page.

Then, late at night, very late, with no one in the streets to see us, we stuck our manifesto to the trunks of some chestnut trees. A few days later we stole past those trees, like fearful criminals revisiting the scene of the crime. No sign of our notices. Even if they had come to the attention of Securitate, who could ever prove we were the authors?

I didn't mention this incident to my father. Why make him worry? He was worried enough as it was.

'Don't worry, Dad. Nothing's going to happen. I am innocent.'

'You don't know anything!'

It was true. I didn't know what he knew, that's for sure. But he had lived through a different age, the years of Stalin's purges. The time when people who did not like Socialism, who opposed collectivization or spoke out of turn were brutally silenced. My father had lived through the era of the Canal, the most dreaded word he knew.

Anti-Communists and nationalist intellectuals by the thousand, people who belonged to or had relatives belonging to the bourgeoisie, people who had or were said to have 'bourgeois aspirations' – all were sent to the Canal, nicknamed 'the Canal of Death', to rub shoulders with the most vicious criminals and slave to build a naval link between the Danube and the Black Sea. A splendid place to cool hot tempers and clear all discontented minds.

I knew little indeed about the atrocious labour conditions in this Romanian *gulag*, with its hundreds and thousands of people killed 'in accidents', burnt to ashes or cemented over in common graves. But that was all in the past.

'Come on, Dad, it's not the fifties any more'.

In the 1960s, the terrifying era of 'Proletarian Internationalism' had yielded to 'National Communism' as Romania started to distance itself from the Soviet Union. Unlike other Socialist countries there were no Russian soldiers in the streets of Romania and the Russian language was not compulsory in our schools. Our new General Secretary of State talked about peace and the 'non-interference' of the great powers in our internal problems, about how proud we should be as true Romanians, about the brilliant future which would be ours once we had overcome the difficulties inherited from our past.

Nicolae Ceauşescu talked also about 'the liquidation of village backwardness' and 'industrial development for the progress of society'. We were fed up with being considered the villagers of Europe for so long, and so this went down well with our young hearts, though I could not understand why anything Western-looking or coming from the West could pose such a threat to us. But at least Ceauşescu was not a drunkard, as his predecessor Dej, who hid in his office, had been. By comparison, Ceauşescu appeared dynamic. Not too cultured, but serious and decisive. We saw him visiting hospitals and schools, in the fields and in factories. He boosted morale and discipline. Those discovered in restaurants and coffee bars during their work hours were harshly punished. That was good. Down with truancy and slackness in our society! And there was something else which went to our hearts.

We always had a complex about being a minor culture, our voices mere squeaks on the world stage. Now, Ceauşescu's anti-Soviet attitude gave our country a new role, endearing him to Western leaders. In 1967, wasn't Romania the first country from the Soviet bloc to establish diplomatic relations with West Germany? Then, a year later, weren't we visited by President Nixon, Willy Brandt and de Gaulle? You see! A new era was in front of us.

'You don't know anything!' my father repeated. 'Remember Ludovic!'

Although the Canal had closed its gates a decade previously, and people were no longer taken from their homes in the dead of night, the fear remained. And for none so much as those who had a marked person in their family. In ours, my father's brother Ludovic was the one.

Ludovic Antal was 'the Golden Voice of Romania'. He was an actor who recited poems like no one before or after. For many years he travelled the country with a theatre company, returning home with his arms laden with flowers. Until one night in the late 1950s. A little bit drunk, instead of acting his part he had started reciting a poem about Vlad the Impaler. The poem asks the *voivode* to come back to life and once again rid the land of villains and madmen – a barely veiled allusion to those who now ruled the country. Ludovic concluded with 'Down with Stalin!' The audience fell silent. No one knew what to do – to applaud, cheer or boo or what. To make things worse, there were some party bigwigs present. It was Bucharest's most prestigious theatre.

Not long after, somewhat surprisingly, Ludovic appeared on the same stage again. Maybe he was too well-known to be silenced on the spot. His role this time was to point a small pistol at a fellow actor, a man with whom he had quarrelled from time to time. When he pulled the trigger, the actor fell down and real blood flowed from his chest. Someone had put a live round in Ludovic's gun. He was never able to prove his innocence, so he was sent to prison.

That's why I never actually saw him on TV, though I could hear his warm, mellifluous voice on the radio after midnight, or in recordings which still sold like hot cakes. That's why when my teachers asked me if I was related to him, I said no, as my parents had taught me.

Having to reassure my father about my forthcoming 'visit' made me feel even worse. As I entered the long corridors of the Securitate building I began to feel sick. They told me to wait in a large room where some other people were sitting on long wooden benches. Everybody looked very nervous, with their eyes kept down, saying nothing.

Just sitting there, in that anxious silence, was enough to put the wind up me. What if they had found out about those stupid A4 sheets? What if they took me for someone else and I couldn't prove my innocence? Maybe I was there because I had such low marks in my 'Socialism' classes. No, that was ridiculous. But what if I couldn't find the right words; what if they discovered who knows what? Would they shout at me?

Finally, a middle-aged officer appeared, and I was led into another room with an enormous portrait of Nicolae Ceauşescu on the wall behind the desk. The officer did not shout; he was very polite throughout. His words were calm, caring, almost parental. He even had me sit in an armchair.

We had a nice chat about school, football and life in general. Who did I consider to be the best footballer in the world? George Best, I told him without hesitation. He smiled. He thought Dumitrache – the centre-forward for the Romanian national team at the time – was better. I didn't comment. What about the best singer? Here I hesitated a little. But there were no threatening words, no reproaches. I began to feel a bit more relaxed, so I confessed my passion for the Beatles. That's how I was at seventeen. If someone talked nicely to me I was ready to open my heart.

By the way, had I written some words on the blackboard one day?

So that's why they'd called me in! I freely admitted it. I didn't see any danger in that.

'And "Freedom!" What did you mean by that?'

I explained. I had no political intention by it. It was just a matter of fashion. The officer smiled again. How did I know about Western pop music? From the radio, of course. Did I listen to Radio Free Europe? Yes, but only the music, I wasn't interested in politics. Just what he had thought, he confessed in his turn. He looked like a decent bloke who had been put in a job which he had never liked. At the end of our meeting he asked me to sign a document admitting that I had written those words on the blackboard and that I listened to Radio Free Europe at home.

'Good luck at school! And study hard! . . . Our country needs well trained people,' he told me as he shook my hand.

Was that it? I left the building almost whistling. I hadn't the slightest idea that from that day forth I would be labelled for ever.

George and Cesar laughed about my experience.

'They are morons if they waste their time on little things like that,' we decided. Nevertheless we agreed to be more careful in the future, though we were not going to abandon our music sessions even if we had to take on the whole world.

But as we grew older, a certain feeling of apathy crept into our souls. Was it just the start of the 1970s fashion, when most Romanian teenagers were chewing gum with that aura of knowing it all? Or was it something deeper?

After August 1968, when the Russian tanks rolled into the capital of Czechoslovakia to end 'the Prague Spring', Ceauşescu became a bit too much for us. From that year all we could hear in the media were his calls for 'the respect of our independence and national sovereignty' and how loved our leader was in and outside the country. Indeed, he was the only Socialist leader who was opposed to the invasion, and that made him well-known abroad. President Nixon came to Bucharest again, followed by other Western heads of state, all of whom heaped praises on our leader.

Then it was time for Ceauşescu to return the visits. In 1970 he went to France, then had a sojourn in New York, met U Thant, the Secretary General of the United Nations, and had supper with Rockefeller. All these men shook his hand. By degrees Ceauşescu was turning into a messenger of world peace and a champion of international human rights; but inside the country things weren't going so well. That year Romania suffered devastating floods which, of course, did not upset the Five Year Plan. Work hard, citizens, we have to establish ourselves alongside countries like the USA, Canada or Japan!

To the outside world, Ceauşescu talked about nuclear disarmament. But there were rumours at home – rumours which soon became stronger than the voice of any national newspaper – that in October Ceauşescu signed a treaty with Moscow strengthening the role of the Romanian secret police to ensure peace in the Balkans. This was also the year in which Elena Ceauşescu was granted a doctorate behind closed doors. She couldn't speak Romanian grammatically, but you don't really need Romanian to have a chemistry doctorate, do you? After all, her husband also stammered and mumbled. 'When he speaks, he keeps a nail in his mouth,' the joke ran; a habit from his days apprenticed to a shoemaker in his youth.

The personality cult was gearing up as young people's enthusiasm began to wane. In schools, new patriotic poems were introduced, which we were forced to learn by heart, each more ridiculous than the last. More and more of the great leader's books appeared in shop windows and our teachers encouraged us to buy them as essential reference works for our History, Economics, Socialism, Geography, Literature and Philosophy classes.

Nobody bothered to read them, of course, and we often invented quotations off the top of our heads. It was all good for a laugh, but still, the whole comedy awoke in us a certain feeling of disgust. Consciously or not, a cynical attitude towards the world was creeping into our hearts.

That was when Bacchus appeared.

On Saturday nights we used to meet in the main park of the town. In a quiet corner were statues of long-haired and bearded writers which fascinated us. No Marx, Lenin or Ceauşescu – just poets. Huge busts, small benches between, bushes and trees. By daylight the park was a hangout for gypsies. They sat on the benches, eating salami, chucking bottles of beer on the paths, spitting and peeing on the statues. At night, the place was deserted.

We used to meet by the bust of Eminescu, our national poet. We still hated school, but how could we resist his poetry? Sophisticated and yet rooted in the folk tradition, his verses touched the depths of our souls. His philosophy stirred our imagination, his love for the eternally insensitive woman made our hearts ache. During the day we threw paper pellets at the literature teacher, when he turned his fat back to the class. At night we gathered round Eminescu and cleaned him of the gypsies' spit, urine and bird shit with a sponge. Then we sat on the benches and recited his poems by heart. On special nights, George used to climb on to his head to recite while we held candles in our hands, echoing the main stanzas like an ancient Greek chorus.

One night we noticed a guy dancing alone in a copse of chestnut trees. We stopped and watched him for a while. At first we did not understand what he was doing as we could hear no music. Gaps in the clouds above threw small round circles of moonlight on to the grass. He leapt from one silvery patch to another as though spotlit on a stage, waltzing with an imaginary girl, his arms spread wide in an embrace. It took us a while to realize that he was actually dancing with the moon.

He was quite well-known around the town. Some people called him 'the eternal student', others nicknamed him Kafka. Our parents called him 'the madman', and to us he was Bacchus.

'Seize the day, boys! Don't let it swallow more than five hours sleep. Remember! Sleep is just another drop of death.'

I see him, in my mind's eye, walking down the street with his curly black hair tumbling over his round spectacles and framing his absent-minded face. He had a pair of tight jeans, a brown coat and a famous diplomatic bag in which he always kept a plate, a fork, a small knife and an orange, 'the essence of my life', as he used to say.

You come across hundreds of people in your life and hardly remember any of them. But now and then you meet a character like Bacchus and never forget him.

When Bacchus started talking about life and love, it was like a huge wave rising in front of us, drawing us in, heaving us up and throwing us down again, spinning and twisting until we did not know where we were any more – then vanishing, leaving us shuddering and bemused, asking ourselves whether it had all been real or just a dream. We could not resist him. His craziness stuck with us like stamps on an envelope.

'Boys, life without craziness is like food without relish. You are seventeen and you mustn't be ashamed of this age of I-don't-know-anything-but-I-do-know-it-all-and-anyway-I-don't-care-and-actually-I-don't-know-what-I-want-*but-I-want*. That's its charm. The time when each and every moment pulsates with life. When the laugh is immaculate and the game is pure. Don't worry! You'll soon reach the age of those who are staring at us. The time of the ironic smile, the age which kills both passion and laughter. *Now* is our time.'

'Let's take a train to see how the sun rises 200 kilometres away! At home it smells of clean, starched sheets, how boring! . . . It smells of iron in the train, a most fortifying snack, I tell you. Let's go! . . . And look here! Wherever we go this night I'll keep this ash branch in my hand to be our guiding light and the symbol of human suffering. Agreed?'

'Agreed!'

And off we went, George, Cesar and Bacchus and I, and at midnight we took a *marfar* to meet the dawn in an unknown park of some unknown town.

A *marfar* is a goods train that carries timber, machines, cement, tanks or animals, but not people. There are lots of *marfare* speeding all over Romania, given priority at every junction and not stopping for hundreds of miles. Once we'd bribed a railwayman to find out where our *marfar* was going, all we had to worry about was the lack of comfort and the risk of six months' imprisonment if we were caught. But who cared? The first rays of dawn found us slowly circling on a deserted creaking merry-go-round in the park of a distant town.

'Isn't life worth living, boys, eh? Look at the plants, the trees, birds, the ponds, its frogs! What splendour! I propose we spend the next hour watching the pond and seeing how the frogs make love. Agreed?'

'Agreed!'

Bacchus was more in touch with nature than any person I ever met before or after. Soon we were completely at one with his world.

He put little caps on our heads and took us to his Jewish canteen. 'No racism, boys. Just look, see and learn!'

And we did. We ate for free in his Jewish canteen, pretending we were Jews. We went to his university and listened to philosophical dissertations on Hegel, pretending we were students. We went with him to literary circles and pretended we were poets. At exhibitions we were painters.

'Where art is involved, there is no race, age or sex. No morality or immorality ... It's art and that's all. That's what grown-up people forget.'

He definitely did not like 'adults'.

'Look at them! Mature people, dragging their carcasses from one compromise to the next. How superior they are! Laughing at Don Quixote and his windmills ... as if those who cannot see a star as anything other than a gaseous body would ever be able to understand anything of life. All those who are different from them they condemn as insane. What do they know about the world's masters and geniuses? Homer was blind, Beethoven deaf, Byron lame, Toulouse-Lautrec a dwarf; Oscar Wilde was homosexual, Baudelaire syphilitic, Michelangelo a hysteric; Leonardo was impotent, Kafka a consumptive, Van Gogh completely deranged, Dostoevsky epileptic. Rilke, Nerval, Pushkin and all the others – drunkards, madmen, sexually obsessed, with suicidal tendencies . . . That's how they portray them. And secure in their "sanity" they laugh at people like us who struggle, suffer, cry, fall, rise and fall again, devoured by passion and tormented by life's mysteries.'

That's how Bacchus talked, with us around him nodding our heads and waiting, as always, to bring the subject round to love.

Because love, as you can imagine, was very much on our minds, and here Bacchus gave us the fuel we needed. For me it was Iolanda, my first true love.

You know how it is at that age, when holding your girl's hand while walking in a park means everything in the world.

Flowers, poems, helping her jump over a stile, climbing the path to the top of the mountain . . . Was there a 2,000-foot sheer drop where the edelweiss grew? So what? The more perilous the climb the more value the flower. Or walking her home in pelting rain, our feet splashing on the tarmac; I had her crying with laughter at my jokes. I laughed too when our boat overturned in the middle of a lake and I was still telling jokes to convince her it was just an excuse – for me to swim with her on my back. She never knew how my heart sank and how scared I was that something might happen to her. On the bank she pretended to faint away but still wouldn't let me give her the kiss of life.

Iolanda was a touch ungrateful, a bit fastidious, playing with the strings of my heart. But who cared? She was the queen. Life without her had no meaning. And I needed her to feel I was alive.

Bacchus was right. We had nothing in common with those wise grown-ups with their cold, contented faces. Reason and moderation was what they preached. But we preferred love's ups and downs.

There were plenty of downs indeed. Iolanda lived so far away from me that all we could do between holidays was write letters to each other. My God, how many letters I wrote! In school, with pages hidden between the covers of notebooks, sitting on benches in a park, at home all day long and during the night, under the blanket with my little torch. Each letter was dozens of pages long.

In reply she would send me notes like: 'Received your letter. It was so nice! I'll write more next time,' which was enough to make me reach for another ream. In fact, there was a time in my life when I remember doing nothing but writing letters to Iolanda.

Maybe that intensity was what put her off in the end. OK! I told myself: hepatitis stopped me becoming a famous footballer, school stopped me being a singer but nobody is going to stop me becoming the man of Iolanda's dreams. Except, of course, Iolanda herself.

Our meetings became rarer, which was painful enough. But I still didn't stop loving her. From time to time I still wonder if I ever did.

Cesar and George had rather similar experiences at around the same time. So we helped each other through the bad times.

We used to sing and laugh just to cover our heartache, but it was Bacchus who really raised our spirits. His words staunched our wounds.

He always knew what to say. And he never gave up his theory of love for love's sake.

'Pardon me, miss,' he'd say to an unknown girl right in the middle of the street. 'Wouldn't you like to open a rest-home for butterflies with me? Here is an orange. Half is for you as a sign of trust and desire for partnership.'

You could say it was only love we were in love with. That we were self-deluding, selfish, romantic rogues. But we were seventeen, and when we loved we loved utterly. Each moment had its own unique intensity of feeling. I had so much love in me that even while embracing a girl I felt sad; missing her, grieving that everything passes and the moment does not hold.

We would give our girls everything: heart, soul, body and mind, caught completely in the world of passion. This was a form of love that could not last. With so many highs and lows it was too exhausting. Someone had to quit sooner or later. If I look back on my past, I would say the girls quit sooner than us. At the end of it, they wanted security and peace. We gave them everything but that.

Yet we didn't give up.

One day I saw a poster which caught my eye: 'GEORGE AARON — LATE ROMANTIC'. In the exhibition hall, the artist started talking to me, though we had never met before.

'My name is Aaron, with a double A.' He grabbed my arm and continued, just like that.

'Look at that guy over there, the one with his belly bulging over his belt! He thinks he's at the butcher's. Look how he gazes at my paintings. You know what he is thinking now? He's thinking that my paintings are pieces of meat . . . That picture-meat is too fat, this one has too many bones He weighs it with expert eyes. Then takes a deep breath, wrinkles his nose and moves on. He is looking for a larger canvas to cover the empty space on the wall he's got. He doesn't like my painting. There is no woman in it with breasts as big as melons. That's what he needs.'

'Oh, no! Look! He's spotted something hanging on a hook . . . Now he is ready to ask: who is the painter? I introduce myself. With my head high and back straight. It's useless. When he sees my dark face and how small I am he thinks I am another gypsy beggar and the price of the painting is already tumbling. The haggling is about to start. Just like in the market. Eventually I give up, happy to settle on any price . . Then it all starts again with someone else. I'm used to it.'

Soon Aaron and I became friends. He lived on the outskirts of a little town surrounded by hills and mountains. It was summer when I first visited his room, the attic in a ramshackle house, where the days and nights came in and out through the gaps in the walls, the cracks in the ceiling and the broken window.

'You should see what it's like in the winter,' he told me. 'Before I go to bed I always put on my woollen socks, my fur cap and my gloves. I cover myself with three blankets but I still wake up like a mummy in the morning, my fingers stiff with cold. I wonder sometimes if I'm not going to wake up in an ice-cube. It's no joke, old man! This is my life. Loneliness, deprivation, and agony . . . They are all here, all the roots of my paintings . . . My paintings. My misery, my revolt and the warmth I need as well. They are my food and sleep. My firmest friend and beloved woman. They are all here and they are all I have.'

Just the mention of Aaron's name was enough to drive my parents close to hysteria. While Bacchus was their public enemy number one, they saw Aaron as the root of all my bad external influences.

I used to meet this Bohemian painter in his favourite coffee-house, where he spent hours watching passers-by, making sketches and notes. His paintings were way beyond me.

'How could you expect to understand them?' he would lecture me. 'You are just another product of our age, a time when everybody eats as much as they can but nobody feeds the spirit any more. How could you or anybody else understand my little monsters?'

He would drink six cups of coffee then rave at me for hours in his manic attempt to communicate the essence of his world. It was a strange world indeed – his canvases were full of all sorts of weird creations. 'Beings of the unbeings,' as he called them, with heads instead of tails, necks as bellies, noses instead of eyes, ears in the mouths, long thin legs writhing all over the place, entering the earth above and coming out of the sky beneath, twisted tree roots, hydra-headed centipedes, dragons . . . all painted with incredibly small, fine brushes, under a magnifying glass. It was painstaking stuff, hundreds of hours of work. But the trouble was, you couldn't see the detail.

'They are the mirror of the world turned upside down, old man. The image of the world as it really is today!'

Aaron thought he was the only one who could really see how it was, which infuriated Bacchus even though we all ended up on his side. But we loved Aaron. He was poor, lonely and miserable and our problems at home or school seemed so minor in comparison with his grinding poverty and daily struggle to survive. And then, something terrible happened in our neighbourhood which proved that Aaron's horrific view of our world was not far off the truth.

In 1971, Ceauşescu and his wife visited China and North Korea. As soon as they returned it was obvious to everyone how much they had been influenced by Mao and the great Kim Il Sung's way of thinking. The cult of personality took deeper root. Suddenly his portrait was everywhere. On classroom walls, in the corridors of businesses, in bookshop windows, on books, on posters . . . His face was always shown in profile, which led to the joke of 'the one-eared President', meaning that he had one screw missing. When the joke came to the attention of Securitate the portraits disappeared overnight – to be replaced by Ceauşescu's full-frontal smiling face, both ears now clearly visible.

From then on Securitate took heed of jokes involving our leaders and tried to stamp them out. You could still make clever remarks, even political ones, but no allusion to the Great Thinker!

Bad times were foreseen for Carlos, 'the king of jokes'. Everyone in my town knew Carlos, a man of thirty, a gambler. He played poker for a living and toured the country in search of other players to cheat. He was not a bad man. He was so good at telling jokes, I guess many players let themselves be fleeced only to hear another good one from the gambler.

The only family Carlos had was an old mother and hundreds of pigeons. All the money he won from gambling he spent on chocolates for his old mother and in building a real wooden castle for his little birds. He did not take much care of himself and, from time to time, he would drink a bit more than necessary. Once he was drunk he could not keep his mouth shut. And, no matter who he was with, he told rude jokes about the President.

One night, in a restaurant full of people, Carlos drank more than usual and climbed up on to the table announcing that as long as his blue eyes still saw light, he would find a way to get rid of Ceauşescu, the root of all our future evil. This was dangerous talk. But not too dangerous, we believed, since everyone knew that Carlos couldn't hurt a fly, let alone a human being. But that night Carlos disappeared. Everyone thought he was off on one of his tours around the country to get money for his mother and his birds.

Months passed. Then they delivered a sealed coffin to his mother's house and told her that her son had suffered a terrible accident. Nobody believed this, so they opened the coffin. There Carlos lay. Instead of his blue eyes, white cotton wool plugged his empty sockets.

Suddenly we were all afraid. Everyone knew Big Brother was watching us, but how closely did he see into our lives? What were the limits? Where did the danger zone begin and end? We were not dissidents. But our minds were tormented by abstract notions and metaphysical things which had nothing to do with our leader's dialectical materialism and the scientific Communism that we were taught in school. We didn't negate the system in its everyday manifestations. We just laughed. Every enormity was condensed into a good joke. But then, what kind of political threat was Carlos?

There is a modern Romanian proverb which says that a person on his own is weak, that two are strength, and when there are three together one is an informer. With Aaron and Bacchus we were already five, and we all trusted each other. This was something to value.

When Cesar, George and I graduated from the *Liceu* we decided to hold a three-day celebration at Aaron's house, a house which was said to be haunted. A man had once lived there who was married six times. A year after every wedding, his wife of the moment died. 'She died happy, at least,' he used to say as he followed the coffin to the graveyard. The police began to watch him carefully. The mystery was solved when they found his sixth wife tied to the bed, laughing insanely. He was tickling her feet with a feather. And that's how he killed his other wives. They literally died of laughter.

Aaron swore he could hear the laughter of these women echoing through the house at midnight. We didn't hear it. But there were plenty of other ghostly noises to be heard.

Between the houses in Aaron's road there was a narrow entrance, where the drunkards peed in the evening. As soon as the tavern nearby opened, you could hear their urine smacking on the walls.

During the day, locals met in the courtyard along with the cats, dogs, pigs, hens and all the beings in the neighbourhood, all joining in the common yelling. Fathers yelled at mothers, mothers were yelling at their children, children yelled at the animals and the animals yelled at the sky. And then there were the two young men who practised their knife-throwing every night. They used Aaron's door as a target. No one dared stop them, of course.

After midnight there were some moments of silence. Then just when you felt sleep embracing you, horrible creakings, scrapings, groans and all sorts of sinister noises came in from the dark. That was the signal for the bugs to come out.

I always hated those cockroaches, with their black-bean bodies and thin, metallic legs, so quick and unpredictable as they scuttled across the floor.

We left the light on and smoked packets of cigarettes in the hope that the insects would keep away. No chance! On the walls black and brown creepy-crawlies; in the corners big grey spiders. And then there were the rats outside. I really don't know what we'd have done without our two full barrels of crystal clear home-made wine.

In those days you could still buy good home-made wine or plum brandy in the countryside. All you needed was to shout over the fence at any house and the owner was ready to serve you at prices that were so cheap that nobody bought by the bottle, but by buckets, basins or barrels.

Over the three days and nights we filled a hundred sheets with our rapturous slogans and philosophical aphorisms. By the time we had drained our barrels we had boiled it down to the three main Ls of our life:

LIVE, LOVE AND LAUGH!

This was to be the motto of our newly formed group, and was henceforth to replace the Learn! Learn! Learn! of our parents. We called ourselves 'Hell's Angels' though we knew nothing then of the American bikers. George had seen these words in a foreign magazine and he liked how they sounded. Besides, we really believed that we were the only angels in that hell of a country. Then we burned our pages, so as not to leave any trace of what was now imprinted on our minds.

Next morning we packed, locked Aaron's room and went out to feel the country's soil under our naked feet. That was how we began our journey around Romania. It was to be our last romantic journey together.

We wandered for days, climbing hills and mountains, cutting through fields, crossing bridges, feet bare, feet shod. We slept in wagons, *marfare* and barns, jumped through windows of closed hostels, slept to the song of crickets, sheltered from the rain under leafy trees, ate biscuits in railway stations, rice in monasteries, danced in the depths of caves. We hitched lifts in lorries, small cars, tractors. We were even picked up by some Danish tourists with whom we talked English. We were so proud of our English. And how confident they seemed to us, long-haired and bearded! One of them had his legs out of the window, just like in the movies. What a car they had! What a life was theirs in the West! And they didn't even ask us for petrol money when they dropped us off! What good-hearted and civilized people they were!

Back home again, Cesar, George and I carried on studying for the university entry exams. Our parents wanted us to be students and that was what I had to work for. To become a student, like Bacchus.

'University destroys real talent. It changes artists into commercial morons. It will force us apart,' Aaron was saying.

We did not believe him. There was only the one year of compulsory military service to be got through and then we could all get together again.

'It's a good thing to do your service before university. I don't see what else could cool you down,' my parents said to me.

'Hm!' I replied. Just one year away and then the world would be ours. We all thought the same. We had no idea how right my parents would be in the end. The Army, Securitate and life in Romania after the mid-1970s cooled us down indeed.

IV

We Are Our Country's Pride

'*One*, two, three, *four*! . . . I said: *One*, two, three, *four*! . . . Halt! . . . A-
bout *turn*! . . . One, two, three, *four*! . . . *T*-urn *left*! . . . Atten-*shun*! . . .
Don't move, soldier!'
     The air is stale and mouldy by the filthy, grubby wall where we stand
to attention in the late afternoon heat. Behind us lies the regiment's
pigsty with its grunting and squealing. Thousands of flies are buzzing
round our heads.
     'Hey! You . . . On the second row! Didn't you hear the order?' The
lieutenant, a thin, middle-aged, jaundiced-looking man, yells like a
banshee. The flies are trying to land on my eyelids, and I move my
head away.
     'Aaaah! So after one month in the Army we still don't know what
"attention" means! Good . . . Something else you'll have to learn! . . .
Sub-machine-gun number two!'
     That was me.
     One month earlier, they had marched us at the double into the
company barber shop. We entered one door as civilians and came out of
another as sheep with naked heads on our shoulders. Then, straight
into a huge shower-room, to be doused in cold water, to remove the rest
of our civilian dirt. We climbed into khaki uniforms which more or less
fitted, put on heavy boots and marched to our platoons where they
handed out the guns. From then on the number of the gun was our true
identity.
     'Yes sir!' I yell in turn. Of course, in Romanian Army language this
was a hundred times more complicated – not 'Sir', but a kind of 'Hail
to you Comrade Lieutenant!' Let's keep to 'Sir!' so as not to complicate
things.

'Step forward!' comes the order.

I turn about, and perform a quick march round the platoon; three parade steps in front of the lieutenant and here I am, stiff as a board.

'Sub-machine gun number two. Tell the others where we are at this moment!'

'Allow me to report!' – that's how we had to start any sentence when we talked to a superior – 'We are on the parade ground, *sir*!'

'Good! And where else?'

'Allow me to report! Near you, *sir*!'

'Very good! And where else?'

'Allow me to report! Near a pigsty, *sir*!'

The platoon giggles. I feel the lieutenant's eyes fixing me in a withering stare.

'Good! And where else?'

'In the Army, *sir*!'

'A-a-a-a-all right!' he shouts, his thunder-voice splitting the clouds above. 'Now, tell the others what you think the Army means! Tell us in a loud voice and use your deep erudite knowledge, right? We are curious!'

I'll tell you what this was all about. We were the first generation of Romanian students to do our military service before university. We were not boys with no higher education who spent two years as 'troopers'; nor were we doctors, engineers or other graduates, who had to endure only six months in the Army after university. We were just boys of eighteen; yet potentially, we were the future intelligentsia of the country. The officers were bent on proving to us that we were worthless.

I kept silent. How should I answer? Army food is something that enters your mouth and goes out through your arse: somehow, I had similar thoughts about the Army itself. The Army was just a place you go to lose your girlfriends, where you are forced to march in a column, your eyes fixed on the nape of a guy more moronic than you whose eyes are fixed on the nape of a guy more moronic than him and so on and so forth. How could I get this across to the lieutenant?

I was thinking. But the Army teaches you especially *not* to think. First you carry out the order, *then* you think. That was the most important rule we had to learn, from day one.

'Well, sub-machine gun number two . . . why are you standing there speechless, like a calf in front of a new gate?'

That was supposed to be very witty.

The guns forced themselves to laugh, with that constrained laughter which comes when your superior tries to make a clever joke. I call it the sheep laugh, since I believe that's how the sheep laugh when the shepherd tells them jokes.

'Well, either you don't know the answer or you don't *want* to answer! You give yourself airs, don't you?'

'Allow me to report! I'm not giving myself airs, *sir*!'

The platoon giggled again.

'Well, well! . . . You'll soon learn what the Army is, don't worry! Until then, quick march to your place! Cigarette break!'

Whether you smoked or not, every fifty minutes of Army training ended with a ten-minute 'cigarette break.' This gave you time to catch your breath after dragging your body through pits, puddles and trenches. You puffed deeply, spitting the tobacco strands from your lips, rubbing your burnt fingers on your thigh – those unfiltered cigarettes were always too small for your young lungs – then it started up again.

'Atten-*shun*!'

We run, search the base, jostle each other, line up one behind the other in perfect order, stand still and wait, tense as loaded springs.

'Sub-machine gun number two!'

Here we go again! Run round the back of the platoon, three parade steps, stand to attention in a cloud of flies; I'm getting quite used to them.

'Yes, *sir*!'

'Today we'll learn what "*Culcat!*" means,' the lieutenant starts yelling again, his hands waving in the air to help him explain.

'Now, this boy who thinks he's clever will show us what he can do. You boys think "*Culcat*" means lie down or throw yourself to the ground. Well, that's not all it means. Atten-*shun*! Sub-machine gun number two, Cul-*cat*!'

I throw myself face down in the mud. It is not good enough.

'Atten-*shun*! Cul-*cat*!'

Once again I'm down flat on the ground, obedient as a dog. It is wrong again. Once more! Not good enough! Cul-*cat*! ... Down on my side, leg bent in front, roll so I can't be seen by the enemy. Not good enough. Cul-*cat*! Wrong again!

The heavy uniform, gun across my back, kitbag, ammunition, water can and the gas mask, the sweat and everything gets thrown down. I'm standing up again, then down. Not good enough. The heat is melting my bones. Stinging tears roll down my face, which is now caked with mud. Down! Up! Down! Up! ... Time becomes a straight line, the distance between head and earth, until I feel I cannot move any more.

'It's not good, sub-machine gun number two, but quick march to your place! Pla-toon! Atten-*shun*!' the lieutenant yells.

I guess the idea of war hovering around him for years had gone directly to the lieutenant's testicles. It changed his normal voice, giving him strength, and a meaning to his life. I bet he used to yelp at home, to his tall, blonde, ravishing wife. I saw her once, swinging her hips in and out of the company's library. We soldiers sat on benches pretending to clean our guns, eyes glued to her legs. What a splendid pair! A challenge to happiness ... I saw her only once, it's true, but that was enough to give me pollution on my Army bedsheets for weeks. Did the lieutenant guess I slept with his wife in my dreams? Of course not. He was too much inside himself to observe anything. What a lion he was, in front of us, his jowls quivering, his chest stuck out.

'Now, you'll learn that in the Army the mistake of one soldier becomes the mistake of the whole platoon! In war it means loss of life. Thank God the Americans haven't invaded our country yet! Atten-*shun*! Cul-*cat*!'

Thirty soldiers threw themselves to the ground. That might have made him happier but it was not good enough. *Culcat*! ... Once again. And so it went on for hours, until dinnertime came.

'Pla-*toon*! Atten-*shun*! ... *R*-ight *dress*! To the mess, quick march! *One*, two, three, *four*! ... Now *sing*!

It was a red dusk that day. I still remember the big round sun sinking below the hills as we marched towards the barracks. It was one of those miracles of nature that urges you to sit and watch. I should have shouted to the others: 'Hey, stop! Don't let the miracle pass! Feel it, let it enter your soul!' But who was I to refuse to sing and march when the lion commands?

> Through the night, wind and rain, Tra-*la-la*
> We march happily to train, Tra-*la-la*!

While we sang the sun went down. No wonder. Our voices were too awful to bear. The moon came up, shy, like a woman. Not that we had time to notice her much, our heads bent over our tin plates in the canteen. Then it was quick march to the study rooms.

At nine each evening, after dinner, we were obliged to watch the news on TV. This was followed by the evening roll-call and the trumpet playing 'The Silence'. An hour later it was lights out, and the snores of sixty soldiers rose from the line of iron bunk beds. Reveille was at five, when we had to run in our white long-johns round the barracks. But that was not the reason we cut short our jokes and pranks at night; it was the Americans who regularly got us out of our beds.

About once a week in the dead of night, a blood-curdling voice would bellow from the loudspeakers: *ALAAARM*!

We all had to leap out of bed, dress in two minutes, snatch our arms from their gun-racks, fasten our ammunition belts and sprint out to parade at a place – I can't tell you exactly where – it was top secret. The American enemy was likely to invade our country at the least notice. And so it was that night. The alarm sounded at about two o'clock and in minutes we were out on parade, fully dressed and panting to annihilate those bloody Americans who robbed our sleep.

There was no sign of them, to our grievous disappointment. Instead, the lieutenant was waiting for us, standing on top of a wooden box, keen to teach us how to dig a hole by torchlight. He looked fresh and very pleased with himself. He was a complete moron and that's a fact. Otherwise he would have been warming the sheets for his ravishing wife.

'Sub-machine gun number two! Start digging here! Get yourself a hole dug before I finish this smoke.'

I took the spade we always carried on our backs – it constantly banged my kidneys as I ran – and started to dig like a badger. By the time the lieutenant had finished his smoke, the hole was dug. He threw his butt into it.

'Cigarette break! . . . Soldiers! Throw your stubs in this hole so as not to mess up our field, please!'

Soldiers? . . . Please? . . . Bad sign.

'Atten-*shun*!' he yelled when the break was over.

'Sub-machine gun number two! . . . Fill in the hole!'

I started shovelling it in. We were already used to this nonsense of digging holes and then filling them in, next day digging other holes and covering them again, so I didn't take much notice.

'Platoon dismissed! You may go back to your beds! . . . Not you, sub-machine gun number two!'

The others returned to the barracks. I stayed, as he ordered, to solve the mystery of the night.

'From now on, little boy,' he whispered kindly in my ear, 'I'll take you personally in my charge! What do you think, eh? You think you are clever, eh? . . . Shut up! Don't interrupt me! . . . I noticed right from the start in the barber shop. Talking about sheep, weren't you, with your long hair? You came here with heart problems on your medical file, right?'

It was true. At my last medical check before entering the Army, they discovered I had extra-systolitis and tachycardia, both mild diseases of the heart. Maybe it was the coffee I had drunk by the litre while doing my university entrance exams. I was also considerably underweight and there was even talk of postponing my military service. But then the doctors decided there was no real danger. If you stand sideways the enemy will never see you, they joked. But they had included a medical certificate along with my Army papers.

'So you thought we'd be easy on you, eh? I'll teach you what it means to be in the Army, don't worry!' the lieutenant went on. Then his voice softened.

'Or maybe you'll do your best and be a model soldier . . . That's a possibility! I don't know whether you noticed, but I lost the butt of my cigarette in that hole of yours. Bring it to me first thing in the morning! And be careful not to mistake it for one of the others! Dig, number two! See you in the morning at roll-call!'

The next day, I went to see the major, complaining of abuse. He listened to me, then he looked in a filing cabinet where he found my papers, which helped him think deeper. He spent some time reading and then he exploded.

'I have your file right here in front of me, soldier! In civilian life you called yourself a Hell's Angel, didn't you? Well, in your civilian life you do what you think is best, but don't come here and waste my time with your pitiful civilian attitudes! It's not heaven here, nor hell. It's the Army! Do you understand?'

'Yes, *sir*!

'Good!' he replied. 'Did you carry out the order? Did you find the cigarette butt?'

'Allow me to report, sir! No . . . Because . . .'

'No?' he yelled. 'There is no "because" in the Army: haven't you got that yet? First you carry out the order; then, *and only then*, may you complain. This is the last time I let you go unpunished! *Out!*'

And out I went, as quickly as I could, not wanting a kick up the arse. I was pretty scared. There we were, me a hundred miles north of home, George a hundred miles south of it, Cesar doing his military service at the coast – just four months after we'd baptized our group, and the Army had the whole thing on its files! My God! . . . I felt sick as a cat.

Before I could reach the barrack room I was puking like a drunkard. Here a bit, there a puddle: my vomit decorated the corridor. I couldn't stay on my feet. They sent me to the regiment's first aid centre. A doctor looked at my tongue and then gave me some pills. I don't know what kind of pills he gave me, but soon I was having diarrhoea, then a high fever took hold of me. The bed began moving in circles. Food poisoning, the doctor concluded. For a week or so I was exempted from training then it was back to learning how to become a real soldier. And I knew that I'd be the platoon's scapegoat from now on.

That autumn seemed endless, with its rainy, misty days and the long climbs up wet, muddy hills after wading through streams and rivers carrying twenty kilos on our backs so we would develop a stronger male stride. We would arrive back at the camp late in the afternoon, with mud in our nostrils, ears and eyes. Then we had to clean our guns until they gleamed 'like the moon on a clear night'.

'Sub-machine gun number two! . . . You call that barrel clean? There's less shit in the regimental latrine. Thank God the Americans haven't invaded us yet to see what sluggards we are!'

'Atten-*shun*! To the classroom, march!'

Late autumn, we field-trained only during the day, since each afternoon had to end with two hours spent in the study room. We had to learn by rote from blood-red books full of half-brained military rules and tactics. In the age of satellites and guided missile systems we had to study in detail guns last used in the First World War, and tactics of the previous century. We committed to memory military maps used against the Germans in 1942. 'Never tell anyone about these secret maps,' they solemnly commanded us. 'Not even your wife.' It didn't seem to matter that the maps were printed in West Germany.

I think now the officers were training us for the absurdity of later civilian life, but I always fell asleep over those blood-red books. Then, when questions came, my answer was never good enough.

'Soldiers! . . . *Outside*! Take the porridge off your brain! Get your arses out in the rain!'

Because of my bad answers, the whole platoon had to slither like worms in waterlogged trenches. 'Don't forget! One man's mistake affects the whole platoon!' The lieutenant was so pleased to remind us of this.

'Sub-machine gun number two! . . . You see that tree on the top of the hill? The second one on the left?'

'Yes, *sir*!'

'Good! The command is . . . wait for it: *Gas*!'

When you heard 'Gas' you had to put that sticky, cold rubber gas mask over your hot wet face and sprint.

'To the second tree on the horizon . . . *Run*!'

I pant, huff and puff and spit inside the mask. My body jerks on running feet which don't seem to be mine. I moan and groan and run round the tree, as hard as I can I push myself down the hill. Back in front of the platoon I take off the mask, the blood running from my nose. The lieutenant laughs.

'That's the way to become a real man and a good patriot, little boy!'

'That's the way my arse,' I mumble into my chest.

'What's that? Did you say something, number two?'

'Allow me to report! I didn't say anything, *sir*!'

'Good!'

Winter came, with its freezing days. But at least now we were allowed to leave the regimental camp once a week, to breathe the civilian air. Everyone waited for the Sunday pass. Competitions were planned to see who'd drink the most in the taverns. I was not usually included. As a punishment for my clumsiness, I had to wash the loos in which my compatriots would puke wine and vodka as soon as they returned.

Alone in the dormitory I read letters from George and Cesar, always complaining of being confined to camp on Sundays. What a coincidence! Nothing to be done. Cross off another Sunday from the calendar hidden under my pillow. Another week would start again.

'Down! Up! Run! Crawl through the tunnel! . . . Keep going! Forward! Turn left and quick march to the river! Don't worry, the ice won't break! Oh! Has it broken? So what? Stand up! Stand up! The Romanian soldier has to be able to light his fag at the bottom of the sea and play cards in the fire! . . . Don't move!'

You would run for hours with the sweat pouring down your body. Then suddenly came the order: 'Halt! Don't move!' You would then have to stand stock-still for five minutes – long enough to feel the strong, icy Russian wind freezing the sweat on your skin. Fingers, toes, legs, arms and brain would start to harden. You felt that you'd topple to the ground and shatter into a thousand pieces if someone gave you a push. But nobody pushes you. No one dares make jokes any more in front of the lieutenant. We are too scared now.

'Don't move! And don't forget Rule Fourteen, you little vermin!' he yells at us.

We all knew what Rule Fourteen meant. If we were not good enough soldiers we could lose our university places, and have to stay in the Army for another two years. Or we could be court-martialled if the mistake was serious enough. That was what happened to the four guys who reported to headquarters one evening that they had lost a tank.

You may wonder how it is possible to lose a tank. Well, it can happen. Let me tell you how.

These boys were in the tank battalion. Early one chilly morning they were practising manoeuvres over hills and endless fields, shooting at imaginary targets with their huge guns and rolling over ditches and garbage piles. It was bloody freezing everywhere, more inside the tank than out. So when they found themselves near a village, they decided to hide the tank in a dip, covering it with snowy fir branches and taking the portable radio with them to the nearest tavern.

There, sitting by the fire, they continued to report on the radio how big the hillocks were while drinking a good, warming *ţuica* – that's what the Romanians call their strong home-made plum brandy. But on leaving the tavern, the boys found themselves heading in the wrong direction. They searched and searched but could find no sign of their tank anywhere. They couldn't even find a caterpillar track.

So there they were later that night, coming into camp on foot while the whole company was on red alert, the officers shaking in their boots. The missing tank had already been reported to other army units, and even Ceauşescu had been personally informed. Planes and helicopters were circling overhead.

'Where is the tank?' The officers were shouting.

'Allow us to report! We don't know, sir!'

It might sound amusing, but things went from bad to worse. The directions they gave us were completely wrong, and next day the whole regiment was searching for the tank at random. Finally, a shepherd rang headquarters to say he had just found a tank. Would it be all right, he asked, if he sold it for scrap? The officers congratulated themselves on their great achievement in finding the lost tank. But the crew were court-martialled, and from that day forth we heard nothing more about them. I should say that we did not laugh too much about it either. It could easily have been one of us.

It was about this time that we all began to feel the fear growing in us. It entered our veins, encircled our brains and waited to consume us, as the spider in the middle of its web prepares for its victim. Four months of Army life had taught us how dangerous life was, and how pitifully vulnerable we were. We all felt under threat of being punished for things we did not understand. I guess that was part of our Army training: to teach us to live under constant fear.

Spring came and the lieutenant still hadn't tired of proving me an idiot.

'Sub-machine gun number two . . . Go and clean the boots of the platoon. The others go to lunch!'

Missing lunch in the canteen was not such a great catastrophe for me as the lieutenant thought. We sat at long tables in that reeking dining-hall waiting for the huge tureens. In the early days the colour of the soup and the smell of the hall made us queasy, but the army had no pity for the squeamish. Soldiers spat in the tureens, took the spit out with the ladle and displayed it proudly. They then put their spittle aside and started sipping from the ladle to see whether the soup was not too hot to serve. You got used to that.

I always seemed to be the last to arrive at the table and there was never any meat left. So I closed my eyes and chewed the usual boiled cabbage mixed with something called 'concentrated food'. Once, with my eyes closed for a second, I found myself chewing a dirty piece of floorcloth. When the officers were not around, the boys were still keen to joke with the others. And what better butt than me, the platoon scape-goat?

One day I found a tiny little dead mouse in the deep soup plate, and from that day on I stopped going to the canteen, except in the mornings, when I took my ration of purple bromide tea. This we were given to keep romance out of the ranks. I preferred to stick to food parcels from home, from my parents, who kept asking me why I did not take more care of myself and why I was so thin. In autumn I had weighed sixty kilos without clothes. In spring, in my boots, I still could not reach fifty-five. My parents advised me in long letters to eat better and get more sleep.

At night there was guard duty rota, and everyone was desperate to avoid the middle shift, from midnight to three in the morning. You had to stand in front of the dormitory door for three hours, ready to shoot any American who dared to infiltrate. Guess who most frequently found himself on duty after midnight, as a punishment for his mistakes that day!

Listening to the snores of the others and the shouts of those suddenly waking from their nightmares, watching half-asleep soldiers shuffling to the bathroom then climbing back on to their squeaking beds, I chewed over the day's events with my eyes and ears peeled to catch the slightest external sound, careful that the lieutenant should not find me asleep. My mind became open to other fears, more metaphysical ones. Absurdity . . . Fatality . . . Death.

To take my mind off the horrors of the night, I started writing short stories, full of unknown creatures invading the world and soldiers who kill themselves at the end of their military service. Somehow, though I wasn't aware of it at the time, I was putting in writing what Aaron had put in his paintings: the dark side of the world. Next day, I would read my masterpieces to my colleagues. Nobody seemed to like them much. There were no jokes in them, no laughs. My comrades were more interested in my love letters. Soon, they found me better themes to write about.

They asked me to write their love letters for them. In the Army, men's bravery is measured by the crudeness of their language; but this language was not to the liking of their would-be girlfriends. So they gave me details of eye and hair colour, height, shape, size of breasts and thighs, hobbies. All I had to do was to put in words the soldier's endless passion, adding a little story as background.

I wrote such good stuff for them that by the end of spring our platoon came first in the competition for the squad which received most letters from home.

This helped to cool the fury of my companions a bit. But after such nights I was a walking zombie during the day. My marching was out of step and I was dim-witted for lack of sleep. My nerves were broken chords, my mind lost in misty clouds. Little wonder that one day I leapt to fight with 'the Bull', a local boxing champion, when he read letters from my Iolanda out loud, making fun of them.

Our girls wrote back on very delicate paper which the soldiers used as toilet paper after they had read them and passed them round. This paper was much better than the coarse thick sheets which the Army used to toughen our arses for hard times ahead. As far as I was concerned the others could make *borsch* with their own stuff but I had my little taboo. I would not let them touch Iolanda's letters. And that was what the Bull couldn't understand.

Despite my threats, he continued to read the letter to the simpering soldiery around him, his voice full of mocking intonation and dirty laughs. I took a small bench and hurled it at the middle of his bovine head. Then I jumped on him and started kicking and punching with all my strength. At one point the hate in me vanished but it was fear that made me continue. I knew that once he was up again I had little chance of survival.

Eventually our comrades pulled us apart, two holding me and four holding him back, and that was how the lieutenant found us. The next day saw us locked together in the same cell for two days and nights. I thought this would be the end of my military career. It was not. It was just another of life's experiences. I learnt what it was like to have to pick blades of grass from between the paving stones during the day and rub your mate's back to help him sleep at night.

Summer came again with its smell of freedom and its long bright days, reminding us that the hot weather makes training harder to endure than the cold. But it was only a matter of weeks before we would be out of this hell. Each day I could hardly wait to hear the command: 'Atten-*shun*! To the camp . . . quick march! *Sing*!' which meant the day in the field was over, and it was time to bury our noses in those blood-red books.

> *One*, two, *three*
> We are soldiers, pride of our country!
> *One*, two, *three*
> That's all we ever want to be!

The pride of our country? Us? It was enough for a dog to bark and we were ready to vanish like birds from the trees. Or maybe I was wrong. Maybe singing with all our might made us not only forget how hungry we were but also gave us the strength which our ancestors had when they faced the Romans, Huns, Turks, Germans and so on. Maybe that was what you needed for war. You sang idiotic songs as loud as you could in order not to hear the whistle of bullets, death whizzing past your ears, not to see pieces of head, hands, legs and guts lying in the mud. You sang with all your breath, stepping over the corpses . . . After the war you returned home a hero. But this was peacetime, for God's sake!

Our last weeks of service were spent with stripes on our shoulders, ready to train the new recruits. The officers were less vigilant towards us and our nights were no longer disrupted by alarms. Instead they were filled with poker, backgammon, charades and other nocturnal jokes of all sorts.

Sewing the pyjamas of a sleeping soldier to the mattress and then shouting: 'ALAAAARM'! He tries to jump up, but can't and yells 'I'm paralysed! Mum! I'm paralysed.' Pouring water from one glass tumbler into another near some snoring soldier's ears, while you whisper 'Pee, my little darling, pee!' so that he pees in his sleep. And if he won't, then pouring water into his bed. 'Shit!' he shouts when he wakes, 'I peed myself again.' Jokes and pranks which proved how well-trained we were.

Oh yes, during the day we pretended to behave as they wanted us to behave. Yet, while the lieutenant sat up front by the driver on the way to the shooting ranges, we sang Gary Glitter's 'Rock and Roll' at the tops of our voices out of the back of the truck as we passed through the villages, in such good English that passers-by must have really wondered whether the Americans had not come at last. Yes, that's how much the Army changed us.

Anything can happen in life; and by the end of my time in the Army I was promoted to full corporal. All the others were sergeants, sergeant-majors or even sub-lieutenants. I did not mind. Napoleon, Hitler and Ceauşescu all started out as corporals, so I had nothing to worry about.

I was put in charge of the new conscripts, to train them in the art of Army tactics. We were on a mission. Behind some trees at the foot of the hill I gave the command:

'Soldiers! Uniforms off!'

You should have seen how scared they looked. They thought I was some sort of pervert; they had no idea in their little brains what I had in mind. Then, when I began to sing the joys of that beautiful summer's day, they finally twigged. We lay on the grass enjoying the sunshine with our uniforms rolled up under our heads. But as it happened, the major chanced to pass.

'What are you doing here?' he asked, so surprised that he forgot to shout at me.

'Allow me to report! We are drying our clothes after crossing the river in pursuit of the American enemy, sir!'

'River? What river? The only river I know is four kilometres away.'

'Allow me to report!' I continued, standing to attention in my green underpants. 'We were concentrating so hard on finding the enemy that we didn't notice we'd come so far, *sir*!'

That's how I got to be arrested for the third time.

The last day finally came. We filed out through the company gate while the lieutenant shook our hands, congratulating each of us on our individual achievements and advising us to be good patriots in future. When it was my turn, he looked deep into my eyes and asked with a smile if I now understood what the Army was all about.

'Yes, sir!' I told him almost reverently. 'The Army is something that you take in through your eyes, mouth, ears and all the pores of your body. You feel it deep in your guts for a year and then it goes out through your arse!'

And off I went, running through the gate to freedom.

I did not have the slightest idea what was waiting for me back home.

V

Filed Under Casanova

The first news I heard back home was that the university faculty at which I had enrolled no longer existed. It was a decision from on high, the dean told me, pointing his finger towards the ceiling, which meant 'talk to the First President about it, not me!'

By the early 1970s Ceauşescu's zeal for collecting more and more titles was in full ascendancy. His most recent accolade was First President – hitherto he, like his predecessor, had been merely General Secretary of State. Accordingly, he had himself pictured with an impressive sceptre for his new portraits. Even Salvador Dalí sent him a personal telegram of congratulation, which the editor of a national newspaper innocently published. But some near-genius must have found the means to explain to the Great Leader that such a thing could only be hugely ironic. When the penny dropped, the editor disappeared.

Not content with already being a symbol of world peace and founder of the Golden Age, Ceauşescu was now becoming an acknowledged expert in every field of human aspiration. He was the country's best architect – he appeared on TV pointing towards blocks of flats, poring over plans for some new city. He was father of all farmers – now he breaks open a cob in a cornfield. He was master engineer – with his hard hat in a steel works. He was a brilliant scientist, doctor of all doctors – in his long white coat he visits a hospital laboratory.

But the Great Teacher – not yet. So he started to reorganize the whole education system.

As a doctor in chemistry, Ceauşescu's wife was to be of great help in this matter. She had already begun to play an increasingly important political role. She had become a member of the Central Committee

Politburo, made up of the twenty-one most powerful people in the country. At the same time she was granted so many honorary doctorates from universities abroad that I could fill pages with their details.

But the truth was that neither Elena nor Nicolae liked teachers, whom they considered to be unproductive intellectuals. Yet someone had to sort them out.

So Nicolae and Elena took to this new task with such fervour and acuity that even Solomon would have been envious. They changed national curricula, educational textbooks, dates of terms, formats of exams, structures of universities and colleges, their places and profiles, even the shape of their buildings. Since both of them left school rather early in life, they must have acquired such skill from their parents: Nicolae from his father, a peasant farmer, and Elena from her father, a ploughman. And the more the rumours spread that they had no education, the more momentous were their decisions.

The Faculty of Romanian and English in my city became the Faculty of English and French overnight. If I still wished to become a teacher of Romanian, I would have to study somewhere in Maramures, one of the remotest areas in the north-west of the country. Otherwise I had to sit another entrance exam, for French, though I had never studied the language before.

The sleepless nights writing love letters in the Army were now followed by my assault on the language of Voltaire. But that wasn't what bothered me most. Nor did the fact that now I had an Army walk and a shaved head bother me much. After all, George and Cesar faced the same problem of readjusting to civilian life. No. What really worried me was that Aaron, the painter, had been taken away because of his beliefs on art, or so it seemed.

The role of art in Ceauşescu's new multilaterally-developed country was crystal clear: art should please everyone and be instantly accessible. A simplicity based on old traditions and the worker as hero were its primary themes.

A new movement emerged and spread quickly throughout the country. This was the so-called Cîntarea României (Hymn to Romania). It started as a competition between poets, actors and folk groups from different cities, who gathered to sing, dance and recite praises to our country and its leaders and to Mother Nature. Soon it became national, and every institution was dragged into it. Under its banner, all those people who had not yet realized their artistic potential were now encouraged to produce art. It was incredible how quickly the movement swallowed all TV, radio and live performances, all music, literature and cinema.

All over the country you could see sculptures of strong-armed workers with determined faces striding unsmiling towards a scrutinized horizon. The smile was left for paintings. When not portraying the wonderful life in factories, they showed idyllic images of the countryside. Clean, uncomplicated people were painting thousands of images of clean, uncomplicated people and that was what society was supposed to need.

Through art, people were to be retaught their traditions and their past, and also to revere the family unit. Women symbolized beauty and the fecundity of nature. Ceauşescu had banned abortion in 1966 and families were now strongly encouraged to have at least four children. You couldn't get contraceptives for love nor money anywhere in the country. In short, the more children around a table, the better the picture.

The awful banality and lack of real values of the new artists, spokesmen of the mass culture, became more frightening day by day. Aaron was one of the few who swam against the tide. That's why we loved him so much. Though at that time we had no idea he had depicted the Great Leader on one of his canvases.

It was strictly forbidden to paint the Great Leader without special permission to paint him, permission which came only after a thorough examination of your past, your parents' lives and the files of close relatives to ensure that none belonged to the 'bourgeois class'. But Aaron painted him regardless, and he did so in his own style.

Aaron's picture showed a hideous tree with skeletons instead of branches, death masks instead of leaves and bloody roots which reached into Ceauşescu's face instead of the earth. It was called 'The Roots of Evil'. Did Aaron start to work on it after Carlos's death? I still don't know. Securitate had somehow heard about its existence, and one night two men in dark blue suits came and took him away.

'We heard his screams as they dragged him down the stairs,' the two neighbours who played darts on his door with their knives later told us. 'He didn't leave any forwarding address. Anyway, it's not our business.'

Now Bacchus's attempts to lift our spirits seemed less effective than before.

'Come on Angels! The worst has passed. We are all students and this is the only time we can be the hub of the universe. Aaron will be back soon. The wide world is still our oyster, boys!'

Was it? My first year at the university hadn't ended and I was realizing just how wide our world really was.

Since I was proving to be a fairly good student, my parents decided to give me a present. Let's spend Christmas in Hungary together and see Budapest! Late that autumn we filled in the travel forms and sent them off. A few days after Christmas we received the answer: my parents could travel, but I couldn't. I went to the Passport Office to find out why. I stepped out briskly along the corridors, waited in one room for an hour or so, was sent elsewhere to wait again, then finally back to the first room, where a young official at last appeared.

'What can I do for you?'

I explained what he could do for me. All I needed was a passport.

'What for?'

What the hell did I need it for if not to travel abroad?

'Where abroad?' he asked, as if he hadn't looked through my application, which was sitting under his nose. I explained, obedient and patient within those dangerous walls.

'Fill in these forms and wait at home!' he rounded off.

That's just what I did. The winter passed. It was April when I went back to the Passport Office. There passed more wasted hours in airless waiting rooms, until finally another officer started in with the same questions as the one before.

'Fill in these forms and wait at home!' he said.

No way! This time they weren't going to have me! I was not going to leave the building until he gave me a straight answer, I told him. Why was I not allowed to travel abroad?

'Wait!' he said, then he left me alone.

You would need to hear that 'Wait!' to understand how bold I was at that age. Just one word, no more, but it was coming from the glowering face of a Passport Office Securitate man. That 'Wait!' didn't mean 'sit and relax while we sort out the paperwork'. It meant, 'You wait here, you little bug, while we thoroughly examine all you have said, heard, eaten and drunk since the day you were born. If you are clean, you'll have a passport.' For a second I thought about giving up the idea. No! I had nothing to hide. OK, I had my shortcomings. But I was not involved in politics. I considered myself clean enough to be able to travel.

Some time later a different officer came into the room. I remember clearly his puckered lips and the black wart on the tip of his nose.

'Let's see what kind of a man you are!' he said, as soon as he had made himself comfortable at the desk. Then he heaved a thick yellow dossier on to the table. Well, I knew that everyone in Romania had his own file in the cabinets of the secret police, but I never imagined they could have so much information on someone who was only twenty years of age.

'Oh, no, my friend! This isn't your complete file,' he said, reading my mind. 'But what I have here should do for the moment,' he continued with a smile.

He started leafing slowly through it. My heart sank. There was a whole novel there. All kinds of declarations, notes, statements given by kids at school, teachers, colleagues, neighbours, maybe even relatives; the officer never told me who had signed them. He read out fragments here and there, and while reading, his voice flat and impersonal, he tilted the pages slightly so I could see that certain phrases were underlined in red, others in yellow and still others in blue. Very patriotic, I thought, since these were the colours of our national flag.

Then came the questions. Dozens of them. Some ridiculous, some frightening. Hadn't I been told that there was nothing to learn from the yells of Western pop music? What did I think of my behaviour in the Army? Where did my jeans come from? Why had I laughed so much on I don't know what Saturday night in I don't know what restaurant? What was the joke? Who told it? What did I mean by going to the American Library? So what if the books were not translated? Couldn't I graduate without reading them? And by the way, what was my opinion of that dirty little Jew who hadn't even managed to graduate? What did I call him? . . . Oh, yes, Bacchus! And Aaron's paintings – what did I think of them?

My voice started to shake. And you know what? He took no interest in what I was saying. I was mumbling my words, confused and bewildered, while he was looking out of the window. He did not need my proffered reasons for such and such behaviour, nor any information I might chance to give him. His role was to pass a message on. And his message was clear: I was far from being clean in the eyes of Securitate. Whether that was because I dared to laugh too much or read foreign books or had dubious friends, it did not seem to matter. He did not bother to tell me if and when I was really in the wrong. But when the meeting ended, I left the room forgetting why I had come.

Back home, I had plenty of time to think, not so much about what he'd said but about what he'd meant. We, Securitate, will not disturb you if you do not disturb us. We, Securitate, know everything about you. And if you want a good salami, a room to live in and a bottle of vodka to keep you happy, that's OK with us. We will do our best to ensure that you live to be a hundred. But if you stray from the path we've laid for you, or if you pester us to go abroad, be sure we will take you to task. That was their basic message.

Well, it did not mean I was going to spend my student days hidden in a corner of my room, trembling in front of a mirror because of those bastards.

We Hell's Angels had promised ourselves a trip to the seaside that summer. But Bacchus was working for his finals, Cesar was having his appendix out, and as for Aaron – he didn't want to be a Hell's Angel any more. Four months spent in prison had been enough to change him. They said they found dollars in his Ivory Tower and an old icon which he supposedly had stolen from somewhere. All lies, of course. Back at home he hardly left his room and, full of suspicion, he evaded all mention of what had happened. He seemed to think that everybody was an informer and even suspected our own little group of harbouring a traitor. Me? George? Bacchus? Cesar? What did it matter? In Romania one person in three carried tales to Securitate. We were already five, weren't we?

So only George and I took the train to the beach. There we could meet Westerners.

The seaside was not the only place where you could see Westerners at that time. They sought out our Transylvanian or Moldavian villages in search of a well-preserved peasant way of life. Even now you can see houses with colourful decorations on the walls and ornamented pillars along roads where you can never drive fast – too many carts pulled by horses fluttering red ribbons on their halters and jingling their bells, too many cows, pigs and goats herded by peasants in white embroided clothes, looking as if they had walked out of the last century. Also, there were the small churches and monasteries of northern Moldavia, with their frescoes and icons and warm intimacy which was so different from the gigantic Western cathedrals.

For those in love with the mountains, there was Poiana Braşov with its ski resort, Sinaia with its castles and villas in which our kings used to spend their summer months, Bicaz Gorge with its high stone cliffs towering above, the spa resorts with their healthy natural curative springs, and the Danube Delta with its unique wildlife. But most foreigners liked best to congregate on the Black Sea coast.

It was not only Westerners who came to soak up the sun. In the early and mid-1970s the Black Sea coast was still used as a good meeting point for our Socialist neighbours. Girls from Poland and Czechoslovakia could meet their Norwegian, Danish and Italian lovers here. The East Germans met their relatives from West Germany, and the Russians met the French. Meanwhile, the eyes of the secret police were watching only the Romanian tourists, though at this time far less vigilantly than in the years to come.

During the day the hot sun tickled your skin and the warm water refreshed your body. At night the air was full of hormones – what better place for a romance? – though I imagine that most women who travelled from the West to the Black Sea Coast at that time had no idea as to what was really happening. Could the women ever really know how many hunters were just waiting for the smallest sign, ready to make their move? Hordes of men observed their every movement, gesture or flash of the eyes. It did not matter who or what or how she was. Short, long-legged, thin, blonde, maybe a cuddly brunette, eighteen or eighty, all were stalked by scores of men everywhere. The receptionist who gave her the bedroom key, the porter, the lift attendant, the waiter, the ice-cream salesman, the lifeguard, the passer-by who apparently did not notice her; all were smiling, and kind, and all were chasing the same thing. All were after a brief, ardent romance and then marriage.

For unmarried Romanian men the thought of finding a Western woman became an obsession. Why risk being shot or imprisoned trying to cross the border illegally? Why ask for emigration and then wait for years, when you could put on your best act for a few days, weeks, months? And then, if the act was good enough, there it was: your passport to freedom.

Among these wolves, people like me and George were 'dreamers'. We took our towels and went to the beach, to lie on our backs and let the sun soak into our rheumatic bodies. Of course we were constantly peeking at the girls around us, with their perilous nuances – we felt a mystical-erotic admiration for all those blondes and brunettes. A gesture, a word floating from a woman's lips and we were instantly transported into the world of dreams. Restlessly turning this way and that in the burning heat, we threw ourselves into the water to caress her, the girl of our dream, the girl born from the sea.

But we could not make love to a dream and, anyway, love is a shared experience, isn't it? She had to be real, a real woman. If we couldn't find her on the beach, where she'd come to enjoy life and have a little romance, then where?

The vulgarity of the wolves around us made us ashamed to appear to be like the others. But for all our different way of thinking, we too were caught in the same net of obsession with the West. We could not resist the Western woman's nonchalance, her lust for pleasure and the healthy image she conveyed when walking in the street, sunbathing or just drinking her coffee. Everything attracted us as irresistible hallmarks of our dream life in the West.

All we knew of life in the West came to us through rumours, other people's reports of banned foreign radio broadcasts, magazines read surreptitiously here and there, full of images of shining tourists in amazing cars and stylish clothes. Our own media assured us that our society was perfect and the West was on the edge of collapse. The reality we met on the Black Sea coast was the complete opposite.

'God doesn't exist,' they taught us in schools. 'Heaven is an invention of the powerful to keep poor people enslaved to the rich. The real heaven is our world,' they said, determined to eradicate the deep need for God inside every human being. But in reality, our world was so grey that young people moved God from a hypothetical non-existent heaven, and placed Him on earth, on this very planet – in the West.

Everything Western had a deity to it. Only there, in the West, we thought, could you find the goodness of the world, in the way that men think, behave and interact. And if I really wanted to meet a goddess, where else could she be found but in the West? Imagine it. We really believed that all you had to do to find perfection in this world was to get on a train and travel a few hundred miles!

I met Lynda, a Finnish girl, while George was in another resort trying to find a hotel where we could stay a few more days. We were going to be kicked out from our own hotel because some German visitors were coming. It did not matter that we had paid for two more weeks. That's how things were at that time: whenever foreign tourists came, the hotel director had the right to throw you out of your room. No apology was given.

One morning Lynda and I took a boat and rowed until the beach was a thin, grey thread stitching sea and sky together. I looked into her eyes and saw the light and waves reflected there. Then we kissed, our eyes closed. Later we sat on the rocks with foaming wavelets splashing our feet while we contemplated the setting sun. It was all so beautiful that I was falling in love with her.

'Let's go to a place that is not on any map,' I whispered. So that night we took a *marfar* high into the Carpathian mountains. There we spent the night in a cave, drinking vodka, singing 'She'll be coming round the mountain', and listening to the sounds of the forest. Just me, her and the stars.

Two days later we were back on the coast and meeting George.

'This is my best friend,' I told her, and she liked him. He liked her too. In fact, they liked each other so much that for the whole of the next day, neither of them was to be found. When we met up again things had become confused. George liked her, I liked her, she liked us. She did not want to choose between us and wanted to keep us both. In her country, she explained, this was perfectly normal, and we were barbarians if we did not take from life as much as we could. Barbarians or not, we were still not prepared to share her.

What were we to do? As we wandered about we came to a miniature crazy-golf park. George's face lit up.

'Follow me!' he shouted. 'I know what we have to do.' Lynda and I followed him and while we were getting our putters, he explained. George and I would play the round and the winner would be Lynda's exclusive boyfriend. She would keep the score. That excited her. We got started.

When we reached the last hole she announced the score: 'Dan sixty-two points, George sixty-two points!' I felt a thorn tearing at my heart. I knew it could not be true. I was way ahead on points. Lynda was obviously cheating! She was no longer my goddess of that night in the mountains.

We played our last strokes of the game. George was sweating and trembling as though the future of the whole world depended on his swing. He did well, but when my turn came I just thwacked the ball into the fence. I was fed up with that mini-game and with everything else.

We shook hands, seeming friendly enough, and George and Lynda disappeared. I was angry with George, though the feeling didn't last long. The elusive West was not going to split up our friendship.

It was 1975, my second university year, when the United States granted Romania 'Most Favored Nation' status. Margaret Thatcher paid us a visit and shared her thoughts on chemistry with Elena, and Harold Wilson also dropped in for a visit. We, the students, began to have hopes. The more important the people coming from the West the better. Surely they'd see how things were going inside the country.

My love for John Lennon had by then switched to Lord Byron. I was reciting his verses to all my girlfriends in the middle of the night. The walls of my college room were covered with English posters, of writers, Big Ben and Tower Bridge. My bookshelves were crammed with *Beowulf*, Keats, Galsworthy, Woolf, Joyce and Yeats. This fact didn't escape the vigilant eyes of Securitate.

Late one afternoon we were leaving the university when a car pulled up, tyres scorching the tarmac. A man in a blue suit got out, flashed an identity card in my face and told me to get into the car.

'What for?' I asked. 'I haven't done anything wrong.'

'Sure. Just a routine check. Will you follow me?'

'No, I will not,' I answered, my heart beating like hell.

It was one thing to go to them of my own free will and quite another to be taken there, just like that. As far as I knew they lifted people in the middle of the night when there were no witnesses about. Curious, my fellow-students gathered round and I took advantage of this. The first thought that came to my mind was to say no to whatever they asked, to escape the immediate danger and then vanish. I needed time to sort out the thoughts which were buzzing round my head. What had I done wrong and how much did they know of my wrongdoings? I needed time to think properly. I'd run away to the mountains of Hagota where they would never find me, I was thinking in an instant.

'Don't be foolish,' the blue-suited man said. 'We'd like you to give us some information about Corobana,' he continued. 'Don't waste my time. You were the last one to see him.'

So that was it! Corobana had been missing for several weeks from the university and hostel. It seemed that I was the last person to have talked with him. As this fact was already noted in the dean's papers, I had no reason to deny it.

I got into the car, although I was still confused, wondering why I had to go to Securitate headquarters to say what I knew and not to the police. Inside the car I recollected all that had happened before Corobana disappeared without trace.

It started of course where all bad things start: in a tavern. Ever since we found out that beer makes you fat we were downing beers every evening at the same tavern. That evening Corobana drank so much that when we left he started weaving about like the bull's pee so that at one point I propped him against a drainpipe and went to fetch a car to take us home. But on my return I could not find either Corobana or the drainpipe.

The next day and the days following Corobana did not turn up to classes. At that time there were big fights between gypsies and students around the town and there were even cases of boys and girls found with their heads cut off, the ultimate punishment for those who did not respect the laws of the gypsy gangs. The police were in the pocket of

Bulibaşa, the gypsy baron, and could not be relied on, so one morning a large group of us got together and went looking for Corobana in parks, taverns, housing estates, anywhere we possibly imagined he might be.

We found him with his head still square on his shoulders, sitting in a tavern next to an old blind man who was playing a ballad on a violin. Corobana laughed off our worries and declared that he had never before felt the meaning of life so deeply, all grace to the old blind man's ballad, a sad song, the essence of Romanian feeling. He had therefore decided to spend some time with that man, from whom he would learn much more about life and about himself than from the university, to which he had no intention of returning.

That's how Corobana was. A sentimental poet, while I was on the way to the most cynical period of my life.

I did not quite trust blind men. One time on a train, I was standing in the corridor, about to enter a compartment where a blind man was sitting on his own. I was watching him, pitying his world of infinite greyness, when I saw him tilt his head back, squeeze some drops into his eyes, look at his watch, then take up his white stick, ready to start begging. It was his way of earning a living. Not much of a one, he later confessed to me, since he shared his earnings with the policemen in the stations and ticket inspectors on the trains.

In a world where children dragged themselves along pretending to be crippled and men with white sticks pretended to be blind, no wonder I became cynical. But this was unfair to Corobana's old man. He really was blind, and when not playing the violin in the tavern he lived and worked in a place called *Arta Invalizilor*, a hostel and craft workshop for blind people. We went there with him and that's where I last saw Corobana.

In the car journey with the Securitate men I tried to prepare myself for what would follow. At Securitate headquarters, the young man in the blue suit took some papers from his briefcase and asked me to write about my last meeting with Corobana.

'Pay attention to anything that seemed unusual or strange to you,' he said. 'And write down anything that might be of any interest to us.' Then he winked, as though we had been friends for a long time. Or might become so. He was my age, I guess.

'Write it down, chum. Don't be shy.'

I started to write, trying to avoid anything that might compromise or endanger my friends.

In the blind man's co-operative, the men and women – all blind – worked together weaving baskets. What I found strange were the screens behind which they changed into their overalls so as not to be seen. Then during breaks the blind people played games. Their favourite seemed to be hiding things: a hammer, a scarf or the beret of the supervisor. I also noticed posters on the walls giving advice on safety at work. The biggest one said: WEAR PROTECTIVE GLASSES TO AVOID SHAVINGS HITTING YOUR EYES! This also seemed strange to me.

I wrote all this down in painstaking detail and signed the sheets. The young man gathered them up and left, not forgetting to pronounce that 'Wait!', now familiar to me. An hour or so passed, then the man with puckered lips and the wart on the tip of his nose entered the room.

'Aaah! Old friends!' He made as if surprised to see me. 'Still the joker?' he continued. 'A man who does not learn anything from his past? Well, well . . .'

Then he started bombarding me with questions, none with any link to Corobana. This time he did not have any dossier in front of him and seemed extremely interested in what I was saying.

'Why do you speak in English with your friends?'

'I'm a foreign-language student.'

'English is for inside the classroom, not outside, don't you know? And where did you get all those English books and magazines that you have?'

'From the British Library in Bucharest.'

'Aha! You admit going to the British Embassy, then?'

'I go to the British Library once a month. It's not the Embassy!'

'Much the same! Your parents work hard as good citizens and you blow their earnings on trips to Bucharest!'

'It's the only place I can find the works of Shelley and Milton.'

'Shelley and Milton . . . Both imperialist spies. They latch on to students like you and infiltrate our healthy culture. We'll sort them out, don't you worry.'

'They are dead, if you don't mind me saying so.'

'Are they? That's good! But we have information that you write letters to . . . What are their names? Let me check! Yes, Tom Stoppard and Harold Pinter. Are they dead too?'

'No . . . They are playwrights who . . .'

'Aha! So you admit to having contacts with foreign agencies, do you?'

'I'm trying to translate their plays into Romanian.'

'Translate them? Why? Do they write about the life of the proletariat? And why not translate our great writers into English? Don't you like our writers?'

'I like them but . . .'

'No buts here, comrade! We'll take care of that too, don't worry! Now, who is John Stedman? Tell us all you know about him.'

I did not know anything about him. I had never heard that name before.

'Are you sure?'

I was not. How could I be sure of anything in Securitate headquarters?

'OK, then . . . What about George and Lynda? I guess you know some things about that, right?'

I knew that Lynda had come back to Romania to see George again, but that was not my business – I was not in love with her any more. And anyway, why should I tell Securitate what I knew about it?

'You don't seem too co-operative!' the man with puckered lips observed. 'Very well . . . We'll bring you in again when the need arises. For the time being, good luck at the university! And study hard! Our country needs well-trained people.'

He then shook my hand and let me go, well-swaddled in the knowledge that I was constantly watched and could never tell how much they knew about my actions, words and innermost thoughts.

The officer didn't know how right he was about our country needing well-trained people. We would need as many doctors and engineers as we could find two years later, when Romania was devastated by an earthquake.

One March night in 1977, people everywhere rushed out of their homes as the earth began to shake. We gathered on open ground near the stadium, most of us still in our night clothes. Some were holding flickering candles in trembling hands; some were in tears, their children huddled round them; others were silent with shock. But we were among the lucky ones. Dozens of new blocks of flats, poorly built almost overnight to fulfil the demands of the Five Year Plan, collapsed like playing cards. Thousands of people were crushed to death. Bucharest, to the south, was hardest hit. And it was like an omen.

About that time, things began to change for the worse in Romania. It became clear to everybody except Ceauşescu and his wife, of course, who were taken up with their travels abroad to collect interminable honours and degrees, that the country was plunging into economic chaos.

For us students it was not the deterioration of food in the canteen, which began to resemble that of the Army, nor the lack of heat in the hostels or other shortages that concerned us most. It was the moral degradation of the country that we were helplessly witnessing; the way people were being brainwashed into indifference, the general deterioration which they accepted as normal.

While the country was regressing at breathtaking speed, all you could see and hear on the mass media was how poor our past was in comparison with our brilliant future, how abundant were our harvests, how productive our factories, how happy our workers.

Most people shrugged their shoulders, accepting it all the same way that they accepted floods and earthquakes. You work for a lifetime to build up a home, then in one night the waters break over you and wash it all away. What can you do? But that attitude made my blood boil. I did not expect widespread revolts; there were too many informers, the secret police were everywhere, not everyone is born to be a martyr. But at least people could have appeared less cheerful at the compulsory mass meetings held every Sunday throughout the year.

These mass meetings were huge demonstrations of patriotism, with carefully choreographed participants performing a sinister ballet. During them, a hundred thousand people would glorify the achievements of Ceauşescu's state. There were thousands of posters, pictures, costumes, flags and bunting; floats decked out with flags, tribunes with silk awnings in red, yellow and blue; red carpets unrolling before the smiling portrait of our leader, as tall as a building.

Yes, there was a time when people could still have put a brake on the galloping madness by simply not rushing to obey with such eagerness. People were scared, of course, that they might lose their jobs if they didn't participate at those demonstrations. But did they have to smile and look so happy as well? Nobody asked you to send letters of thanks to the leader. So why were there hundreds of thousands of them?

People were concerned only with what was going on under their noses, and shrugged their shoulders as the country at large sank into moral indolence. Those who had always thought about things – teachers, scientists, philosophers – seemed now to stop thinking. The Big Lie became institutionalized, part of the unassailable normality.

Why did our Big Lie not face a strong underground opposition, as in Poland or Czechoslovakia? Maybe because fear was stronger in Romania than elsewhere. After all, Romania was already on its way to becoming the most dictatorial country in Eastern Europe. It was not an open dictatorship, but a much more subtle and insidious one. On the surface, we were given certain liberties: not much, but enough to make the system even more powerful and efficient.

Our 'Latin island surrounded by a Slavic sea', as Romania is called, was the only country in Eastern Europe which had no Western neighbour at its borders. And Communism wasn't imposed on a Viennese civilization, as it had been in Hungary, but on people who had suffered a history of oriental despotism. We remained a peasant society, agrarian people who now lived in block of flats but still had the sentimental and obedient mentality of our ancestors. From the days that the Romans occupied our land the name 'Romanian' had a deprecating sense, that of a peasant tied to the land.

One day you would see workmen digging up a road. Surveyors would be measuring, engineers shouting their commands, workers breaking up the asphalt, everyone working hard. The next day, you would see steamrollers flattening the asphalt, and the new road would be ready as quick as you could wink an eye.

A month later a new lot of engineers and workers would start in on the same bit of road. The road plan had been completed, but they had forgotten to lay the water pipes. So again they would dig, excavate, drill, bore and put the asphalt back. Then along came other teams.

Something was wrong with the electricity cables underneath. Now huge piles of earth lined the same avenue which was reported finished the year before. It's just life 'as normal'.

Three blocks of flats were put up overnight in the middle of the city. They were tall enough, wide enough and standing proud in a triangle, just as on the plans. Then they realized that they couldn't get the crane out of the building site. So they pulled the first block down and built another one in another shape overnight for everything to be 'normal'.

'Two load and two unload' was a saying current at this time about how work was done everywhere. It seemed funny, but it was painful if you thought about it.

As part of this 'normal' life actors in my city made coffins, as nobody came to the plays approved by the censors. The income from the coffins was reported by the Director to have come from the sale of tickets for performances of brilliant plays.

This kind of absurdity was rich material for writers. One story described a percussionist in the city orchestra who was suspended because a visiting Party official noticed in a performance of Beethoven's Ninth Symphony that he hit the tympani too hard. Could he not be a bit more careful with state property? Eventually the director had to replace the symphony with a traditional folk song. No one knew if the story was true or not. Reality was becoming stranger than fiction.

And nature itself went by the board. One late autumn Ceauşescu announced he would pay a short visit to our neighbouring city. He'd baptized it 'the City of Spring', and its mayor was very proud of that, but what would the Great Leader make of trees with naked branches or yellow-red leaves? What to do, what to do? The whole district was in despair. Then the mayor came up with an answer. For days you could see men, women and children perched in the trees, sewing leaves to branches and spraying them with fresh green paint. Part of normality. Ceauşescu was so pleased by his visit.

'LONG LIVE COMRADE CEAUŞESCU!', 'FACTS NOT WORDS!' Every morning on my way to lectures I saw these signs hanging over the main entrance of the meat factory. At the end of the night shift, rows of labourers, civil servants and engineers queued in front of the gate for the usual checks before leaving. Women left through the women's gate, men through the men's gate, as the porters searched everybody and everything. Bags, sacks, purses, waists, breasts, bottoms and legs all went under the scrutiny of their big palms. Where is the beefsteak? Where could it be? . . . Hey, you! Stop there! What's that down your trousers? Guards, surround him! . . . Let me see! Wow! Excuse me! It is not our meat. Keep it like that for a hundred years, boy! Next!

Such searching was normal, be it at the meat factory, at the doors of the department stores, at the exits of the libraries. There was too much stealing going on everywhere. The state's goods had to be protected. Just as normal were the cats and dogs wrapped with fresh meat and trained to jump over the back fence of the factory and wait further down the street, where they could be stripped of their loads and sent home.

To lift bits and pieces from the state, which takes everything from you anyway, is not stealing but 'short-term borrowing'. Everyone seems to accept the idea. That's life. Is the chemical plant drenching the town in thick smog every afternoon, so that people are coughing like mad in the streets, their eyes wet with toxins? The Five Year Plan has to be fulfilled, the factory chimneys' filters have to be imported from the West, they are too expensive, we have to meet our foreign debt repayments. The buses carrying people-sardines from one station to another have long cylinders of methane on their roofs – just one of the new inventions to reduce petrol consumption. What's that? They explode from time to time? Well, what can you do? Make a joke about buses with real bombs on top and shrug your shoulders. After all, there are accidents everywhere; our TV is always reporting catastrophes in the West. This was the only news coverage we ever got from outside, except when our leader was receiving his titles.

Are waiters playing football with the meatballs in restaurant kitchens, then putting the meat on the plate and serving it to the customer? What can you do? The waiters have connections with Securitate, do you dare to complain? Anyway, nobody obliges you to eat in a restaurant; you could drink beer, it's so cheap and foamy. Do they put soap powder in it to make the foam even bigger? Come on mate, you won't die of it, they've proved scientifically that you have to drink more than ten pints before you'll puke it all up on the fence near the restaurant.

If you are really squeamish, why don't you drink milk? What milk? The milk you find in the shops, produced under the Five Year Plan, just a little thicker than water, but not much. Did anybody complain that the bottle had no cap when you bought it? Be serious, man! There are more important things in life. Ceauşescu is being given flowers by groups of child-pioneers: the thorns of the roses have to be removed, the stems disinfected and cellophane-wrapped. Who's got time to worry about the milk?

We students had our exams to think about; our minds were supposed to be focused on higher things. But our teachers indulged themselves in formulae and arid distinctions; we had to write down their phrases like parrots. The teachers were more concerned about our presence in the compulsory patriotic field-labour squads than with the real pursuit of knowledge. They recited endless political speeches, while the boys were sleeping with their eyes open and the girls were ingratiatingly nodding their heads. 'Ye-e-e-es, ye-e-e-es,' their looks said. 'You are right dear teacher, look how well we understand what you say. Our foreheads almost hit the benches, we so approve and understand.' From Socrates to Marx, all I was taught to remember after one whole year of this spinach-cabbage philosophy course was that some philosophers were dialectical materialists – they were the good ones – while the others were idealists and were useless. Diogenes was masturbating in the main square; Epicurus, who talked about happiness but in the idealistic manner, was vomiting twice a day; Nietzsche went mad. What more could we expect from idealists?

Wanting to know more of the great minds of the past, I began to spend more and more time studying on my own. What I was discovering from the Rig-Vedas, Plato or Hegel, Erich Fromm or Alvin Toffler told a different story. I found my refuge in the world of literature. I really immersed myself in it. This wasn't the literature taught in the university, of course.

I remember how we gathered round the French teacher when she returned from Paris. 'What is Montparnasse like?' we asked. 'Full of filthy hippies slouching over their easels. They make you sick,' she answered. 'What does Baudelaire's tomb look like?' She did not know. 'What's in the Musée d'Art Moderne?' She hadn't gone there. She did not like modern art. 'Tell us about the Louvre.' She hadn't had time to visit it. She only had time for the market-place where she had bought that gadget for peeling carrots. That was all she had brought from Paris to show us.

The literature I was discovering in the library was recycled in long talks with like-minded friends in taverns and coffee houses. Marcel Proust came up with the steam from our little cups of coffee; Camus drifted in the smoke of our cigarettes. Plum brandy brought Oscar Wilde to sit with us – complete with quips – and we were drinking wine with André Gide. Overstimulated by these talks, I came home at night and wrote letters. Dozens of them written to living people, dead ones, to things and ideas. Endless letters.

I wrote to Unamuno, Sartre, and Salinger. I wrote to Hemingway, asking him why was he so awful to Scott Fitzgerald, to Countess Walewska telling her what I thought of Napoleon, to Romeo and Juliet assuring them that Shakespeare had killed them at the right age, to Poe. I wrote to Quasimodo, to ask how much I resembled him: me always with my obsessions, either too thin, too young, too old or too ugly to be loved as I wanted to be. All during the hours of night. It seemed I was the last in the city to go to sleep.

My friends were right. A doctor could cure me of any illness but the night. And I still believe that the moon, white, yellow, grey, red, shy, jealous, tired or full of passion, is the only one who really understands the shadows around my eyes.

When I was not writing letters I was making plans for my next weeks and months. 'If not now, then when? If not me, then who?' was written on my wall to make me write more. I wrote short stories, essays and plays. Some I started and left at page three, others I finished and read to the university literary circle, of which I eventually became president. I knew full well that my works would not be published. I never talked about the happy Romanian workers. But the words on the wall encouraged me to read more. I read books, poems, newspapers, foreign magazines, anything I could get hold of. With what veneration I stored away some issues of the *Sunday Times Magazine*, three or four years old, just near Orwell's *Animal Farm* on the bottom of my bookshelf! Well hidden, I thought. Or were they?

I was kidding myself that Securitate did not know what I had in my room or what I said to people after I had had a bit of vodka. They summoned me time and time again. Did they torture me? Did they stub their cigarettes out on my skin, as they did to others? Not a bit. Was it because of my uncle, that high-placed person in the Central Committee? I do not know. All I know is the mental torture I suffered at the time.

They put more or less the same kind of questions each time, curious to know everything about me, my colleagues and teachers, Romanians and foreigners. Especially foreigners.

'Write it down! Anything you know about Rod.'

Rod Wheeler. He was the lecturer in Modern English Literature, sent by the British Council to teach at our university. Our one and only joy. Girls almost fainted when he entered the classroom, as he threw the register away, put his arse on the teacher's desk, asked us to sit on the floor and started talking about Robert Frost. He had a beard and long hair.

All the boys in our class had beards and long hair. Mine was the longest of all. As a student, I thought I would be free at last to wear it as I wanted, though it seemed many people could not sleep because of my hair. Neighbours, teachers, relatives. As for my parents, best not to mention their torments. Oh my God! Their only child. Look at him! . . . What a bad future he will have! . . . Not entirely sane, by all accounts! Looks like a hippie. And all because of my hair.

'I'm not complaining,' my mother frequently told me. 'But think what other people are saying about you . . . about us!'

That was it! It was important to look like everyone else. If I looked different, it was dangerous. For me, for them, for everybody. I tried to explain. It was not a question of fashion but of attitude, I told my parents; it was the symbol of my inner freedom. Not to mention that it made me look like a Westerner. Little they understood, though. Years of trouble, a sea of tears from my mother's eyes.

Rod always smiled when I talked about my fight to keep my hair long. He gave me advice. I was his best Romanian friend, or so he said. How could I tell Securitate what we talked about in his kitchen with the taps turned full on? Me scared of being sent to prison; him scared of being refused permission to marry the Romanian girl he was in love with, and later married.

'Yes, we admit he is a good teacher. But haven't you noticed the way he tries to influence you?'

I did not notice what Securitate prompted me to see. One day the police lifted Rod and me from the street and took us to the police station for a haircut. They let us go only when they realized who he was. We wrote a letter of complaint and sent it to Bucharest. I told Securitate that this had been *my* idea, not his. They did not like that. In fact they never liked whatever I wrote down. Once, an officer tore up my 'explanation paper' – that's what they called it – right under my nose.

'I called you here to give me real facts, not to pull my leg!' he shouted at me.

Another time, they made me write the same declaration in two ways: first using small letters, the second time using capitals. I guess they were checking whether my hand didn't shake while repeating the same version of my story in a different style. My hand didn't shake, but they still didn't like what I was writing. And they had doubts about my future.

'You still go to restaurants with black students. Do you really feel any affinity with them?'

Not especially. Later I almost hated them for the way they swept up our girls with their dollars. But when the first groups of black students came to my city, it was painful to see how people gathered round them. They came from Kenya, Ghana, the Congos to learn Romanian before studying medicine at our universities. There were also Arabs from Iraq or Qatar, but they were lucky: their lighter skins didn't attract so much attention. When the black students went into the street, hordes of children followed behind, old women pointed long fingers, laughing or making the sign of the cross. I felt so ashamed of my fellow countrymen. I had to convince these foreign students we were not all savages. And the Germans visiting our country, surrounded by teenagers asking for blue-jeans and chewing-gum, what did they think about us? Wasn't I right to tell them we studied Goethe here in Romania?

'My, my! What a patriot you are,' one officer told me. 'You

almost make me weep! And since you are such a good Romanian, tell us what you know about John Stedman!'

'I swear to you I don't have a clue who the hell he is.'

Did I sound genuine? Did they realize that I was not so dangerous after all – that they could let me be for a while? Then, in my final year, they struck a new note with me.

It was the year of Ceauşescu's sixtieth birthday. A grand book of homage was published and for weeks the TV was full of him and his wife. Ceauşescu attended a gala reception at the American White House, and had a trip down Whitehall in the British Queen's royal coach; the couple were so pleased to receive Her Majesty's gifts and hospitality. Mrs Thatcher again praised the personality of Our Man, who had lunch at Number Ten; and there was a reception at Westminster Palace. Every little detail of this trip was reported in our newspapers and TV. It was about this time that I met the infamous Securitate officer Major Doroş.

Major Doroş was the chief officer in charge of all students' files. Years later I would discover that colleagues, friends, girls whom I had made love with, people I knew and some I did not, teachers, Army commanders, Securitate officers, all had signed the bottom of each report on me, before handing it over to him. Even today, I only have to think of his swarthy, brooding, thick-set face and I instinctively look over my shoulder.

There were many rumours about Doroş. In his own outfit he was all-powerful. It was said that he carried out executions himself, with his bare hands. Nobody dared question or defy him. He was so commonly featured in black jokes that when he appeared in front of me I was in no doubt as to who he was.

He first led me into his room with its comfortable leather armchairs, surprisingly courteous. He gave me a glass of whisky and out of the blue started talking about a brilliant future for me. He had looked through my file, he said, and realized I was a bit eccentric, a bit naive, maybe, too inclined to see the good in people. That was probably why I had so many friends everywhere, he confided, patting my shoulder. Then he told me what good citizens my parents were; he talked about my uncle, my Hungarian name and my mother's descent from

Vlad the Impaler. Remember! Your illustrious ancestor sacrificed his life to free our land of foreign domination!

By the way – how was my Hungarian? And what did I think about our bad Hungarians? Not all of them, of course, but those who wanted to hand over Transylvania to the Huns. 'With your knowledge of Hungarian and good family background you could be of great service to our country.'

Then he told me about the passport he could obtain for me if . . . A wonderful improvement in my social life if . . .

To cut it short, he wanted me to be an informer. This was not the first time I had realized they wanted me as an informer, though I never understood why were they so keen on me. Was it because I had so many friends in every walk of life? Was it because I never talked with my colleagues about the meetings I had with Securitate, so that Securitate thought I might join them? Anyway, they had never been as blunt with me as they were being now.

How was I to answer Major Doroş? To utter a definite no was a frightening prospect. To say yes was equally scary. I immediately expressed my gratitude – but 'I have problems with my drinking,' I confessed. 'Half the time I can't keep my big mouth shut. I'm sure I'd blow it.'

'Blow it? Blow what? You Casanova, you . . . little joker,' he patted my shoulder again 'Think about it anyway!'

I thought about it all right. They knew everything about me, even every detail of my love life, it seemed.

I was still thinking of Iolanda when Felicia appeared in my life. Felicia had big black eyes, and her skin seemed to turn to fire when I touched her. What a pleasure to hear her say 'I love you', a warm shiver running through my body from the root of my hair to the tips of my fingers. When I was eighteen she stayed the whole night with me, my jaw trembling with the fear of doing it wrong, and hip, hip, hooray! She made me a man. I could not sleep, for caressing her body and worrying all the time whether she had enough blankets.

A few days later a pain started there, in the lower part of my body. At first I thought it was normal, what you felt when you become a man.

But no, the pain grew worse and soon it started to drip. I had to face it, I had a venereal disease. So off I went to the hospital, burning with anger and shame, watching the nurses giggle as the doctor injected me. Nobody would believe that this could happen the first time.

You feel sickened after an experience like that; I started drinking more beer with the boys. Beer is cleansing and time is passing; sunny days come again, you are cured and again feel the call of love.

Veronica was thin and delicate. Her palm quivered when resting in my hand. She had a heart disease, and I felt strong and ready to protect her from the wicked world which so mocks the weak. She was fragile, and yet not like the others, who always say no when you tell them to live life to the full. Veronica was more than ready to say yes to life. She went with me to Eminescu's statue, where I poured out my heart's philosophy, opening her eyes to a world where one and one is not always two – there are other spaces and times, my darling. I gave her books with notes in the margins, told her about Penelope who waited for ever, and Tristan, faithful to the end.

Youth is full of stupid mistakes. When Arabs first appeared in our university it was obvious that my true love was about to leave me. I had poetry, but they had the money. I had love, a kind of continuous delirium, but Veronica had other plans. One evening I saw her in the arms of an Arab, kissing him passionately. When she saw me, she lowered her eyes and tried to explain. To explain what? She'd found the other worlds I'd spoken of, with their Kent cigarettes, and whisky, and Alfa Romeos.

Back to beer, then, and the jokes of my colleagues.

Thinking of George and Lynda, I tried the seaside again. In the morning light, lying on the beach, the girls looked soft, a little bit curious, full of sun. In the evening they were predatory birds. I tried my chances in the discos, chewing gum, my collar turned up like the others, pretending I was a foreigner. I remember once I asked an angel sitting at a table if she would like to dance, in my best English.

'Why not?' she answered ethereally in English, morning stars in her eyes.

'Where are you from?' I asked her while we were dancing together.

She was superb. She was glued to my body, we were one. I felt her heart pounding through her T-shirt.

'From Romania,' she whispered. 'And you?'

'Me too,' I answered. I couldn't lie any more. I was already in love with her. She moved away from my body. Her eyes dulled, her heart went back inside her T-shirt, she stood stiff and apart. The song ended. When I asked her for the next dance she turned her back. Vanished.

Mary came into my life just as I thought I might become a confirmed woman-hater. I was discovering Shakespeare at the time. I was on my way from the library to my room, with a great pile of books in my arms. I looked deadly serious. Lost in my world. Mary reminded me of Iolanda; I noticed her in passing but pretended not to. No girls in my life any more! *Richard III* was on my mind, but she was so pretty. And so full of life.

Life was exactly what her body was shouting for. From her toes to her long black curly hair. '*Te iubesc!*' (I love you) she said with a lisp, through the small gap between her front teeth.

'Daniel, girls with a gap between their front teeth are harlots,' Veremia, a white-haired man in our class, was telling me.

At twenty-one, Veremia was the only one of us to have had an affair with a married woman. He had plenty of bed stories to tell. One morning her sailor husband came home unexpectedly to find them in his bed, somewhere on the tenth floor, with nowhere to run, nowhere to hide.

'Sit down, my boy! Don't be afraid! I know that my wife is the guilty one, not you. Let's have a talk. Woman, bring the *ţuica*!' And the sailor husband started drinking with Veremia.

At dawn they were almost crying on each other's shoulders. Just before he left, the sailor asked a small favour of Veremia. He did not like bearded men, and wondered whether he could shave his new friend. He took out his cut-throat razor. The student was short and thin; the sailor was a mountain with tattoos on his arms. He started to shave Veremia, slowly, without shaving cream, as real men shave at sea. Then he let him leave. From that day on, Veremia had white hair, and became obsessed with unexplained mysteries of the world: flying saucers, Easter Island, Mexican airfields and the bizarre world of insects.

Girls did not understand Veremia and he was a difficult boy to be with. But in the end he met a thin lady, who excited him because she had a dark wart in the middle of her forehead. It made him think of India, with its fakirs and submissive women. They were happy together until she started to clean his room while he was out drinking coffee and talking with the boys about the Bermuda Triangle. She scrubbed the floor, wiped the pencilled lines off the walls and killed all the spiders, including Mitica, the one Veremia had his eye on. The lines on the wall were the spider's pathways and he was studying its journeys in relation to the moon's volcanic eruptions and Bach's violin partitas. Veremia did not strangle her when he returned, but from that time he became convinced a woman was incapable of understanding the depth of man's thought. He laughed like a drain at my eternal search for love.

What did he know about it? Mary became a woman with me, and only the two of us knew. When she graduated from college we kissed in the middle of the street for everyone to see.

'I decided to get rid of it!' she told me.

She wasn't talking about the *Bacalaureat*, but about our child. She never asked me what I thought, and I instantly felt like Veremia must have felt when he found out about what his girlfriend had done to his spider, Mitica. We quarrelled and fought like they do in Italian movies until people came out of their houses. Next day she went to Bucharest to visit a fifty-year-old university teacher whose private lessons were famous. I never saw her again.

Then Lina came along. She was a pessimist, her head always hanging down: 'What is the point of living?' I felt the need to awaken her lust for life and set to work slowly, with patience, grain after grain, as Romanian countrymen feed up their turkeys. I took her everywhere to discover the joy of nature. What Bacchus had taught us, I taught her. Every night I came home exhausted. It was a useless fight with her mind. The doctors finally diagnosed schizophrenia, an illness which had started when she was a child, maybe from the time when her mother used to tie her to a chair in the middle of the room and leave the doors and windows open so that the draught should punish her stubbornness.

I could do nothing to help, but still I continued to visit her in hospital, upset that we were unable to communicate.

I began to envy my colleagues. They were so practical and optimistic in their adventures, while the girls I fell for always seemed to have problems. Why was I so drawn to the weak? Why this desire to be a saviour? Even with animals, I never cuddled flourishing pets, but took vagabond mutts home with me after midnight, to feed and talk to in my room.

Mona seemed like a godsend. She had no weak heart, no wet palms, no pains in her liver; and she knew how to put the boys in their place. In a Latin society where life is extrovert and boys whistle after girls in the street, you had to know how to handle yourself to keep your cool and not get laughed at. That was what I first admired in Mona.

At the beginning of each university year, the girls were forced to see a gynaecologist who checked whether they were pregnant. The doctor loved to tease the blushing girls, asking them all sorts of embarrassing questions. He would write down the girls' answers to his questions and pass them on to guys interested in a girl's past. One day, he asked Mona how she had lost her virginity.

Coming down a mountain on her skis, her legs had started to open. And they opened and opened until SMACK! She crashed straight into a tree-stump. That was when it happened, she answered. Mona was that kind of girl.

Mona's eyes sparkled when we sat drinking, talking about Malraux and Camus, me rubbing my leg against her leg under the table. The evening was warm and I suggested we walk in the park, going where nobody could see us, to kiss until our lips hurt. She let me prop her against a tree trunk and we did it there, at the foot of a tree which might have reminded her of her stump. She made real noises.

Later that night, a whole group of us, boys and girls, came to that tree to pay homage. Finally, we decided to sleep in its branches. It was a big chestnut tree with plenty of room, so we stayed there till the rain came.

The next day, my tonsils hurt. It was not the greatest pain of my life, agreed. But three months later, I had suicidal thoughts as I watching helplessly while my pride was larded with all sorts of creams. The doctors concluded I had a kind of vegetation, a wart on my penis with its root somewhere deep inside the channel and only its tip peeping out into the light. It drove me crazy.

Twice a week I had to sit on a white shiny metal shield while the doctor cauterized the wart with a kind of whistling biro, blood spurting on to his white coat. It had no effect.

The next day the monster just appeared again. So I went back on the shield with the whistling biro, trying not to yell. I was so ashamed.

Six months later, it had still not disappeared. God only knew how I was to be cured. Doctors, nurses, old women and old men looked at my lower part, giving advice, herbal remedies, exorcizing techniques and new cauterizing methods. I really began to wonder whether anything would remain of my pride. Eventually the doctors fixed on the idea of cutting it open, just a bit, to take out the root of the wart. So off I went to hospital, after writing to Freud that I was going to kill myself if I lost my best friend.

I did not have to. But it was there in the hospital, during the operation and afterwards, when I had to pee down a tube coming from me, that I learned about the reality of physical pain. It was like the pain Romanian girls must feel when they insert a plastic tube into their cervix to make the foetus abort, an imprisonable offence.

The doctors assured me that everything was fine, but my friends joked that the end of my sex life was in sight. Like any imbalance in the human system, illness provokes a crisis in the mind. For a time I lost interest in philosophy and *belles lettres*. My all-consuming urge was for sex. Sex at all times.

My poetic vision of romantic love had brought me nothing but disappointment and venereal disease. The diseases were cured, and so was my romantic outlook, now replaced with the advice of my friends. 'Do it now, Dan, before it's too late.' I took them at their word. And that's how I came to be known as Casanova on my Securitate file.

It wasn't difficult to have sexual adventures in Romania. The fear of Aids did not exist, the other venereal diseases were curable. And, after all, with life as it was, what else was there to do?

But soon there were other matters to concern me. I was in the final stage of my university career; a dissertation on Saul Bellow took up all my time. At that time we could still find Bellow's books in the American library. That very same year Bellow visited our country; his third wife had been born in Romania. But soon after he published his critical impressions of Romania in his novel, *The Dean's December*, Bellow became an 'enemy of our people'. He was removed from the academic syllabus. It was just my luck to become an expert in a subject which no longer existed.

VI

Enough is enough

Finally, I became a teacher. Commuting daily twenty miles north of my city, I was carrying out my duty to the country. That was the law: after graduating, most students had to do three compulsory years in a village school specified by the authorities. In my case the village was not far away from my home in Băcau, though sometimes twenty miles in Romania could feel like the distance between a city and the end of the world.

Each morning at six o'clock I had to face the same madness at the railway station.

First, we gather on the platform to find out whether there's a train that day, and if so, when? I crane my neck to read the announcement panel, an auger in the swarming crowd. Round me, all sorts of creatures weave, twist, turn, shove, push, appear and disappear, leaving their stench behind. Ah! There is a train today! Good! I can buy my ticket. I hold my breath and enter the eddy towards the ticket hall. In the hall, other people jostle, gesticulate, clamour, elbow and finally harangue an official behind a ticket window, grey with spit upon dried spit.

'Make it quick, miss! The train is here!'

Through the holes in the perspex, Miss is mumbling her answer, something about not having ten hands. A second of silence follows as the men fall into melancholy. A woman with ten hands! Just enough so that two can be spared continuously to caress their temples. What an image! But the train is tooting at the platform. Men start yelling: he who yells loudest is the first to be served. Soon, everyone is flooding out of the booking hall, cramming and pushing, surging on to the platform, and thence on to the train. No one feels disposed to make space for anyone else.

'Please, you lady with the child, after you!' No question of that. Everyone is in such a rush, you'd think it was the last train of his life. We bump and knock, one against the other, then weave between bags and cases, demijohns, parcels and the forest of legs. Make room for yourself, grit your teeth and push, one-two-three! Hopla! Shoulder forward, squeeze, thrust your elbow into a fat belly, step on a foot nearby, pinch the skin in front of you, ram, one-two-three! Hopla!

If you are lucky you reach a compartment. If not, there is room in the corridor, standing on your toes in the space between the carriages, in the small toilet. The timid ones are left behind, with hands hooked around the stepping rail, one foot on the running board, one in the air. *Crrr! Poc! Crrr! Poc!* . . . The train starts moving at last.

The rails clatter, people shake, the town is left behind. Inside we are like sardines and only our heads have room enough to jerk up and down, up and down while the train moves slowly onward, slower than a bike. You feel it would be better to jump out of the window, if only you could reach it.

Finally, the train stops at the village station. Sometimes the doors don't open, maybe for fear that all the sardines might tumble out together. Other times they open uselessly since, caught somewhere in the middle of a corridor, I have no way of getting out. A hundred times I vowed never again to use a train but then, what else could I do? I had no car; my parents had one but petrol was rationed. The monthly quota was exactly the amount we needed to get to and from Hagota once a season, so the car was up on blocks, washed and cleaned every Sunday by my father.

I could have gone by bus and did so now and then. This was a different kind of hell, especially in the summer.

There is a hot sun burning down, and a human bunch of grapes is running across the street towards the bus coming over the horizon. What number is it? Shit! It's the wrong one. The bunch of grapes deflates, returns to the pavement. The peasants and gypsies cluster round – women with long dirty skirts, men with puke on their trousers. They shout, scream at each other, spit, swear, press against you. Your stomach is turning upside down. But hooray! The right bus is coming.

The bunch of grapes rushes into the street again. Some fall down, those behind jump over them. The driver finally manages to get the door open; the bunch contracts, the juice flows into the bus.

Inside, there's no room to throw a needle. You are pickled, crushed, squashed. All sweat, your tongue is aflame, melting your fillings as the bus rumbles down the road. The driver is yawning. His tonsils appear in the mirror above his head, and finally you end the journey by cursing your mum that she ever brought you into this world.

It was better to hitch-hike, which brings us to another story. You could stand for ages on a road leading out of town, jerking your thumb up and down. The lorry drivers already knew our faces, impoverished teachers who paid under the odds for the journey. Small cars did not bother to stop either.

For a time I carried a placard. 'I'M A SHITTY TEACHER BUT I PAY WELL!' It seemed to have some effect; lorry drivers stopped more often. They let me into the cab and the same conversation began each day. 'How much you earn a month?' they asked. I always answered with the truth. 'But that's what I get in a week. You know that?' Yes, I knew. That was just another thing which got me all hot under the collar before they dropped me at the school gates.

It seemed I had punished my brains for nothing at the university. And now, even if I wanted to be a driver, it was just not possible. If you refused to do the three years' teaching, you had to pay back the state for your schooling, which no one could afford.

So I had to go through with it, day in, day out, leaving my house at five to start the working day at eight. For the first time I really envied Cesar. He was an engineer – not like Bacchus, George and me, all teachers now.

Cesar had a job in Electroputere Power Station, just ten minutes from his home. He was dead keen to make a real career of it, though he was starting to have his doubts.

After several months he was still clocking in at seven in the morning and leaving at four in the afternoon, spending his entire day doing nothing. Nobody told him what he was supposed to be doing, so eventually he went to the Director.

'I didn't come here to waste my time. I want to do something constructive for our country. I'm highly skilled, but you don't seem to have any use for me.'

'Don't we?' the Director pondered. 'Well, let me examine your file and I'll call you as soon as possible.'

Cesar was patient for a month then tried again.

'I specialized in energy technology, and I have some good ideas for improving electricity supplies . . .' he began.

The Director cut him short.

'Let me see . . . I'll give you a week to check the street lighting on Estacada Avenue! Some bulbs are faulty there. Would you count them please and make a thorough report?'

It was not exactly what Cesar was waiting for, but nevertheless, he did his survey.

'Well now, I see you are good at it,' the Director told him at their next meeting. 'So could you go and count the faulty bulbs on May 1st Street? You'll notice this one is longer than Estacada, so I'll give you two weeks to make a thorough report.'

Things went on like this until Cesar resolved to make a formal protest at the next *Sedinta*.

Sedinta. A magical Romanian word. It means 'Management and Staff General Meeting'.

You went out to buy some bread at midday and found the department store closed. '*Sedinta*' was posted in the window. You went to a restaurant, to gulp a beer. The doors were closed, '*Sedinta*' stared out at you. Your tooth is aching like hell, you rush to the emergency dentist. The dentist is not there; '*Sedinta*' is written on the door. You arrive at the ticket office: two minutes before the train leaves they shut the ticket window, there's a long queue. *Sedinta*! You drive past rippling cornfields at harvest time but no one is out there. Where are the farmers, the workers, you may ask. 'At *Sedinta*,' the field answers.

Once a week, sometimes once a day, every factory, farm, shop, every school suspended its activity for an hour or two. Why did time stop so? It was *Sedinta*, when all workers, team leaders and directors met to chew over and affirm the latest political handouts and circulars. It was like a religious meeting, reading from Party documents instead of the Bible.

Cesar's meeting fell due. Chief engineers, sub-directors, staff were talking passionately about computers and other new technology they needed for the plant. Cesar was just waiting for his moment; he was going to tell them exactly what he thought about those light-bulb reports. Suddenly the Director stuck his head round the door and shouted:

'Tomorrow everybody will report to 23 August Farm to water the fields. Everybody to bring their own mug!'

The engineers at once put away their ideas on new technology and went to spread the news to the workers.

It was normal for patriotic labour activities to take precedence over any other work. It did not matter that it was late autumn and the sky was full of rain-clouds. The next day, in pouring rain, busloads of workers crowded round the gate of the farm, each one carrying a mug in his hand and quarrelling with the farm manager, who did not want anyone to trample across his fields with their watering order from the Director. It took Cesar quite a while to understand that there was little use for his skills in a work culture where everything was imposed from above, the directors blind apostles of a mad God. The Old Testament had been replaced by the New Five Year Plan, and the words of Ceauşescu became the nation's Bible.

On the face of it you might think that Cesar had more reason to envy me, or Bacchus, or George for that matter. At least we were able to apply our skills in the classroom. But to teach what? And when?

Three out of the four seasons each year were taken up with political celebrations. Spring was the time when the infamous 'Hymn to Romania' began, that huge national competition in which cities, towns and villages with all their factories, enterprises, farms, hospitals and schools had to compete in reciting poems, dancing and singing songs of praise to 'the most beloved man' who had now become 'the incarnation of the highest aspirations of all Romanians'. We teachers had to drop the curriculum to train the children for their part in this crazy hullabaloo.

Then came the Great National Festivity days, like Ceauşescu's birthday, Women's Day – which soon became Elena's Day – First of May, the Day of Liberation . . . for which we had to make children learn still more poems and songs on the theme. In autumn, the compulsory patriotic labour began. Whether we liked it or not, we teachers had to drop the curriculum yet again, take the children out into the fields and set them harvesting until the sun went down.

The only time you could get any serious teaching done was in the winter months, when travelling was at best uncertain. And then there came the winters when we could not commute any more. The horrific winters of the 1980s. Bacchus was lucky. He escaped them.

Bacchus became a teacher of philosophy. A very serious one. If you saw him in his black suit and red tie you'd never guess he was once the same crazy eternal student I told you about. There was no impassioned talk about love, no wild notions of making a crusade to Don Quixote's tomb any more. Now he talked rarely, and always chose his words carefully. It nearly drove me mad. One day, in the secondary school where he taught Marxism, an important teachers' meeting took place. The village mayor and some city inspectors were present. The Director was in mid-flow, praising Bacchus for his good behaviour, when Bacchus suddenly stood up and interrupted the proceedings. He politely asked the Director to keep quiet until he got back from the loo.

'I'm going to have a long pee and don't want to miss your pearls,' he told him. All the others sat there with their mouths open.

Bacchus never came back. Later, I found out that he had arranged with a lorry driver to hide him in a truck delivering clothes to Turkey, where Bacchus already had some friends waiting for him. He entered the truck one night, soon after it was loaded but before it was sealed by the clothing factory inspectors – fearsome, tough men, though open to a bribe if it was high and trusty enough. It needed guts to sit hidden there, surrounded by boxes, jackets and overcoats, for three days, to keep your breathing quiet when you cross the border, drinking water from your can and shitting where you were, all along Romania's roads and then Bulgaria's much smoother ones. It was risky, it's true, but not as risky as trying to hide in the holds of a ship to reach Turkey by sea. Too many people were denounced by the very ones who had taken their money; there were too many rumours of people thrown into our warm Black Sea. You couldn't trust sailors. Veremia's experience had already convinced me of this.

And hiding in a lorry was less risky than attempting to go by train, squashed in the small space between the ceiling and the roof, hidden under the benches or outside, tied to the underframe between the wheels. Sealed lorries were less often searched, and so here was the small chance, small though it was, for those with real guts. People would hide in lorries carrying furniture to France, Norway or Sweden; they hid in refrigerating containers, wrapped in meat destined to become German pet food, until they reached Hungary. They hid between eggs, properly sealed, those eggs which were used for making shampoo. Some succeeded, like several members of Phoenix, big pop stars in Romania who fled hidden in their own loudspeakers, to rise from their ashes in Belgium later. Many did not make it.

Bacchus was lucky. He finally arrived in Tel Aviv, more dead than alive, I heard, but with enough life left to send ecstatic postcards to me.

'I'm in the free world! Fly to me!' was written on the first of many. Completely insane. As if he didn't know what awaited me once Securitate had read them. Of course, Securitate wouldn't put me in prison because of his bloody postcards. They were added to my growing file in Securitate's cabinets. They let me receive them, hardly interfering with the text – occasionally a mark here and there, to let me know that they were watching. But what really interested them was not so much who received correspondence from abroad, but in how you responded.

Bacchus was always ending with 'Write to me as soon as you can!' Maybe he had chosen to forget just how things were in Romania. I didn't mind that much. What really hurt me was that he had said nothing about his plans. Not a whisper. As though I might be an informer.

Bacchus was the first of the Hell's Angels to get out of Romania. At the time of his escape we were only just embarking on our decade of horror.

In the early 1980s, Ceauşescu suddenly discovered that the world's energy resources were limited.

Romania itself was never short of petrol, oil, coal or wood, though it seemed that these were always destined for other countries rather than for us. Before the Second World War, big American, French and English companies bought our oil for peanuts; during the war, the Germans took it for free, and after the war the Russians continued the tradition, even during the time when Ceaușescu seemed to turn his back on the Soviet Union.

On the international stage, Ceaușescu struck an anti-Soviet attitude. That made a good impression on the West. At home, hidden pipes under the sea and long trains of tankers were secretly carrying our oil to the big, bottomless belly of the Soviet empire. That kept the Russians happy. Let this little man talk against us. It's good for the West to believe we have a voice of discontent within our Communist puppet satellites.

But at home, as the leader of the Party, the Army and the secret police, with all ministers reporting directly to him, Ceaușescu could finally put his Stalinist views into practice. At home, the media talked only of how rotten the West was. All we saw of the West were its natural and unnatural disasters and its reckless attitude towards the world's energy resources. Ceaușescu was keen to contrast life in the West with life in Romania, thus showing Romania as a marvellous and unique example of how things should be done.

'If the West can't see the danger of its irresponsible energy policies, let it suffer the consequences. I have to look after Romania, the future Switzerland of Europe,' the President announced at the end of one of his televised speeches. The country's mayors, local Party leaders, dignitaries and deputies loyally stood up and passionately applauded.

Back in their leather armchairs in spacious offices, the country's leaders set about putting the President's views into practice. They turned off the lights.

Some mayors and district Party officials thought it was enough to turn off half the city's neon lighting. Some switched off even more. And the rest were sure that a city needed illumination only above restaurants, cinemas and supermarkets. Within a couple of years, while the West was reportedly heading for collapse, my country was striding towards a brilliant future which had no need of artificial light.

It was not enough. Ceaușescu felt that his people's response was insufficiently serious minded. A further order from on high decreed that henceforth just one street lamp every three hundred yards was quite enough to prevent passers-by from bumping into obstacles – like unlit lamp posts. Because in private homes only one 40-watt light bulb was permitted per room, at night you could see small groups of men gazing skyward, looking for law breakers. The Militia and civilian patrols were authorized to enter any home where there was suspected misuse of light bulbs.

For anyone who insisted on using an electric iron or washing machine, oven, heater or a radio while eating, electricity bills were so high that no ordinary person could afford them. Soon people went back to the old traditional methods which worked without a plug: washing by hand, cooking on the hearth, pressing your trousers with irons heated in the fire. Instead of listening to music, people sang.

And it did not stop there. All institutions, factories, collective farms, hospitals, schools, places of entertainment and every office in the city had to reduce its power consumption first to 70 per cent, then 60, then 50 and less.

The President was still not satisfied. Inside the country, he continued to appropriate palace after palace. Former museums became his properties; he tried all manner of kingly beds but still he could not find his sleep. He had to do something big, something monumental, something that would amaze everybody. So in 1984 he began building *Casa Poporuli* (the House of The People) an immense white concrete and marble structure brooding over Bucharest. It was to be the largest building in the world, with more than a thousand rooms, including sixty-four great halls. Built in French neo-classical style it rose for twelve floors on a man-made hill, like a giant wedding cake. Below ground were other floors, ending with a huge anti-nuclear bunker at the very bottom.

To raise that Mussolini-style abomination, a dozen churches, three monasteries, two synagogues, the remains of two palaces and seven thousand people's homes, not to mention parks, gardens and hostels, were demolished. Within months, the bulldozers had flattened the most beautiful sites in Bucharest. Thousands of workers, master craftsmen and architects combined their talents to create that building. It was meant to dwarf people and inspire fear. A glimpse of it was enough to chill your blood.

After the events of 1989, a BBC reporter got special permission to enter this building, and he took me along as his interpreter. We saw its unfinished marble pillars, the gold inlaid ceilings, and the enormous crystal chandeliers. When lit, the building would consume in one hour a quarter of Bucharest's electricity for the day. From the presidential balcony we looked out over the 'Boulevard of Socialism,' an avenue that is exactly a metre wider than the Champs Elysées in Paris. The boulevard opened into a square with room enough for 300,000 people to come together and celebrate our leader.

But still the President was not content. He wanted a great river to flow through the city. Vienna and Budapest were on the Danube, so why not Bucharest? The Danube was maybe fifty kilometres away, but isn't the Dîmbovita a tributary of the Danube? So Ceauşescu would have the Dîmbovita diverted through the heart of Bucharest. The city was riven with bulldozers.

Paying off our debts was already one of Ceauşescu's main concerns. North Korea had no foreign debts, so why should we? Now exports were boosted, and imports were cut completely. Was Romania second only to Britain in European sheep farming? It was indeed, but towards the middle of the 1980s you could find no meat in the shops, be it sheep, cattle or pig. And when some scraggy chickens appeared, people queued for ages. There were queues for bread, potatoes, eggs, soap, paper. Queues everywhere and for everything became another part of 'normality'.

Still, the President could not find his sleep.

'People in this country eat and drink too much,' he declared in one of his interminable Five Year Plan speeches. The fat politicians and leaders, half drunk and half asleep, staggered to their feet and started applauding in a frenzy.

The decrees on how much, how often and for how long a Romanian should eat followed soon after. Food rationing was part of everyday life in a time of war; and weren't we as a Socialist country in a Cold War with the West? Six eggs, half a kilo of flour, half a litre of oil, half a kilo of salt and a quarter of sugar, a kilo of beef and two of potatoes were more than enough to feed a person per month. The Central Committee immediately approved the quota.

And still the President didn't sleep any better. To become 'the new Switzerland of Europe', he decided, Romania had to reduce its petrol consumption forthwith. At a time when TV broadcasts were reduced to two hours a day – after all, Ceauşescu had to keep an eye on it, and his time was of the essence – petrol was rationed to twenty litres a month and driving was banned on Sundays. And then driving was banned on Saturdays as well.

And still the flood of decrees did not abate. Each month brought new waves; there were so many new laws and decrees that no one could keep up. No one understood anything any more. To end the confusion, driving was banned completely during winter, and large areas of the cities were subject to unannounced power cuts of indefinite duration.

You would be reading a book or mending a torn shirt when suddenly the lights went out. Outside was just an ocean of darkness – pitch black in the room inside. You might be at the theatre: Othello can't find his hands, Desdemona survives. Or in a cinema perhaps: the bombardment of Stalingrad ends in a groan, an uncensored kiss dissolves into night. You get your candle out and wait. How did the movie end?

By the light of candles, architects drew the wrong lines on plans for a new block of flats, engineers calculated wrong numbers, directors approved the wrong plans. A new ten-storey block of flats appeared in the city, perfect in every respect, except that the block had no entrance staircase. Knock it down and start again, but this time there's no ventilation in the toilets.

Factories, hospitals, railway stations, restaurants: everything was plunged into darkness. As you watched the shy light of candles begin to flicker here and there, you knew there was nothing to be done. Your plans were now in ruins.

Did you want to take a bath by candlelight? Well, you can't; at least not if you wanted it wet. The water supply was interrupted as well. Hot water was limited first to two hours a day, then to two hours every two days, then once a week. In my city everyone had their bath on Thursdays. Then it became chaotic. The water supply, hot or cold, was no longer subject to any rationale. It just came when it came.

Back home, covered in grime, I rush to the bathroom, turn the tap on and *Trrrst*! ... *Pleoc*! ... *Trrrst*! Nothing but gurgling from the pipe: no water to wash my hands or teeth. Shit! And there's real shit in the toilet bowl; it has to dry there till next morning. Hell! No toilet roll; cover the shit with the newspaper! The queue in the shop for toilet paper was just too big. And I'm thirsty and it's late: everything's shut, closed by decree. Shops, restaurants, any place where you could buy a bottle of mineral water shut their doors at nine p.m., to be sure they are empty by ten as the law now requires. I have to hike over to my parents' place. They are more careful than me, they always save their water in jars.

At my parents' place, people had already sunk water pumps between the block of flats. You could see men, women and children filling their pails and then climbing slowly to the tenth floor. No one dared use the lifts, of course. Once the power was cut you could be stuck for hours – and it was dark as a coffin in there, unless you had a candle. But with all the candles in restaurants, candles in cinemas, candles in the hands of passers-by, there were soon no more candles to be had.

So people sat in the dark doing nothing. And when you do nothing, you think. Darkness became subversive. Questions were raised. Even directors, managers and mayors dared to complain. Because public transport had been reduced to half, then a quarter, there were no commuters any longer: people were coming in to work late or not at all. In factories, sudden interruptions of power caused machine tools and instruments to break down daily. How could we be expected to fulfil the Five Year Plan?

The complaints sent to the capital made the President furious. Those who were not capable of understanding their country's vital interests were thrown out of office. They were replaced by others who were keen to report the incredible achievements of their outfit. 'This year, our factory has achieved 120 per cent of its target.' 'Japan is still ahead of us, it's true! But in two years time our car industry will have closed the gap, our word on it!' 'Now our agricultural productivity has reached 400 per cent . . .'

That's the sort of things the papers I used in the toilet had in them. All lies of course, but without them, the paper could not have been published at all. The headlines used to shout at me from the bowl.

As greater and greater achievements were reported upwards from the provinces to the centre, so plans for still greater attainment were issued from the centre downwards. It happened like this. As soon as Ceaușescu and his wife achieved absolute power, they surrounded themselves with relatives and idiots, cronies who in turn chose other relatives and idiots to carry out their orders. The whole social pyramid became a huge waterfall of lies, pouring down on the heads of ordinary folk. There was nothing left for us but fear and the lie. It entered our life. You could not survive without it.

I remember a timber factory in my city whose machinery had broken down. So the director had sent two-thirds of the workers home. Yet this director continued to report to the centre that everything was OK; output each month was up 20 per cent on the previous month, the quality of the planks was much improved.

But one day Ceauşescu himself decided to visit the factory, to offer a little of his good advice. For among all the other things our great leader could do, he was also an expert in woodcraft.

Panic hit the factory. Then, overnight, things were miraculously sorted out. When Ceauşescu arrived all the workers were in place, bent over noisy machine-tools on busy production lines. Engineers were drawing non-existent plans, workers were carrying long, planed boards from one hall to another; everyone seemed happy and bursting with confidence as the presidential couple examined the well-polished timber, praising the manager for the lack of dust and giving a few additional tips on how to surpass this impressive work. 'I want your factory to be the best in the country and all the other factories of Romania to follow your excellent example,' Ceauşescu said, before leaving.

Two hours after the Ceauşescus' departure, a fleet of trucks arrived to transport the wood and tools back to the timber factory in Comăneşti where they belonged, thirty miles down the road. Workers streamed out of the gates, homeward bound or making for the nearest tavern, to swig a few beers and bet on the director's next fantasy percentage.

'Next month we'll top the plan with 25 per cent. *Noroc*! Have another beer!'

'I bet on 30 per cent, comrade! *Noroc*!'

Things were like that more or less everywhere. You might think it was funny. In reality, it was a dreadful disaster.

In a few years Romania had become the most backward country in Europe.

Foreign tourists were discouraged. They asked too many questions, they took too many pictures, they proffered too many suggestions; this was not what Ceauşescu needed to help him sleep. They might turn sweet dreams into nightmares, those Westerners. Men with two faces, you can't trust them. Years before, Jimmy Carter had been so pleased to shake hands with Ceauşescu. But then, the Americans had started a crusade to win human rights for our religious minorities.

What do they mean, the Helsinki Treaty is not respected in Romania? Rubbish. Ceauşescu is giving his people the most basic human right – the right to work. The rest is just Western propaganda. Instead of reading Ceauşescu's brilliant books, reprinted by serious Western publishing houses such as Robert Maxwell's Pergamon Press, the West read books by dissidents like Virgil Tanase and Paul Goma, both banned, beaten, arrested and exiled to France. France was also where the Romanian playwright Eugène Ionesco, father of the Theatre of Absurd, and the Romanian thinker Emil Cioran, lived in exile.

Did Securitate bungle an attempt to kill Paul Goma in Paris? Why so much fuss? Any secret police in the world has its failures. In 1978 Pacepa, the head of Securitate, fled to the US after which Ceauşescu had to restructure the whole of the secret police. His former colleague talked about the family parties, Ceauşescu's obsessions and habits, all of which he published later in his book *Red Horizons*. But he was a traitor. Why should the West listen to his lies?

How dare the West put its nose in our *borsch*? So, a whole army was trained up to put a stop to the intruders. Not suddenly and officially, but subtly and efficiently. Customs officers kept Western tourists waiting for days, checking and double-checking. Receptionists suddenly had no rooms in their hotels, or if they had, the price was exorbitant and to be paid in dollars. Waiters treated foreign customers like public enemies, Militia men watched them with frowning eyes. In the seaside or mountain resorts, restaurants and hotel bars were closed for the night at ten o'clock sharp. There was no music, no dancing, no lights. Just drunkards staggering along, with bottles in their pockets.

Even in the streets, tourists were studiously avoided. It wasn't that we, the ordinary people, didn't like them any more. Far from it. But there was a decree in force according to which you had to report any conversation with a foreigner within twenty-four hours, no matter what it was. You pointed out the public conveniences? You had to report it to the police. And why did you presume to tell them this, then?

Is that a foreign tourist on the street? We would hide in shop doorways. Even those visitors who were eager to visit our beautiful mountains had to give up their quest. They met everywhere the same look, the same grimaces, the same nervous gestures. In the buses, row upon row of resigned worn faces. There was no chat any more. None at all.

I don't know how much the catastrophic drop in living standards had changed people's mentality, but it was certainly enough to change the way they walked in public. With heads bent towards the pavement and hesitant steps, people walked with the gait typical of a thinking man now forced not to think.

Now that foreign tourists in Romania had become rarer than toilet paper, Ceauşescu was beginning to sleep well at nights. Everything in Romania was perfect. Romania was left splendidly alone. The Western democracies turned their faces away; Russia ignored us. And the unbearable winters began.

We shivered with cold in our blocks of flats. The heating was turned off whenever the air temperature was above ten degrees. But it seldom was above ten degrees – even the weather reports were lies. But we were the lucky ones in the bosom of our families. In state orphanages, children abandoned by mothers denied abortions clawed at blankets in unlit dormitories.

In hospitals, things became horrific. Most major drugs were thrown into the export drive, leaving hospitals criminally undersupplied. Doctors were systematically bribed. Scores of young people were infected with hepatitis B from unsterilized needles. While swelling voices sang ever-new praises of the leader, 'Our greatest national treasure, for our homeland's sake you must live forever,' babies died in their incubators when the power was cut. Patients died on operating tables. Microbes fed on life-saving serums in thawing refrigerators; donated blood supplies rotted.

The worse things became, the more vigilant were the secret police. They had eyes and ears everywhere. Whenever I rang a friend, I could feel a third ear listening in – there would be a tell-tale echo, a click or a cough. Men or women who became too strident in the queues were lifted out and taken away to somewhere nobody really wanted to know about.

I remember a story which circulated in my town, about two sisters who met to celebrate New Year's Eve together, just the two of them, hidden inside the walls of the flat.

'How are you, my dear?' they started their chat.

'As always, sickened by Ceauşescu,' the other one replied.

A week later, the woman was summoned by Securitate. She was asked to stay in a room and wait for five hours, then she was told to go home. No reason was given as to why she had been called. Then, a week later, she was called again. The same story. Then called again, nights and days. She cried and fell on to her knees, but they were silent. After a month they finally told her: 'We hope your sickness is over now.'

I don't know how true that story was, or who started it. But rumours like that had their effect. They shut the mouths of any discontent. If you were convicted of a 'subversive' act, your parents, children, brothers, sisters, wife and in-laws would all be punished, according to the gravity of your 'crime'. This was a clever piece of state terrorism, as most Romanians, good or bad, are deeply sentimental folk.

There were undoubtedly some few brave souls who openly refused to go along with it all. And there was no shortage of others who, their hearts fired up with dirt-cheap vodka, said 'To hell with this stinking life! I don't give a damn what they'll do to me. I'll fight.' But in the cold light of dawn your strength ebbs away as you think of the misery that you'll visit upon those you love.

Fear gripped our hearts from early in the morning to last thing at night. And the examples of Hungary in 1956, of Prague in 1968, of the crushing of Solidarity in 1981 constantly underlined the universal threat: keep quiet and be good or the Russian tanks will arrive.

After 1944, Romania had to pay 'war compensation' to the Soviet Union though we ended the war fighting with the Russians against the Germans. Whole factories were dismantled and carried to the USSR. Cows, cattle and horses were taken away as payment for the armistice.

Our mineral resources took the same route. The Russians also took Bassarabia, Bucovina and Moldova to form part of their new country.

The Russians drained us economically. But what people remembered most vividly was how the Russian soldiers behaved as liberators. The inhuman treatment of prisoners of war, the rapes, the looting and stealing. As liberators, the Russian soldiers behaved worse than the Germans in occupation. People could not forget that.

My dreary, fraught days in the schoolroom had passed into years. Winter had come round again, and now all traffic was banned. Trains still came now and then, but you had no way of getting on them. There were no cars, no lorries, no taxis, no ambulances, not a single bus in or out of town. All motorized travel was prohibited – due to weather conditions, they said. That's why there were no traffic accidents for three months in Romania – the only truth ever reported by our country to the media abroad.

I had to choose between getting to school on foot or renting a room in the village. Eventually I took a room with old Tamba, the French teacher, who was a drunkard. Tamba's house stood halfway between the school and a tavern, but that didn't stop him bringing his tipple into school. He would put the bottles under his desk, where they clinked when he moved his feet. Sometimes, he had to prop himself up on the blackboard while teaching. The children laughed at him. I did not.

Tamba was our symbol of the general depression. When no one was around, he'd grab my arm and whisper furiously in my ear: 'Don't kid yourself, young man! We are victims, no doubt about that. Every last one of us! Most of all we teachers. And there's no way out. Not here in this Socialist shit-heap and not under capitalism either. I should know. I've lived through them both!'

After school I sat with Tamba in the village tavern, warming our bodies and brains. I looked around at the locals with sinking heart. Where was the proud, courageous, land-loving peasant I had read about in books? Where was the man who featured in my grandpa's stories?

In the old days, Romanian villagers had many feast days – weddings, saint's days, Sunday and birthday parties. There were days to celebrate the joys of spring and the depths of winter; there were thanksgivings for Mother Nature's bounty. People in the countryside lived for them. When a celebration started it lasted for three days and three nights; that was the custom of every village. They would kill a pig, and then eat, drink, dance the *Hora* and care about nothing but having a good time.

But the new centralized laws now threatened the peasants with starvation. City bureaucrats came knocking on doors, demanding ever more drastic quotas. People had to slaughter the family cow, the last pig, the last goat. And the old traditions were banned. Even Christmas and Easter were cancelled and proscribed. Rather than proud, bold countrymen I now found men too tired to fight for riches that would never be theirs. On their faces, I could see a deep, ineradicable hurt. These men and women had sent their kids to us. We were their last hope now that life on the land was all but defunct.

'Don't kill yourself with the kids,' Tamba was telling me between brandies. 'No one is going to put up a statue to you. For the money we are paid it's not worth waking up in the morning. What are we, we teachers? Gendarmes with pens instead of guns, with our hands and feet roped to the desk. Did you give your kids low marks? You are publicly criticized in *Sedinta*. You give them A's? They fool around and jump on your head. What power do we have? To award gold stars to those who lug their empty bottles to the school collections, and that's it. I wouldn't be surprised if the little monsters started throwing stones at us.'

The children did not throw stones at us yet. In winter they trudged three miles each way, struggling against deep snow and biting winds to find their place on small, hard, narrow benches where they waited with wide eyes for our words.

They were good children, sitting shivering in the classrooms with their calloused little hands clutching the unwieldy pens. How could I have sat there, cynical and careless at the teacher's desk, while the children laboured to memorize and recite so many empty, pointless things?

My job was to teach these children English. They did not know how to count or read too well; their minds were already stuffed with patriotic poems. English was what they needed most!

And yet, I brought my guitar and played some songs, John Lennon here and there. We pored over old English magazines together and the walls of my classroom slowly began to fill with images of that wonderful Western world.

This was what offended the authorities most. The village mayor – a former tractor driver – had the right to enter my classes whenever he liked, to check the quality of my teaching. He didn't like my 'imperialist' approach and threatened to report me to the centre. I defied him. As soon as the winter was over, school inspectors started turning up. First, they banned my posters with their pictures of English castles. 'Put up images of our own beautiful country instead and write short English texts beneath them,' they ordered.

Next they directed me to stick to the textbook. No more foreign magazines. So what if we were only looking at a face in a picture? It was obvious that the magazine hadn't been printed in Romania. I bit my tongue over that!

Then they forbade me to play English songs.

'But I am a teacher of English, for God's sake!'

'All right! If you really want the kids to sing, play Romanian folk songs translated into English! But you are supposed to be teaching a language, not music!'

Then even my role as an English teacher was put in question.

Ceauşescu himself doubted whether foreign languages should be part of the curriculum. His minions were quick on the uptake. The Minister of Education, Suzana Gîdea, appeared on TV with an important announcement for teachers.

'The curriculum has to be altered . . . As for foreign languages, are they so important in our lives? Allow me to set an example. I am your Minister of Education and I don't know a word of any foreign language,' she said proudly.

Since I was so good at music, they gave me music classes to teach as well. 'The children love you?' they asked me, accusingly. 'Good! You can teach chemistry as well.' A few months later, I got physics too.

The following spring a new law appeared. The village needed its doctors, engineers and teachers. They were too often late at work; things could not go on like that any more. Henceforth, anybody who worked in a village had to live there. Commuting was prohibited.

The mayor called me in – I was going to school by bike at that time – and, smiling, gave me a paper to sign. It was a kind of indefinite leave to remain in his village. There was a new identity card on the way, stating that I was a permanent citizen in that place. They had to be joking! Soon I'd have to apply for a passport to get back to my own city. Of course, I refused to sign.

'You'll not be allowed to teach any more!' he threatened.

'So be it.'

In fact, that law was barely put into practice before my teaching career in any case came to an end.

A few nights after my meeting with the village mayor, I heard the door buzzer go. I was back in my city, in my small bachelor flat on the tenth floor. At first I thought it was one of my friends. We used to pay each other late-night visits, never ringing first as we knew the phones were bugged.

I opened the door. Two young men in blue suits flashed their identity cards in front of my nose and pushed me backwards into the room. I watched speechless as they went through my drawers: throwing everything out, tapping on the floor and walls, leafing through books, magazines, newspapers. Finally they found my writings.

'Where is the stuff about biscuits?'

'What biscuits?'

'Ah! You pretend you don't know! Come with us!'

I went. What else could I do? I hadn't had a brush with Securitate for quite a while. What was it all about? Was it the biscuit manuscript? No, not possible. Was it because I had refused to move to the village? Ah! The turkey farm visit – that was it. Or so I thought.

A while back, Ceaușescu had visited a turkey farm a few miles from my school. They loaded us all, teachers and children, on to a tractor trailer and took us to our allocated position on the presidential route. We found our place, carefully marked out with chalk, and for six hours, we rehearsed our appreciation of the president. At last the real cavalcade came into sight. Everybody started cheering, applauding, waving flowers and shouting 'Long Live Comrade Ceaușescu!' At least, everybody did except for me and my band of kids.

To tell the truth, we thought it was just another practice. The President couldn't have noticed that we didn't wave – the car swept past at speed. But I had noticed a man taking notes.

My interrogation began at three o'clock in the morning, in a room with clean, white walls and a table and chair in the middle. I sat on the chair, the other two kept walking round me and the table.

'So, you insist you don't know who John Stedman is . . .' the blond officer began, showing me a typed sheet of paper.

'Recognize this letter?'

He put it in front of my eyes, so close that I could not see anything. When I managed to read it I finally realized who John Stedman was.

There was nothing to worry about. John Stedman had just been someone who wanted to exchange ideas on literature, and had put his name in the penpals column of an American writers' magazine that I had found in the American Library. I answered his ad and he replied. That was all there was to it. I felt a wave of relief.

'Ah! So, you finally admit knowing him. Answer!'

'May I tell you that . . .'

'Shut up! You answer yes or no to my questions.' The officer bellowed as if I was deaf.

'Yes, but . . .'

'No buts! Do you admit to having links with this man or not?'

'Yes and no . . . I mean . . .'

'Shut up! Yes or no to my questions! Answer!'

I became confused.

'You don't know what to answer, eh? . . . Do you want *me* to answer instead? You want some help?'

'I don't . . .'

'Shut your mouth! Answer my questions, nothing else! What organization is Stedman involved in? What is your role in it? Tell us now what you know, and we might make life easier for you. Answer! Speak, or I'll show you what the Devil looks like!'

I kept silent. I did not know what to answer; neither did I want to find out what the Devil looked like. My confusion mounted. Then the officer held John Stedman's letter up to the light bulb so that I could see through the paper.

'What's this? Explain yourself!'

Behind the typed words were the faded traces of a watermark. It was watermarked paper, nothing else. I tried to explain. The officers were not convinced.

'Do you pretend there's no organization involved here? Do you think we are stupid?'

And before I could answer, the overhead light was switched off. In a second, the beam of the table lamp was focused on my face. It was like in the old movies, when the Germans interrogated spies.

'Answer, you bastard! I heard them yelling at me.

'Where is the typewriter? What did you write in the hotel? . . . Where are the papers on biscuits? What's this connection with Bacchus? Who went with you to the American Library? Answer! Don't lie! Don't hide anything! We know everything about you!'

Have you ever been interrogated with a lamp shining on your face? I can tell you, no matter how tired you are and how poor your memory, when the lamp is burning before your eyes and fear reaches its peak, you have moments when you remember everything. But the thoughts spin so quickly and in such detail that your brain refuses to clear. You get stuck on one small thing. My mind was fixed on the typewriter decree promulgated a few months before.

To have a private typewriter you needed special permission, which was obtained from Securitate. Once it was granted you were required to give a monthly report, providing pages typed on your machine and a synopsis of what you had typed during the previous month. Renting or lending your typewriter out was strictly forbidden. I didn't have a typewriter permit, but my father did.

My father had broken the law by letting me type my writings on his machine. I was typing a novel on which I had been working for eight years, a couple of plays and some short stories written in the hope that one day a miracle would happen.

Maybe nobody would ever have found out about this if I hadn't received a letter from an editor who lived in the vicinity of the town of Piatra Neamţ, who was keen to publish a short story of mine. Let me tell you what happened that day.

I had been glad that this editor was not part of any of the literary circles of my own city. These circles were full of informers and arse-licker writers who made me feel sick. At that time, Bacău was proud to have its own 'dissident' writer, Calistrat Costin, who 'dared' to attack the life of a Communist activist family. But many of us suspected that

Costin was one of those dissidents who wrote with the blessing of the secret police: that he was collaborating with Securitate, informing them of what was said during the heated discussions around his circle. While those caught in his net were picked up and interrogated, Costin was spending time in Belgium, France and Italy.

I hoped this editor was not that type of man. And my short story did not have a political subject, and there were no political allusions in it. So I packed my father's typewriter, took a train to Piatra Neamţ, rented a room in a hotel and met the editor the next morning.

As I had expected, he wanted to make a few small changes here and there in my story. We started talking about what, where and how we could do this.

I will never forget the beginning of that short story of mine.

Midnight. Elena was walking slowly down the path which wound between the old university and the new graveyard of the city.

That was how it started. Believe it or not, we talked about that beginning for the rest of the meeting.

First of all . . . 'midnight'. Did we really need the story to start at that time, the editor wondered. Aren't people of our country supposed to be asleep at midnight? Did I want to encourage life at night? Well, literarily speaking it was OK, but from the ethical point of view, shouldn't people make efforts to get a good night's sleep so that they could work efficiently during the day? We, as writers, should never forget our responsibilities, didn't I agree?

Then 'Elena'. That name was to be changed immediately. The character was not very positive, and there could not be the slightest possibility of confusing it with our President's wife. Good.

She 'was walking slowly'. Nothing against it – but doesn't it give rise to psychological interpretations? 'Walking slowly' might suggest indecisiveness, lack of interest, lack of involvement. The character was a Socialist of course, a member of the Party, right? Couldn't she be a bit more purposeful, more decisive?

And where was she walking? 'Down a winding path'!

'Let's be serious! Nowadays, when our country is in full industrial development and thousands of new buildings and avenues are being erected, when the widest, straightest boulevards of Romania are everywhere being constructed – you are talking about winding paths? Imagine if the story is translated into a foreign language. What would the foreigners think of us?'

Not to mention where the winding path was going! 'Between the old university and the new graveyard of the city.' What did I really mean? Why a new graveyard right near the old university? Weren't lots of educational buildings new? And anyway, he wondered again, why was I so keen to leave room for unfavourable interpretations? Was I implying that people who learn things are closer to death than others? Or was I implying that in Romania people first go to study and then die, with nothing happening in between?

I wrote down all the editor's advice in my notebook, went back to the hotel and started the new version of my story.

Noon. Mary was striding confidently along the wide boulevard built in the years of Socialism, an avenue that clearly separated the new university and the old church.

And I continued in the same vein until I felt a need for refreshment to help me in my creation. I went down to the hotel restaurant for a bottle of wine to take up to my room.

The restaurant was empty. The orchestra was playing loudly to an empty room. A waiter reminded me of the shortage of bottles in Romania. He was not allowed to let me take one out of the restaurant unless I brought in an empty one beforehand. So I went out and bought a bottle from a gypsy, who was selling empty bottles at the side entrance of the hotel.

Back in the restaurant, the waiter told me that my bottle was not the right size and shape. So out I went again. This time I managed to get a good bottle. It was full of mineral water. I also bought some biscuits, the only food I could find at that time of day in the city, except for cans of beans. With the bottle and biscuits in my hand – you never find carrier bags in Romania – I went back into the restaurant, where the waiter told me that only empty bottles were accepted. I went to the toilet and poured the water away. The waiter then confessed that the last bottle of wine had just been sold.

I returned to my room with the biscuits, all set to continue writing about healthy people in a prosperous country. Not an easy job, you must admit. As I munched and pondered, it came to my mind to write about biscuits. After all, they had qualities which nobody could deny: they eliminate acid from the stomach and can be consumed regardless of the state of one's teeth; they can be dipped in water for those who have only gums. They are easily transported over long distances, can be eaten, unlike most other foods, without using electricity and you could get them without queuing for hours. In short: a fine theme for the censors.

So I continued my story with Mary, but now Mary was concerned with biscuits. There followed a long discourse on the history of biscuits, from the beginning of time up to the present. It clearly pointed out how biscuits had been frowned on in feudalistic and capitalist societies, and what a new era had opened up for biscuits after Lenin; how much they helped the Russian Army to defeat the Germans, and what a brilliant role they could have in a Socialist society if people would have a bit more respect for them.

I got really carried away. I was just writing about a perfect way to fight social inequality by convincing people to eat equal quantities of biscuits – drawing attention to the standing our country would enjoy in the world if it would only produce biscuits in the shape of white doves – when the bell-boy knocked at my door.

Standing in the doorway, he looked me over, then whispered that he had valuable information for me if I could give him something in return. How much? We started haggling. Finally, I gave him a tip. He told me the hotel chambermaid had overheard the clacking of my typewriter and had called somebody. It did not require too much imagination to guess who.

I thanked him, packed and left as fast as I could.

Later, I read the polished version of my 'essay' on biscuits to some close friends. They liked it. They liked anything that was mocking or absurd.

There was not much samizdat literature in our country at that time. There were pieces translated from George Orwell or Solzhenitsyn, typed pages passed from hand to hand in a great hurry, but they were few, and we were too scared to share our views on them. Instead, we devoured anything which dealt with the Absurd. Kafka, Camus or our own Eugène Ionesco, whom you could still find in certain libraries if you had the connections, were our idols. Unable to criticize the system, we sublimated our frustration by exaggerating our experiences until they became 'absurd'. My short story was 'absurd', almost a long joke. That's why my friends liked it.

Jokes which cynically satirized everything were our real samizdat literature. We had hundreds, thousands, millions of jokes: long, short, cultured, allusive, blunt, said in one breath or whispered out of the side of a mouth. I doubt there can be any other country which created so many jokes in such a short time. A political event was happening in the evening; by the next morning we had dozens of versions of it, all mocking. The jokes were the only things that Securitate could not stop.

My 'essay' was taken as a good joke and, in spite of my precautions, someone copied it and passed it from hand to hand. I guess eventually it also passed under Securitate's scrutiny. No cause for laughter there. Not when you are guarding the country from so many hidden enemies.

With that blinding lamplight in my face, Securitate seemed determined to find out more about my writings. Then about other people's writings – like the people I used to meet in the local literary circle. Then about my connection with Bacchus, 'the traitor'. Then about George. What relations did he have with foreign agencies? Who was he meeting and where?

I refused to talk further. Not that I had much to say, but each word I uttered could later be weighed and weighed again and turned against God only knew who. Even my 'yes' and 'no' could endanger people. I kept silent.

The overhead lights went on again.

'So that's all the help you can give? Very well!' They smiled as if we'd just finished playing an amusing little game. Then they left the room. I sat there for hours, quaking and nauseous. The next thing I remember was the dawn chorus of little birds outside the window. Major Doroş, fresh from his breakfast, was talking to me.

'We see the time has come when you finally need our help. As a student you were an exhibitionist. Yours was a world of love and mockery. Adolescence is confusion, we understand that. But now you are a teacher. You have a duty to our country, which has spent so much educating you! I advise you to put your childhood behind you and become a responsible man. A good *Romanian* teacher of English, that is what we expect you to be now. Take life more seriously, settle down, find a good woman, start a family. My colleagues want to persuade me that you are not worth saving . . .' He closed his eyes and was silent for a moment.

'But I don't believe it,' Major Doroş continued. 'Look! I will turn a blind eye to all the unanswered questions in your file, if you promise to do better . . . Go and be a good teacher and don't pester us any more about travelling abroad. We won't give you a passport until you've carried out your duty to the country and proved yourself a good, reliable Romanian citizen, as I still believe you are.'

My God, how clearly I understood I would never be allowed abroad, just from his intonation at that moment.

'One more word . . .' he declared, before shaking my hand. 'We are confiscating your father's typewriter. We will be waiting for you to bring it here tomorrow.'

The next day, I lugged the typewriter to their office. My eyes were wet when they covered it with a nylon sheet and wrote I-don't-know-what on a piece of paper.

'Don't be so sentimental, mate! You fill in a form and you might have a new one,' an officer told me, thinking I was going to cry just because I was losing a typewriter. How much they knew about my acts, and how little about my feelings.

It was not only that the machine had somehow become part of my life – I now loved it as you love a pet. But it was also part of my inner freedom, as my long hair was, during my university years. While the officer was burying the typewriter under wraps, I knew exactly where I stood. I had refused to be an informer. There were reports in my Securitate files that could deprive me at any time of what little freedom I had left. The last warning had been issued.

After that night, something else happened to me. Whenever my heart felt touched, I could not stop tears coming to my eyes. Sometimes they came late at night; at other times they came early in the morning, in public or alone. Sometimes they came without any reason at all.

'It's a sure sign of a nervous breakdown. A tendency to depression you inherited from your father,' a psychiatrist told me two years later.

Maybe he was right. I often saw my father standing at the kitchen window late at night, smoking a cigarette. Sometimes he had tears in his eyes when he stubbed the butt out on the window-sill.

'What's wrong, Dad?'

'Nothing! Just this depression I inherited from my father. I hope you won't . . . Don't worry about me. It's something that comes and goes.'

Maybe it was something else, something deeper than a personal depression. Whatever it was, after that interview with Securitate I felt a deep numbing grief.

There were no Hell's Angels any more. Cesar's problems with his electricity seemed remote to me now. Aaron remained aloof in his ivory tower. Bacchus had gone away. Then George upped and went.

From the time we played football together – him Pelé, me Gordon Banks – I always considered George my best friend. While students at universities in different cities we met only during our holidays, but the distance did not affect our friendship. OK, we had our crises. Sometimes we quarrelled, sometimes we loved the same girl – as happened with Lynda – but we didn't fall out over it. We had too many things in common. And more than anything else, we continued to trust each other. We shared our views on the few true dissident writers still in Romania, like Noica, the banned philosopher living secluded in his house. We'd recite short verses from Ana Blandiana, the courageous young poet who didn't give up her convictions despite the threatening world around her. We talked about Ceauşescu and his clan, and we would even exchange experiences we had with the secret police, although we both knew how dangerous that was. Reporting conversations with a Securitate officer was strictly forbidden. 'Not a word outside these walls, not to your best friend, your parents, your wife.' We defied this. At least for a while.

We used to meet in the park, after midnight. In summer we would drive off somewhere in silence. There were rumours that the police had powerful tracking stations that could pick up even a conversation in a car. So we parked, and chose a place on a river bank, with no bugged trees around. Only then did we talk about our secrets. George knew as much about my meetings with Securitate as I knew about his.

As I understood it, George's run-in with Securitate was over Lynda.

She had come back to Romania a year after that crazy-golf game I told you about. And the next year after that. Suspicion fell on George. 'Why does she come here so often?' they asked him. 'It may be because of love,' he told them once. 'What do you mean . . . love? Either you are married or not! Don't lie to us, you little creep!'

George, with his beard and watery blue eyes, looked like a traitor; Lynda, blonde and with a Finnish passport, looked like a spy. Then, without any explanation, Lynda stopped coming to Romania. 'Aha! . . . She doesn't come here any more! Why not, creep?'

The creep, who meanwhile had become a teacher, did not know what to answer. That brought still more questions, needing still more answers. Why did he go to Bucharest so often? Why was his name on the American Library register? Who did he meet there? Why was he translating books on yoga? Why had he asked the children in his class to observe a moment's silence when John Lennon was shot? These are the sort of questions to which you can never provide the right answer when Securitate is doing the asking. How could you answer them?

Officially, you were allowed to enter any foreign library in Bucharest, including the American one. But the building was surrounded by cameras, and from time to time you could see flashes from the windows of the block of flats facing the library's entrance. Inside there were Securitate men pretending to read, their eyes searching all around. Even the library's Romanian personnel gave you the books with a look that suggested you were not behaving well by taking them home. The British Library wasn't much more hospitable. The policemen guarding its gates were always looking at your identity card. 'You again, eh?' Yet, as students and teachers, we went there again and again. Now we were to face the repercussions.

But George fell into another of Securitate's nets. In the late 1970s a transcendental meditation movement was allowed to start in Romania. In Bucharest, a surprising number of teachers, engineers, doctors, directors of enterprises and psychologists joined the fashionable circle. But when the movement grew to a certain point, the government declared the members 'dissidents'. All those involved with the movement were thrown out of their jobs. Some faced prison, and an onslaught against anything close to transcendental meditation began throughout the country. George was frequenting a yoga circle in Bacău, and had written a book on the subject. His name was on the list. From now on, George knew he would have no future inside Romania.

'Someone's invited me to the UK. I'm going, be sure of that,' he told me one Thursday night in his bathroom, all the taps turned full on, water gushing everywhere to drown out any bugs. I never asked George who that someone was. We had an agreement that our confidences would only go so far. It wasn't that we didn't trust each other, but what if they used the truth serum in one of our meetings with Securitate? We took great care.

I thought George had lost his mind. Who the hell was going to give him a passport?

But George had lost his patience, not his mind. He had no intention of filling in forms and waiting on Big Brother's mercy. He kept asking for audiences with lieutenants, majors, colonels, insisting on being heard. Each time he received the same 'Wait!' I have already told you about. But his nerve was stronger than mine. Day after day, week after week, month after month, he was back at Securitate's offices.

'Why do you want to travel to the UK?'

'I'm a teacher of English. I want to improve my English.'

'That's not a serious reason.'

'It's all I want to do'.

'That's *all*? And if we don't give you a passport?'

'You can't refuse. According to our constitution I have the right to travel wherever I want.'

They made threats about his teaching career. He didn't care. Then about his family. George did not give up. Things got worse. They raided his house, turning it upside down in their search for subversive literature. That happened a year before my own flat was searched. They took his diary, his work on yoga and a book he had been writing since he was a student.

Next day, George was back at their offices asking for his passport, with a funny smile on his face. Did he receive threatening phone calls in the middle of the night? Next morning he would be back at the same door, smiling still, as if nothing had happened during the night. All the officers knew him by now. They called him 'the lunatic'.

Suddenly, out of the blue, George started to avoid me. He did not come to my flat any more; he was never at home. I went to his school but he was evasive. He pretended that he was too busy to see me. 'There are things you must not know,' he whispered, ushering me out of the door. Then George disappeared. I had no idea what had happened to him. His colleagues had no idea where he was. His parents couldn't tell me either. Had he been arrested? I had no word whatsoever. Then, one year after that conversation in his bathroom I received a long-distance call.

'Dan! It's me, George . . .' I heard his voice through a swarm of interference. 'I made it! I'm in the free world. I'm calling from London.' Then the line was cut.

I could not believe it. Had I dreamed it?

Soon after, I received a postcard with Big Ben on it, and on the back George's signature. It was a real bombshell. How the hell had he done it? Legally or illegally? Did they just hand him a passport? Couldn't he even have given me a hint? So much for our great friendship. I felt deeply hurt.

I found myself more and more alone.

As for my new friends, at one point I was surrounded mostly by doctors who liked to kid me about the operation on my penis and the future of my sex life. 'Forget poetry, Dan! How long do you think that little thing of yours is going to survive after such an operation? Five years? Then it's all up for Willy! Plenty of time for poems and chess after that!'

The doctors cynically shrugged their shoulders each time a patient died on them. 'What can we do to help anyone? Two hundred patients a day, that's what the plan says. And for what money?' They took me to the hospital morgue, and to a special laboratory where monsters born instead of normal babies were kept in sealed glass jars. 'That's the result of radiation from the chemical plant. People don't know.'

More and more sickened and depressed by all I was seeing, with no glimpse of a better future before me, I started drinking in earnest. Not drinking for pleasure as in my student days, but long nights of heavy boozing, mixing wine, *ţuica* and beer so I could finally get to sleep, spending my days in a poisonous cloud where nothing could touch me any more. Afterwards, I would go straight back to the bottle again. More beer, more vodka. My new friends were Tamba, then Teddy, a doctor who kept his bottles in the emergency room at the hospital, Trifan, a dentist who used to lock out his patients so he could drink with me, and a lawyer who used to stagger while defending his clients.

I was sinking. But now and then, like a sleepwalker almost, my footsteps took me back to Hagota. Dark and despairing as my life had become, Hagota remained unspoiled for me.

Sometimes I went there alone. I took a train, then a bus, then one of the two paths which cut between the mountains, to the house we were so lucky to have. There I could recharge my batteries. There I could eat real cheese, drink real milk from the shepherds' huts, draw real water from the well. Other times, in summer, my parents and I took the car, using the petrol coupons saved up during the year. Sometimes I stayed for weeks, free to sleep on sweet-smelling hay in the barn after unburdening my true thoughts and feelings on to handwritten sheets of paper. Hagota was the only place where I could write. There were no bugs, no suspicious eyes. Nevertheless, before leaving, I always wrapped the pages I had written in plastic bags, hiding them in a hole at the bottom of the garden. I guess they must still be there.

One autumn night in Hagota I sat drinking with my father. He was as panicky about my future as he had been at the time when I was a child and was sent home to die. After a while, my father started talking about George, singing his praises. 'Look what can be achieved,' he was telling me, 'if you really set your mind on what you desire.' My father wanted me to take a leaf out of George's book etc, etc. It was then that he told me the full story.

George was lifted off the street one evening with a gas mask on his face. He was doing yoga – he told the men in blue suits – and he couldn't take chances with pollution. They locked him up in a room with barred windows. The next morning, Major Doroş looked in on him.

'How are you this morning, my friend?' he greeted George, cordially shaking hands with him.

'How is your father? Your mother's well?' the colonel asked, as if George had just arisen from his own sweet bed.

'I'm OK, thank you. My mother is happy as usual, and my father prayed again this morning for our President's health and welfare,' George answered, smiling in that special, peculiar way. The colonel pointed to the window. Did George like it? Should it be larger or smaller, what did he think? With curtains, or without? And generally speaking, would people jump out of it if the bars were not there?

'You'd be a fool to jump out of this window, then die with nobody knowing what had happened to you,' George answered in a friendly manner. 'There are so many other windows, better places to do that. I'd suggest the building opposite the American Embassy. Reporters could take pictures of your body so that the world could find out what had happened to you, don't you think?' he asked, genuinely earnest.

'That's enough! Aren't you just a tiny bit scared, George?'

George's eyes rolled in his head and he started to stare transfixed at the far top corner of the room.

'Of course I'm scared, sir. Only madmen are never scared of anything and I'm as sane as the next man. If I may dare to ask, can you tell me if you see a fly over there, in the corner?'

The Major, perplexed, turned his head to look. There was indeed a fly.

'Well,' George continued in a low voice, 'that fly is the thing that scares me just now. You see, sir, I believe not only in metempsychosis, but in the transmigration of beings into things too, and right now I'm thinking if that fly suddenly turns into a train, this very minute, the train will come thundering down on us. Like this!' And he jumped up from the chair, making gestures and noises to show what it would be like – noises that my father tried to do as he told me George's story.

'So you can see, sir, how an innocent, insignificant fly can kill us in the next instant. Of course I'm scared. How could I live without being scared?' Then George calmly sat down.

A week later, he was granted a visa to go to the UK, my father told me.

'They'd rather have a madman outside than inside the border.'

'How do you know this?'

'It's obvious.'

'No, I mean, how do you know all this stuff about George?'

'But Major Doroş told me,' my father let slip.

'What!?'

He went and got another bottle, pouring himself a stiff one while ignoring my empty glass. It was the only time in my life I ever saw my father more tipsy than me. And then he confessed. He knew Major Doroş from the local philately society. My father was a stamp collector, and so was Major Doroş. They met every Sunday and sometimes the whole group would go off to a restaurant to stand Doroş a drink.

'You know how things are. We've all got kids . . . We give him a drink, and he might be a bit more understanding with you.'

No, I did not know how things were. Until that moment I had no idea that my father was on such terms with Doroş. And how could Doroş share such a thing with my dad? I had a horrible feeling in the pit of my stomach, maybe the darkest premonition of my life.

I cornered my father. I yelled at him. I wanted the whole truth. And he told me. He had tears in his eyes as he spoke. He said it had all started when I was a student. My father was so scared about the future of his only child that he bent over backwards to be Major Doroş's friend.

'So you became an informer?' I shouted in horror.

'No! How dare you . . . ? How could you think that?'

He took the Bible he always kept in the bedroom at Hagota and swore with his hand on the book that he had never said a wrong thing about anybody in his life. But his voice was shaking terribly. He told me how he had used his connections to get hold of wine, salami and Kent cigarettes to take to Doroş every month. Doroş's wife would always invite him in for a brandy.

'Yes, I bribed him. There was no need for you to know that. If he had asked me to lick his arse I'd have done it . . . If he'd only let you alone. So that you could have a future.'

I felt the sky falling in on me. That Hagota night sky, splashed with stars like nowhere else – as if God had thrown a fistful of salt on it every night – now it was suffocating me.

So that was why my father's eyes were wet when he smoked in the kitchen at home. He had had to compromise himself for his son. And I had no idea about what was going on behind my back while my parents were protecting me. How far had they been compromised in this way? How much had they really suffered because of me? And what could I do from now on? I knew how much they loved me but what was I to them if not a continuous burden? And how could it be otherwise as long as I lived?

Later we cried on each other's shoulders, my father repeatedly reassuring me he had never said a thing to Doroş about my friends. He knew how hard I had tried to protect my friends whenever they had hauled me in. So how could he betray my faith? But I was not convinced. And my doubts made my father feel worse. It was a bad night for both of us.

The next morning, I woke to a sound not usually heard in those parts. Workmen with chainsaws were cutting down the trees at the foot of the mountain opposite our house. They were not locals, but came from God knows where. I went and asked what was happening. Not that I was very curious, but I was ready to do anything not to have to think about the previous night.

'Nothing unusual, mate,' the ganger told me. 'We have to cut a square kilometre and send the trees to the timber factory to be made into matches for Sweden.'

'What can you do?' the chief said more to himself, shrugging his shoulders. 'These are orders from above.'

What could you do? What could *I* do – against this, against anything else? In fact, what could I do against anything that was happening in my life? Securitate had made a dog of me, chasing its own tail. I was a burden to my parents no matter what I did. I would never be allowed to travel abroad. I would never be published. I was forbidden to teach as I wanted. Too scared to speak out, my head was bowed for life. Enough of this hell! Enough is enough.

VII

A Hot-Air Balloon

A few days later I presented myself at Securitate headquarters and asked for emigration status. This was not as easy as you might think. Applying for emigration in the 1980s was perfectly legal. Thousands of people dared to do it. But most of them had close relatives abroad, so they could put down 'family reunion' as their reason for wanting to go. In a state in which a person could be 'disappeared' for making a joke, how could anyone dare to have political reasons for leaving the country? Not even those with relatives abroad were safe from harassment; but at least they were unlikely to suffer 'unexpected accidents'. Their relatives made enquiries at the foreign embassies. Their voices were now heard in the West.

After the mid-1980s, the Western democracies finally stopped thronging to give Ceauşescu prizes and honorary degrees. His internal policies had at last begun to offend the free world. The long list of complaints made French diplomats consider closing their embassy in Bucharest. The US Ambassador to Romania, David Funderbunk, resigned in 1985, subsequently alleging corruption within the embassy and bribery of US officials by the Romanian government. Funderbunk's disquiet was further provoked by the ex-Securitate chief Ion Pacepa's book *The Red Horizons*, which was later published in the US. Pacepa talked about sophisticated surveillance methods, about a whole country tightly controlled by the secret police. The West started to listen to more than Ceauşescu's empty words.

Ceauşescu still had a fiercely loyal Securitate, and he had a strong Party which had infiltrated everywhere. Elena was at his right hand. Nicu, his son, was an important Central Committee member. Lieutenant-General Nicolae Andruţa, his younger brother, was a key figure in the Interior Ministry, and Ilie, his older brother, was Deputy Minister of Defence. But abroad, Ceauşescu was losing his friends.

The Chinese still backed him. Honecker, Zhivkov, Gaddafi and Saddam Hussein were still on his side but, in comparison with the past, his popularity was fading fast. Even the new leader of the USSR, Gorbachev, was talking about changes. And Gorbachev made it clear that he didn't like our leader.

Ceauşescu realized it was time for him to compromise a bit: enough for the West to see that he was not 'Dracula', as they had started to call him. The polite trickle of requests from Romanians abroad, asking for their families to join them, was turning into a flood. So Ceauşescu arranged for a few hundred people per year to be granted emigration. The list was approved only by him.

I had no relatives on the other side of the Iron Curtain. 'I am not allowed to travel, I don't have any future here and my reasons are not political,' I told Securitate. But who was I fooling?

At first they wouldn't accept my application. I insisted. I said something about the Helsinki Treaty, Human Rights, the American Embassy. I tried to be as bold and 'lunatic' as George had been, though I was a bit late in my timing. When George had played his card, Securitate preferred to have the insane outside the country. This policy had changed just a year later. Now they preferred to keep them within the borders. I knew this, but I continued to insist.

'Every bird perishes by its own song,' a Romanian proverb says, and I was determined to fulfil it. My God, how adamant I was in those days. My steps were decisive, my eyeballs enlarged, always fixed on something in front of me. Past, present and future folded down to a single horizontal line: I had to leave Romania.

Of course, I was over-acting a bit. Every night I studied myself in the mirror and worked at the look I had to wear the next day. A look of insanity, if you told me I was wrong to leave my country – and a sane one, if you talked to me about other matters, like the world of Shelley or Socrates.

I don't know how much I impressed Securitate, but they finally gave me a registration number. This was my first victory. My new status was officially established. I had a new number, didn't I? Not the one in the dossier with the pages dutifully signed by schoolmates, teachers, Army officers, colleagues, relatives, people I knew and many I did not, all pencilled in red, yellow and blue. But a new one altogether.

I was classified in a separate file. Different officers had to deal with me from now on. And this new number gave another dimension to my life. It did not imply half-truths and whispers of discontent any more. There I was, true to myself, standing against the tide.

Emil Cioran, the Romanian thinker, once said that while the Americans say 'yes' to any possibility, the French start by saying 'no'. And the Romanian is in two minds right from the start, because he wants to profit from both 'yes' and 'no'. I no longer wanted any part in this.

'Don't rush things! Time solves all problems and truth always rises to the surface.' Relatives, friends, teachers and writers I knew were always whispering such things to me, looking over their shoulder to be sure they were not being overheard. I got to hate that snaky kind of thinking and the cowardly wisdom of cultured non-resistance. I hated that discrepancy between avowed morality and everyday compromise, and I could no longer lull my spirit with fine-sounding words and noble sentiments. Now that there was no going back for me, I needed a fierce spirit, a spirit even of hate. That gave me strength.

After a while I started being summoned to endless meetings at which different officials tried to make me change my mind. The Chief of the Education Department, Major Doros, the local Chief of Securitate, the Mayor, the Party Secretary of the county . . . Sometimes I had the whole lot of them in front of me, all in a row at a long, rectangular table with a red velvet cloth. It might have made you blush. But not me, with my look carefully planned.

What was worse was that my parents were now also interviewed and threatened by turn. They couldn't lose their jobs now since they were both retired, but the embarrassment of those meetings was hard for them to bear.

'The man is thirty-three years old,' my father protested. 'I can't interfere in his life any more.'

My poor parents. They always backed me. In the days to come I would surely not have survived without their love.

One day, unexpectedly, my influential uncle dropped by. He had never visited us before, but that evening in my parents' living room I found out he was not as distant as I had believed.

'Do you think you'd ever have been allowed to change university course after the Army if I hadn't put in a good word for you? The dean! . . . Yes, that's right! Do you really think you wouldn't have seen the inside of a cell if it wasn't for me? You don't have a clue how much I helped you, and you'll never know it all. If you don't care what happens to yourself, think of the shit you're getting us into, your parents and me.'

What did my uncle want me to do? To continue my life as a puppet in the hands of those above me? To change my views and start enjoying life in a paralysed society, able only to wish its President 'to live for ever for the homeland's sake'? Maybe he was going to help me become a Communist Party member now, was that it?

This would not have been an impossible thing to accomplish. In the poorest country in Europe, a quarter of the adult population were Communist Party members. This was the biggest percentage of all the Eastern Bloc countries, bigger even than in Russia. Was my uncle thinking that I could even become an activist in time? A Securitate officer perhaps. Or an informer, with a card for the Communist Party shops in which you could find goodies no one dreamed of, it was said. No thank you!

Nothing was going to make me change my mind. My parents just shrugged their shoulders, as they did with everybody else now. There would be no talk about their son, if you please. They had disinherited me. They didn't recognize me as their son any more. Not that they really meant it – scared as they were, they were secretly still proud of me – but that was how all three of us decided they should act. That way, at least Securitate would go easier on them.

Six months later, my papers were sent to Bucharest and I was given a registration number in the Central Emigration Office of Romania. Now my number had a life beyond my county's borders. This was my second victory. And the last one, as far as Securitate were concerned.

From now on, all I had to do was wait for the answer from on high. Two, four, six years – Virgil, a doctor I knew, had been waiting for nine years. Virgil too had no 'family' abroad. He too had asked to leave

Romania when he was thirty-three. But once he became a symbol of courage for people like me, and a good subject to be talked about for others, he had become complacent.

Repercussions? Instead of being able to open an acupuncture clinic in a city hospital, Virgil was now sent to be a GP in a remote village. His fame as 'the man with golden hands' kept him safe from unexpected accidents. At forty, when I met him, he was secretly carrying out abortions for the daughters of Securitate officers.

I was not Virgil. I was going to push hard. I didn't have golden hands, but was I not a descendant of Dracula, after all?

Meanwhile, I was thrown out of my job. With my emigration papers submitted, I had not the moral integrity and patriotism required for a teacher. I had expected it. Still, when I said goodbye to my kids and saw them crying, I felt a lump in my throat.

The consequences were scary. As I said, it was legal to ask for emigration from Romania, but it was illegal not to have a job for more than six months. You could be sent to prison for 'parasitism'.

Who was going to employ me, with my emigration status? I felt like a fly caught in the web of Securitate. The spider didn't need to bother with me much now. All he had to do was to wait until I broke a law in one way or another. Then he could have his fly for lunch. When despair reaches its peak, it gives you moments of surprising lucidity. I became more foxy than a fox, I can tell you.

I happened to know this man, Rugina, from my drinking days in the restaurant. We'd sit at a table, right up close to the orchestra, splitting our ear-drums with their Birdie Song. We didn't talk to each other. In that din you had to shout and use your hands a lot. Between songs, we did not speak. What should we talk about? The weather? The local football team, which was sponsored by Securitate? So we'd say 'Hello' to each other, drink our bottles dry – and say 'Goodbye'. Not much of a connection, it's true, but a rapport was there.

As luck would have it, Rugina was the Vice-President of a local co-operative which had just opened a language tuition and translation unit. I went into his office with a ten-litre canister of *ţuica* and two big salami, in the hope that he was the only influential man in town who didn't know about my emigration claim. He didn't. He locked the door behind us and after two hours we agreed I was a brilliant teacher, the best translator ever, life was a shit, cheers, old mate!

'*Noroc*! But don't forget! We have to fulfil the plan.' I promised to do so while signing the contract.

I guess the Vice-President did not have time to finish the canister of *ţuica* before Securitate told him all about me.

'You bastard! Why didn't you tell me? I am not going to fire you, but the orders are clear! You can stay on as a translator and teacher, but you won't be allowed to translate anything technical. What if you wilfully translate a wrong screw for a machine-tool and the factory blows up? Who will be responsible, eh? And I am not allowed to let you teach anybody over the age of seven. Nevertheless, the Securitate officer and I have decided that a child younger than that won't be influenced by your lack of patriotism. I'll give you six months to prove yourself, otherwise you are out.'

It wasn't very rewarding to have to repeat in English 'this is a pen', 'kite', 'cow', 'tractor' and 'Socialism' a hundred times a day. Or to help my four-year-old students from the office crèche to go to the loo. But I had a job. In fact, unexpectedly, I had a lot to do. Working hard helps banish desperate thoughts. It was James Bond who kept me busy during those days and nights.

Like every institution, theatres had to fulfil their own financial plan. With no one interested in the plays approved by the censors, and their coffin-making bringing in too little income, theatre directors were happy to turn a blind eye when black-marketeers turned up with pirated videos of Western movies.

Outside the theatre, posters showed a frowning Romanian soldier. You bought a ticket ostensibly to find out what psychological problems he suffered during the Second World War. Inside, when the curtains rose, instead of the actor wrestling with his political conscience, you saw two large colour TVs waiting for you. The lights went down and the video began: Bruce Lee or 007 came out fighting. And it was my voice on the dubbed sound-track which turned James Bond into a Soviet double agent mocking imperialist spies. The story no longer made much sense, of course, but that was the only way to get the films approved. And I added a few embellishments of my own.

I was translating three movies a week, sometimes just by listening to the sound-track – though Sylvester Stallone's muddy mumble was a bit of a challenge. I had to use my imagination. Rambo cries in the lap of his former Army commander, disappointed by the public's reaction to Vietnam: 'I'm weeping because people do not realize how good Socialism is,' my translation shouted from the loudspeaker.

Sometimes the movies were pirated from Western TV and cut with advertisements. A beautiful blonde girl was shaking her hair after using I don't know what shampoo. I was supposed to keep quiet but, as the Romanian saying goes, my tongue was itching. 'Don't use this Western product, it makes your hair fall out!' my voice admonished from the screen.

The ad showed us teeth too perfect to be real, then a gleaming tube of toothpaste. 'Use this toothpaste and your teeth will rot,' my voice boomed in the dark.

The audience didn't care what the translator was saying anyway. At a time when we had only two hours a day of approved TV, to see cars flying through the air or the guests of the Great Gatsby dancing at his parties made people happy enough. Men, women and children crowded into the theatres as never before. Now, just imagine the uproar when the power was cut in a hall of 400 seats filled with a thousand people or more.

The fun went on until Securitate found out whose mocking voice was doing the dubbing, and then I was banned from those translations as well. Not that I had a future in that freelance job anyway. A few months later the West complained about pirated videos and Ceauşescu finally found out what was happening behind his back. The theatres were empty again.

Time passed and nothing happened with my claim, though I did not just sit and wait. I went to Bucharest, I demanded audiences with the National Emigration Department, I knocked on doors of houses that I had not even dared to look at before. I mingled with the other 'emigrant status' people who were crowding the gates of the foreign embassies, all of us well aware that we were being photographed. What did we have to lose? I wrote dozens of letters to the British, Australian, American and Canadian embassies. Somehow, I had got hold of the idea that if I could get my name put on a foreign file, I would have more chance of success. You never knew what might come up.

I always posted my letters from other towns. Most of them came back to me unopened. I did not give up. I threw letters over the closed gates of foreign embassies and sprinted away from the Romanian policemen fiercely guarding the diplomats. One day I stopped a black American limousine coming out of the US Embassy. Before the policemen swooped on me, I had time to thrust my plea through its half-open window. The car disappeared and the policemen caught me, searched me in a second, then slapped my face, right there, in the middle of the street. Then they let me go, their faces hard and cold. I guess they met hundreds of people like me.

Soon after that experience, a man was posted at the entrance to my block of flats. For several weeks he followed me, everywhere I went. Was I going to my job? He was there, opposite the co-operative, drinking a beer on the restaurant's terrace. I could see him from the office window. Was I going to my parents? Whenever I left them, that man was there, on a bench. Sometimes I saw him, other times I just felt his presence. One day, rushing out of the rain, I almost bumped into him. He smiled. I smiled too. He never touched me, never said a word to me. I began taking him to bed with me. He became part of my nightmares. That was his role.

I stopped going to Bucharest, and the man disappeared.

Another year passed. No harassments. My boss didn't throw me out of my job. Even the midnight phone calls, with brutish voices shouting, 'Traitor! I'll fuck your mother if you don't watch your step,' stopped. It all went dead. It was as if Securitate had completely lost interest in me. Had they decided that I posed no threat? Or were they sure I had no chances? Was it because they believed I wouldn't dare to break the law?

The law decreed that once every two years, all employed men had to go to the Army for ten days to learn again to be good soldiers. Nobody minded as your salary was still paid and you had the opportunity to play with some guns. Nobody minded apart from us, the 'emigrants'. If you refused to go, there was a court-martial waiting for you, then six months to a year's imprisonment. But the law also said that after every

Army stint, be it only for a day, you were not allowed to travel abroad for the next two full years, while you might still remember official secrets. That law was hardly enforced, except for people like me. Yet if we opted for imprisonment instead, no Western country would accept us – or so we believed.

Fingers were pointed at me in the streets, and all sorts of rumours were spread about my sanity. Yet people knew that I was no informer. A director of a big enterprise, a bishop, well-known doctors, the pastor of the Baptist church, each contacted me in turn, secretly wanting to learn English. I would go to their homes late in the evening, by long, devious routes, always making sure that I was not followed. My students would put me in rooms which they were sure were clean of bugs, and then the English lesson would begin. I didn't need to take too many precautions when meeting the bishop. The Orthodox Church had submitted to Ceauşescu's policies and notoriously, many of its priests betrayed confidences given during confession. To reward the Church's submission, Ceauşescu let its officials travel abroad.

I could hardly complain of hunger at this time. I knew many who were in far worse situations than me. By the end of the 1980s even the tight control of Securitate could not halt the rumours that many people were close to starvation. Doctors in the villages sent in false reports about the increasingly high infant mortality rate. Nowhere was it stated that the babies were dying of malnutrition, but we all knew what was going on.

Yet 'Hymn to Romania' continued as before. In 1987 the USA withdrew 'Most Favored Nation' status from Romania. Ceauşescu retaliated by announcing that we didn't need it anyway; Romania had no more foreign debts to pay, and it didn't need foreign credit. While posters of Ceauşescu were being enlarged to unbelievable sizes, Doina Cornea, Dan Petrescu, the poet Mircea Dinescu and the other dissidents left in Romania were put in prison or under house arrest. In the windows of the photographic unit of my co-operative, Ceauşescu's smile replaced even the wedding photos of young couples.

The waiting closed in on me. 'Long disease, sure death,' another Romanian proverb says.

In former days I had liked to observe the people in the streets, imagining what their lives were like. What was hidden behind that smile over there? Now, while I walked the streets, my head was bent down and my hands were thrust deep into my pockets – there were rumours that they put dollars in the pockets of undesirables in crowded places, so you could be searched and sent to prison for possessing illegal currencies.

I went to Bucharest again, believing that Securitate had forgotten about me. I even managed to arrange a meeting with the English priest of the Anglican Church in Romania. It was Easter time, I remember, and he invited me to his house, next to the church. The street was full of construction workers' caravans. The men were supposedly digging up the road, but you could see the cameras sticking out of the windows.

The priest, who was actually Irish, told me right away to watch my mouth; his house was bugged. He looked dubiously at the parcel I was carrying – some Easter cakes made for him by my mother, I explained. He didn't want to taste them. I took one at random and swallowed it whole, so that he would see they were not poisoned. It didn't convince him.

'You ... Romanians! You smashed up my car, cut off my phone, send me threatening letters.' I nearly wept trying to convince him I was not one of those. All I wanted from him was to post two letters for me when he went home. One was to the American Embassy, and one was to Margaret Thatcher. He laughed at my naivety.

'There are hundreds like you every Sunday at the door of my church. You are incredible dreamers, you know that?'

Then we talked about religion. Now I was at home in that subject. I invited the priest to Hagota, to see the piety of real Romanians. He promised to come one day. Before leaving, I placed my letters on a small table in his entrance hall. He didn't say anything, but I had a feeling he would post them for me.

About a week later, two men approached me near my block of flats, asking for a light. I instinctively felt the danger. All I could do was protect my face with my hands when they started belting me. I didn't scream or try to react. I threw myself on the ground and lay there while they kicked me. Only short hiccups responded to their knocks.

'Don't kill him! Let's see whether he's got any money,' I heard one of them say while I pretended to be unconscious. They searched me, then came one more blow of the boot – this time right in my liver, making me scream. They ran off. I dragged myself to my flat. There was no water to wash away the blood pouring from my nose. I let it dry on me, covered by dark thoughts and fear. How could I have fooled myself that Securitate was not watching every step of mine? What next? One more wrong move and I was going to be at the bottom of it. That was the message, as clear as day. That night, I decided: if there was no legal way out of it, I would flee.

As you can imagine, informers were flying round me like wasps around a cake. Sometimes they came to my office, pretending they wanted me to translate I don't know what communications. Other times they knocked on the door of my flat. Some of my visitors had emigration status like me. Others were young blokes who had already experienced prison after being caught trying to flee. Some had managed to reach Yugoslavia, only to be caught there and sent back. For every Romanian returned to the country, it was said, the government was paying a wagon of salt. That was the price for a good example to be shown to the others.

They weren't all informers, of course. Some told me their stories, and I believed them. The beatings they suffered from the border guards, the inhuman treatment they had received in prison as traitors; their words are deeply imprinted on my memory. Others lied, showing me all kinds of escape plans. I showed them the door.

How could I know who was who? I guess the strong premonitions I had during childhood and adolescence had been later replaced by a sixth sense. I grew to rely on it for spotting informers. With all the practice it was getting, my sixth sense became as strong as my premonitions had been. And my sixth sense told me to trust Dudu.

Dudu was an architect – he was the only friend of mine who wasn't afraid to meet me in full daylight. The others found all sorts of excuses. Cesar was now an important engineer in his plant. He had married well, and had learned how to play the game. I guess he was now correcting the reports on faulty bulbs made by others. He was busy all the time. But at least he was frank with me: 'Dan, I'd like to see you from time to time, but understand me. I'm scared.'

Even Aaron rejected me, though his reasons were different, or so he pretended. 'What the hell are you trying to prove, eh? That you are bold? That you are true to yourself? Well, you've proved that you are a complete moron. Nothing else. You focused the whole of Securitate on you for nothing. You must know you don't have a hope. You've stopped drinking now, eh? . . . Well, how much do you want to bet that in five years' time you'll be sleeping in the streets, begging for a glass of vodka? And even if, by a miracle, you're in the West, what do you think you'll find there anyway? Milk and honey? It's a world of robots, everywhere. Picasso killed painting, nobody cares about literature any more, art itself is meant to perish. Computers have swallowed it up. Robots everywhere have replaced individual sadness and anguish with serial, uniform ones, easier to be endured. A world of robots, here, there . . . everywhere!'

Dudu did not give me any lectures.

'Well, Dan, you chose your own future and I respect you. Look here. I have close friends working in Securitate. But I swear to you I'm not an informer.'

He didn't need to tell me, I could feel it. And I knew I could share my plan with him.

It all started when I saw pictures of a family who had escaped from East Germany by hot-air balloon. I cut the pictures out of the German magazine, carefully translated the detailed story, and began working on the idea.

It was not difficult to convince Dudu about my plan. At his architecture institute, he had to work four months a year on the congratulations to be sent to Ceauşescu on New Years' Eve. At home, he dreamed up all sorts of houses where he would live when he'd discovered some treasure hidden somewhere. He was a true visionary. The idea of making a hot-air balloon went directly to his heart. We were not in East Germany: materials in our country were of low quality, we had no idea how to fly a balloon. But if the Montgolfier brothers had done it with the technology of two hundred years ago, why should *we* not be able to do it today, even in Romania?

We spent a lot of time in libraries, looking through old books and magazines. How does a hot-air balloon work? How is it constructed?

We investigated sizes, dimensions, weights, the amount of heat needed to keep it afloat. What could we use instead of proper balloon material and the gas burner?

We began making prototypes in Dudu's flat. Dudu was certain that his flat wasn't bugged – he sometimes gave the keys to his married Securitate friends to meet their girlfriends there! We assembled miniature balloons, then bigger and bigger ones, using whatever kind of nylon we could find in order to calculate the ratio between the balloon's size and its carrying capacity. According to our calculations, we needed a balloon that was ten metres in diameter and fourteen metres high to carry 300 kilos, no more.

Making the basket was easy. The blind people from *Arta Invalizilor* co-operative were happy to make us a huge linen basket. They did not ask any questions.

We convinced two peasants who used bottled gas for cooking to sell us their cylinders. We did not need more than two 30-litre containers, which we estimated to be sufficient for six hours in the air. Some workers made the pipes and the tap for the gas burner. For good money, they secretly welded the equipment in a plant workshop, no one knowing what they were for.

The real problem was the balloon. It seemed impossible to find the right material; everything was either too heavy or melted in the heat. Finally we found a factory that was making jackets for Italy, using material which was much closer to what we needed. We bribed engineers, supervisors and guards to get our hands on the brightly-coloured material, but we couldn't get enough of it for the whole balloon. So we decided to have a go with what we had. Our balloon had sides of all colours of the rainbow from the jacket material; its top was made with another kind of nylon. A village girl in Hagota did all the sewing, far from the prying eyes of Securitate. It took her three months.

The plan was to flee across the Danube to Yugoslavia from the south-eastern corner of Romania. We would do it the following year, 1989, at the end of spring, when a national cycle race took place in that area. Dudu had a good friend who was the local cycling champion. For two days the area would be teeming with cyclists, and with their friends and relatives come to cheer them on. We'd be among the enthusiastic supporters, hiding our equipment in the cycling paraphernalia, with two bicycles in the basket. Then Dudu and I would camp in a small field a few kilometres away from the race. During the night we'd get closer to the border – a densely forested hill with a bare patch near the top – and there we would assemble our transport, using the car exhaust to inflate the balloon before lighting the gas burner. Just a few kilometres distant, the Danube awaited us.

April 1989. We had four weeks to go. The world of Communism in Europe was in great upheaval. But this wasn't our concern. Dudu and I decided to try the balloon for the first time, in Hagota.

One morning, before anyone was awake, we carted our balloon to a clearing in the forest. It was chilly, I remember. And we had a few hiccups. At first, the whole thing was a mess. We'd managed to borrow an air compressor, run on petrol, but we couldn't get the hang of it. Then there were problems with the burner which was supposed to heat the air.

Eventually, we got started. Seconds passed like years. Then, slowly, the balloon started to grow. Then . . . there it was, quivering in its ragbag of colours, hovering above the ground. We screamed, embraced and kissed each other. The plan was working. My God! It was working!

From now on, nothing would stop us: we'd enter the West through the front door. We'd . . . A small flame appeared, somewhere towards the bottom of the balloon on its left side. Did it take five minutes, ten minutes or more before our balloon had turned to ashes? Let's call it a second.

In a second, our dream had vanished. That was it.

Now, while writing, I take that event as a symbol. At the time of experiencing it I took it as the end of everything. All my mental and emotional energy had gone into that stupid balloon.

Dudu at once started thinking of another plan. Something a bit more realistic. But I had no time for that, not me. I was almost finished.

So I decided to take my last chance. When the summer came, I bathed in freezing mountain rivers and ran five miles a day to strengthen my body and mind. I was going to swim across the Danube on New Year's Eve. All I had to do was banish from my mind the idea that I could be caught, imprisoned, tortured or shot, greater fears than that of drowning. I was a bag of nerves by the end of the autumn. Crossing the street whenever I saw a policeman or Securitate officer; looking over my shoulder all the time; my nerves like coiled springs whenever I talked to anybody.

No wonder I could not sleep. My body was fit, maybe, but I was really cracking up. I needed medical help. And where better than in the wolf's lair, the Party hospital in Bucharest?

So I went to see my uncle, convincing him that I was now a changed man. He got me into Elias Hospital in the middle of December, just three weeks before my deadline. And there I was, biting my nails down to stumps, and slinking through the corridors, when the uprising happened.

Christmas 1989 in Romania made for good TV and newsprint all over the world. 'Tracer bullets crossing the sky like fireworks and the rattle of automatic guns instead of carols . . .' reported journalists. Teenagers defied death, shouting 'Down with the Dictator!' Tanks rolled on the blood-stained streets, shooting into flaming buildings. Young people in lorries waved flags with holes in the middle, cheering, embracing each other and shouting again, this time with joy, '*Libertate! Libertate!*'

Romania was suddenly on the world stage. I too had my own revolution. My new role in life seemed clear to me. Meaning had come to me. No, not in the first moments, but soon after. The fact that I then went on to lose it again set me adrift into even deeper water.

VIII

The Rose That Did Not Bloom

Had you been in my city on the second of January 1990, you would have seen hundreds and thousands of people queuing in a certain street. They were not queuing for bread; they were flocking to the dread Securitate and Passport Office, animated and full of excitement.

'If you want a passport,' the provisional government had announced, 'you can just go and collect one.'

'It can't be true,' people were saying. 'We dreamed of this for so long. And now, today, can it happen just like that?'

It happened just like that. The dread doors opened and hours, days, weeks later, men walked down the street with nothing in their hands but a shiny green passport. They bore it aloft, even religiously, as though that passport was the guarantee of personal well-being and good luck.

It was really true. We were free to travel wherever we wanted, those very same officers who had tormented my youth were pleased to assure me.

'What kind of passport do you want, Dan? A green one for tourists, or one for emigration?' Major Doroş asked smiling, when I chanced to meet him in the corridor.

I was astounded. So Major Doroş was still there? He was smiling that same smile, which said he belonged to that place, that it was his and would be forever, revolution or not.

All the other officers I knew so well were still in their jobs too. Just one week after that Christmas of blood, they were carrying on with their work as if nothing had happened. Except that large smiles and polite words had replaced their cold eyes and shouts. I could not believe how quickly the officers appeared to change their attitude.

People round me seemed not to care. They simply took their passports and went away. No questions were asked, inside or outside the building. What was going on?

Ten days later, I returned to Bucharest to join the Liberal Monarchist Party. I didn't know much about ex-king Michael and his royal family, but a constitutional monarchy and government sounded better to me than a presidential republic, which we had already experienced. Besides, of all the opposition parties which appeared overnight like mushrooms after rain, the Liberal Monarchist Party was the one furthest removed from Communism. It was time for action; others could sleep on if they wanted to. But someone had to continue what the young people had started, I thought.

Bucharest, I found, was still not sleeping. Fever and tension were in the air. Teenagers handed out written or typed sheets to passers-by: lists of those in prison, missing or still unaccounted for. The first opposition party newspapers were now being sold in the streets. People were asking questions in loud voices. You could hear them in a café, waiting at a bus stop, in the street, everywhere.

General Milea was declared a hero because he had refused to fire on the people. But what of the actual victims, those who had been shot by the Army? Why were former Communist activists still in their offices? Who really were Ion Iliescu and Petre Roman? How was it that they were right at the top of the National Salvation Front?

And why on that night when they appeared at the balcony of the Central Committee building had all the shooting miraculously stopped? 'The terrorists' were firing on the building, then Iliescu and Roman appeared on the balcony. The shooting stopped. They announced that Ceauşescu had been arrested, gave a short speech, and went back into the building. Lo and behold! The shooting started up again. Were the terrorists taking a tea-break?

During the Stalinist era of the 1950s, Iliescu was head of the Young Communist League, one of the inquisitors who decided which student could continue his studies and which was to be thrown out because of his 'bourgeois origins'. Iliescu's merciless attitude towards 'capitalist infiltrators' helped him climb quickly up the Communist Party ladder.

Between 1968 and 1971, he became one of Ceauşescu's protégés, a member of the Central Committee with responsiblity for cultural affairs. His career suffered a slight setback when he dared to criticize some aspect of Ceauşescu's policies in the early 1970s but he continued to be a district Prime Secretary, the highest ranking Party official of a region. He then held other ministerial posts until 1984, when he finally lost Ceauşescu's favour.

Petre Roman declared to French journalists that he just happened to be in front of the people, 'carried by the wave' onto the Central Committee balcony on 22 December. He did not say a word about his previous relations with Ceauşescu, or about the fact that his father, Walter Roman, was one of the founders of Securitate. The terrorists knew better than to shoot at their own.

When I left the Liberal Monarchist Party's tiny office – it was somewhere on the second floor of a block that took you ages to find – I had a paper in my pocket designating me as their representative in Bacău county. For the first time in my life, I was not only a member, but a key official, in a political party. I felt proud.

As I walked through Romana Square, down Magheru Boulevard, towards the university and the Intercontinental Hotel, bunches of fresh flowers still marked the places where people had died. Wreaths had been placed round simple crosses, with small photographs of the dead pinned to the wood. There were handwritten messages in polythene packets, and there were poems, like 'The Letter of the Little Orphan' which I copied into my notebook and now try to translate:

> I was an orphan
> and the guilt was mine
> in the Golden Epoch
> in the Big Tyrant's time.
> They made me promise
> to grow big and strong,
> and they fed me nothing
> in a cold dark home.
> Brother and sister,
> as you pass by,
> take my wish with you

don't let it die.
This world must never see
a little orphan like me.

Melting candles flickered at the foot of the walls, which were covered in fading inscriptions:

Dad, tell mum she mustn't cry.
I went to sing carols,
But I couldn't stand aside
Tell her to be proud, not sad.

And there were new ones, which I hadn't seen before.

IF CEAUŞESCU WAS WORSE THAN HITLER,
THEN THE COMMUNISTS WERE WORSE THAN THE NAZIS!

DEAR NEW LEADER, WE BEG YOU
DON'T STEAL OUR REVOLUTION!

It was evening when I heard rumours of people demonstrating against the National Salvation Front in Victoria Square. The truth is starting to come out, I thought. There were too many impostors up there, too many former Communists concerned for the country's future welfare. People who had witnessed the traumatic events of the last weeks and had friends and relatives among the dead were not going to let the old guard steal the revolution. I hurried to join the crowd. Outside the NSF building, men and women of all ages were shouting and booing.

'Where are the terrorists? Who killed our children?'

'Murderers! Communists out!'

It was like coming back to life. I don't know how many hours I spent there in the middle of the crowd, but I clearly remember what I felt when I saw a familiar face. He was a blond man, about thirty. We recognized each other from the streets during the revolution. Now he was here, at the country's first big demonstration against Communism. We shook hands and swapped phone numbers. His name was Dumitru. I had a deep momentary sense that we were supposed to meet in that place, our footsteps guided by I knew not what.

Back home in Bacău, a day later, I watched the TV commentary on the event. A bunch of violent terrorists and fascists paid in dollars by foreign agents were out to destabilize the country, they said. Where was our free television? I asked myself. No one had paid me a cent to join the crowds in Victoria Square. What were they talking about?

Then, with no eyes for the present, 'the first free television ever' – that's what they called it – focused on Romania's past. For days to follow, the whole country was glued to the TV.

For the first time, we could see the 'Golden Epoch' revealed for what it was. More than anything else, we saw images of Ceauşescu's palaces and treasures. We saw the scales of pure gold on which his imported meat was weighed, the diamonds on Elena's shoes, the swimming pools, the fantastic luxury in which their children lived . . . Now, in retrospect, I know that this was just another clever campaign to make people think only about Ceauşescu; about how much harm he, his wife and his children had done to the country. But nothing was said about the system.

Next was the trial of Ceauşescu's four top advisors. We saw how these once-powerful men behaved behind bars. A month before, nobody had dared to pronounce their names. They had only to frown and we were pitched into terror. Now they had tears in their eyes and asked for mercy, denying everything, or finding excuses. They were only carrying out the orders of *Odiosul*, the 'horrible' man who had given them power. They did not know what they were doing. One of them, Emil Bobu, the former Prime Minister admitted that he could barely sign his name. Can you believe it? A whole country ruled by a bunch of illiterates! Thank God, they had us all saying to ourselves, thank God it was all over now!

It was announced that Securitate had been disbanded, the whole apparatus with its five divisions. The first division had to suppress any kind of political dissent. The second kept control over factories, farms and every social institution. The third had been concerned with counter-espionage, which actually meant dealing with those who had correspondence with foreigners. The fourth had looked after the Army; and the fifth one, composed of orphans, had been taught to regard Nicolae and Elena as their parents, and were trained like kamikaze soldiers to act as Ceauşescu's personal guard. This fifth division, the fiercest one, had 20,000 praetorians, it was announced. The whole lot had ceased to exist, we were told. From the first division to the fifth, they all disappeared overnight. Just like that.

We saw the rooms where mail was opened and phone calls tapped, although there was no explanation of what had happened to the officers who had manned them. Now we had the Romanian Intelligence Service to guard us from foreign intervention.

But was this not the same old Securitate under another name? . . . Come on! Iliescu and Roman promised that former Securitate officers would not be part of it. And anyway the trial of the twenty-one members of the former Communist Politburo had just started. Were they not charged with genocide? They were. You see! What more do you want? people in my city were saying, though the trial was obviously turning into a huge farce, its judges using the old tactic of long-drawn-out legal proceedings to give the impression that something was being done while avoiding the real decisions.

A year later, the genocide trial collapsed in a shambles. Six of the accused were set free. Others received two to four-year sentences – for minor offences. Dumitru Popescu, a former propaganda boss, received five and a half years, while the former chief of Securitate, Iulian Vlad, accused of 'complicity to genocide', was sentenced to a mere three years.

Of course, I could not confidently predict the outcome of the trial at the time. But I felt the sham. Even during the trial of Nicu Ceauşescu, son of the dictator, notorious for his depravities, I felt it. There were a hundred people killed in Sibiu during the December uprising, while Nicu was Prime Secretary of the city. But the court found excuses. He had a liver disease, he was drugged all time . . . He was too ill to stand trial. Poor lad. Now, as I write this, he is a free man.

'Things cannot be done overnight. Give them a chance!' people told me. 'You are too excited. Let time solve the problems; what can you do anyway?' It was the same old slave mentality, which I could not accept. The dead would not let me.

I started a petition to get the former Communists out of the Town Hall. I talked to everybody I met, whether I knew them or not, about the futility of replacing the word 'Communism' with 'democracy' if the system which had created and supported Communism remained as it was. I could no more believe in a Militia and Securitate who'd changed only their hats than I could believe in the 'today's truth' of those who had yesterday served the lie, in the 'honesty' of those who yesterday stole and cheated, in the 'love' promoted by those who yesterday acted out of hatred.

I talked first with my small circle of fellow translators and teachers, then with other workers from different section of the co-operative where I was employed. More than a thousand people worked in services for the community – hairdressing, manicure, carpentry, photographic and laundry services, making baby clothes and toys, and they all knew me. A month before they'd all avoided me because of my emigration claim. Now, my black dossier was proof that I had not been an informer, and suddenly, my earlier deranged views had become heroic. The days spent in the streets of Bucharest added to my aura.

I spoke openly, from the heart and without resentment; I still believed in our future. It seems I spoke so well that several weeks later I found myself elected president of the whole co-operative. Just another strange thing which happened in my life. Or was it so strange?

After the revolution everyone needed change. In Bucharest, Timi-şoara, Sibiu or Braşov more and more people asked for real reform, both politically and ideologically. In cities like mine, where the revolution was only images on TV, what happened in Bucharest or even in the Town Hall for that matter, was too much to think about. It was in the small circle where you worked that change needed to take place. That, I supposed, was why they shrugged their shoulders when I talked real politics, yet wanted me to be their president.

More than eight hundred of the co-operative workers were women. Dear women! It seemed that among women, my honesty counted for more than my managerial skills.

At first the authorities declared my election illegal. They refused to hand over the keys to my new office. Everywhere in the city there had been elections but in most enterprises the directors had kept their positions. In my co-operative, the new boss had come from nowhere. Those above didn't like it. Town Hall representatives, even Army officers, came to intimidate the workers, who in their turn threatened to strike.

If several hundred women act with one thought in their mind, they can change the world; I speak from experience! The women marched me to the central administration, broke down the doors, turfed out the secretaries, clerks and other former president's people and demanded that I be recognized. In the windows of the hairdressing salons notices appeared:

CLOSED UNTIL DAN ELECTED

The Town Hall faced more pressing problems. My co-operative was in the town centre, providing essential services. The thought of a city full of men with long hair and uncoiffured ladies was not what they needed right now. So I was allowed to squeeze to the top.

I did not pass up the chance. Why should I? It is quite a change for a nobody to become a somebody overnight.

Early each morning, a black car waited outside my flat to take me to the office. There, new secretaries guarded the door lest any unwelcome visitor should disturb me while I contemplated the future of the co-operative.

Now I am poor again, as always. But for a few months I had the taste of power. I was the same man, yet I felt more confident. I started walking differently. My steps were firmer. I was quite relaxed in the leather armchair. Even my language changed. One word was enough. Actually, the fewer words I spoke, the better. I quickly learned the language of power: you do not need to kill your brains to convince people. Those around you always agree, whether they like it or not. At the end of the day I carried all my colleagues' smiles home, as a pillow to help me sleep. Not for long, though. Any miracle lasts for three days, the Romanians say.

One afternoon, I visited a unit where sixty women at sewing machines were embroidering cushion covers. In Ceauşescu's planned economic system, their handiwork was sold to factories, which used them as rags for cleaning machine-tools. And everyone was happy, since the plan was thereby fulfilled.

The impossible taca-tac noise stopped when I entered the work room. The workers stood up saying 'Good morning, Mister President!' like children scared of the new teacher.

'Sit down for God's sake! And don't call me president! My name is Dan!' I said, despite the warnings of my vice-president. 'Don't let people use your name!' he had told me. 'You'll lose their respect and they won't have the necessary fear to work.' But I did not give a damn for his advice.

I sat on the nearest table and started talking about the damp walls, the noisy machines which needed replacing, about those awful cushion covers and how they would have to become real craftwork if we wanted to make millions in the European market. I spoke staring at the walls, too shy to look directly at the submissive adults all gazing at me. Turning towards them for a moment I saw fearful tears in the older women's eyes. Suddenly the whole truth came to me.

How could I really change anything? When a worker was told to turn a screw clockwise and that was all he did for forty years, how long would it take him to learn to turn it the other way? And what could I do with these women, with their hungry children at home? What was going to happen to the millions of workers like these throughout the country? Should they be made redundant for ever, to bring about the prosperity of a co-operative like mine?

And even if a miracle happened and people changed their skills overnight, I still could not be a real president.

In theory, my signature was enough to open and close a new unit, to hire and fire, to approve or disapprove all section plans. But in practice, my hands were tied by the central administration of the co-operative. My word had no value without the signatures of its accountants, chief engineers, lawyers and the vice-president who formed the so-called TESA personnel. They did not sign anything without approval from above. Above was the Town Hall.

You might think this made sense. After all, I was new to the job and could wreck the whole co-operative through lack of experience. But that was not the reason. It was the mentality of the centralized system I had to fight with. The TESA personnel, all old staff – crooks bribed from head to toe – did not move a finger without explicit directions from the Town Hall. The idea of personal responsibility was against their set of mind.

Before now, things had been simple enough. TESA received the orders from the Town Hall, which received its orders from the Union of Co-operatives in Bucharest, which received its orders from the Central Committee, which received its orders from Ceauşescu. But now, above the Town Hall was a provisional National Salvation Front with a provisional president. The instructions the Town Hall received from above were too vague, so the Town Hall passed nothing on to my co-operative. As a consequence, everything was paralysed. No plan, no work, no worries. Chaos in the service units. What inspection? What order? We're free now, aren't we?

Completely drunk, some of my hairdressers were falling over their clients. Did a manicurist cut a lady's finger? Well, that's life! . . . And that lady was the wife of an informer, didn't you know that? It's what she deserved! . . . Life is hard, dear President. We elected you because you have a heart of gold and you do not protect criminals. Isn't that so?

For a while I tried to persuade the Town Hall to let me open new sections. My financial plans showed how profitable these new sections could be. But I didn't impress any of them. They were another bunch of crooks.

In endless meetings, the Town Hall talked about ways of keeping discipline and order. Instead of looking for ways to promote reform, they were looking for ways to prohibit strikes.

'These workers think they can do anything now Ceauşescu is dead! We have to show them the country is not in chaos and they have a duty to the state!' the Mayor declared towards the end of one *Sedinta*. Ceauşescu was gone, but his *Sedinta* remained. All the others approved.

'How are we to keep order?' someone asked. 'Wait till the elections,' the Mayor replied. 'Meanwhile, put the names of those who shout too loud on the list. All these beggars. They will soon see what's coming to them.' The Mayor's complicit audience was wreathed in smiles.

I felt alienated and useless, like a cloth puppet caught between a hammer and the nail. On one side, there were the employees: some good, others bad, but all of them wanting me to increase their salaries, with no work at all if possible. On the other, there was the Town Hall, asking me to submit a list of trouble-makers. In between, I was surrounded by TESA personnel, who were leaving parcels full of coffee and Kent cigarettes in my office. That was one thing that they knew well how to do.

'How dare you!' I shouted at them.

'Dare what? It's the customary thing. Don't be stupid.'

I really had to fight to keep my integrity. And soon, even the workers who had elected me turned against their president. Not because I could do so little for them; they knew I had no real power, and now I'm thinking that they even liked that. It was something else they really did not like. It was my Hungarian name and my political commitment. When the inter-ethnic fighting began, I was caught in the middle.

There came a time when I had to travel to Bucharest almost weekly, as a part of my duties as president. I had to go to important meetings, where I had to shake hands with other bosses, directors, ministers, each of them fatter than the other, and each of them reminding me of the patients in Elias. Some of the *Sedintas* were held in the former Communist Palace Hall; others were held in the Central Co-operative Union building, which was still fiercely guarded by militiamen and soldiers. 'The country is full of *agents provocateurs*,' they said.

I don't know what the others thought when they looked out of the window and saw soldiers ready to shoot anyone who dared to disturb their thoughts. But I strongly felt that my place was not with them. They must have become used to being guarded while they did absolutely nothing. I was not. I preferred to walk in the streets, seeing how life pulsated in the capital. My allegiance was with those who had died. I kept going back to the places which bore the signs of the dreadful events. On one of these walks, I met Nick Rankin.

Nick was a BBC radio producer, out to discover culture in post-revolutionary Romania. Now that we were free we'd all rush to the libraries and read books, he thought. He was a bit disappointed, I must say.

We went together to visit the House of the People, that fascist erection which had flattened a quarter of Bucharest. It was closed and guarded by the Army, but Nick was from the BBC and had special permission to enter, so we were allowed to wander through its empty halls. My God, what experiences life has put my way.

A short while back I had been at rock bottom, trembling with fear while Ceauşescu was giving the order to shoot in Timişoara. Now, only three months later, I was walking through Ceauşescu's rooms, and talking in English without looking over my shoulder. I opened the door on to the front balcony. How much I regretted there were no phones there.

I wanted to ring my parents, you see. 'I'm looking down the Boulevard of Socialism, mum. Ceauşescu is dead, I am living.' That's all I wanted to tell them.

It was late evening when Nick finished the first ever programme recorded in Ceauşescu's House of the People. It ended with a bark. The soldiers looking after us had brought a dog with them into the room. His barking echoed strangely in the huge marbled halls. Nick was thrilled. Soldiers, dogs, a descendant of Dracula at his elbow in the empty palace of the late true Dracula . . . We looked around for bats in the high vaulted ceilings.

That was the end of the House of the People, we believed. It would be kept as a museum of the dark age, if not blown up, so that a thousand years later people would not think of it as we think now of the Pyramids. At that time, I had no idea that the monstrous building would ever be peopled again.

But work continued on the still-unfinished monument. And now, as I am writing, I hear that the new government has plans to move in.

Continuing his interviews, Nick came to my city. When he entered my bachelor flat in Bacău he could not believe how much of England he saw there. My bookshelves were groaning with English novels, I had a Union Jack on a stand, and the walls were plastered with National Trust posters.

'May I invite you to see the land of your dreams?' Nick asked.

These English with their 'May I . . .'! Didn't he know that without such an explicit invitation, my green passport was useless?

We travelled back to Bucharest together, where Nick helped me to get a visa from the British Embassy. 'Don't worry about money,' he told me. 'I'll help you out.' I promised I'd come later that summer. He was a bit taken aback when I hugged and kissed him at the airport.

Back at work I struggled to hold on to that intense feeling of love and forgiveness I had experienced while we were all shouting '*Libertate!*' But as the brutal reality of the aftermath became clear to me, I could feel it fade away.

To the outside world, our new leaders portrayed Romania as a free country. But those who did not share their views were still called 'enemies of the people', and former dissidents became dissidents again. Doina Cornea, the little old woman who had raised her voice against Ceauşescu, was now a 'notorious fascist'. Father Tökés, whose actions had triggered the events of Timişoara, was now found guilty of lack of patriotism, dirty dealings and of secret relations with foreign powers. He was so guilty that later he had to ask for protection from the West.

They did not even bother to change the old language. While Iliescu told the West how much the country was open to economic investment and trade, at home, just like Ceauşescu, he promised that Romania would become the new Switzerland of Europe if the workers would only let him protect them from capitalist evils. 'Western investors would replace you, dear citizens, with robots and computers,' he said, his eyes almost wet.

During the run-up to Romania's first free elections in May, the NSF seemed ready to protect the country from everything: shortages, bad weather, bad foreigners – and mainly Hungarians. In Bucharest, people were less impressed by their promises. But in the provinces, old hostilities were rekindled.

Under Ceauşescu, nationalism had been used as one of many instruments of oppression. *Divide et Impera!* Rumours spread by Securitate divided Romanians from Hungarians, workers and peasants from intellectuals, Romanians from Romanians, until eventually we were all afraid of each other. Now, under Iliescu, the old nasty rumours about your neighbour were back in circulation. And this time, they were backed up by nationalistic newspaper editorials.

In March 1990, two months before the elections, violent and bloody fighting erupted between Romanians and ethnic Hungarians. It started when a group of Romanians were attacked by Hungarians in a village near the Transylvanian city of Tîrgu Mureş. Or so it was said. Later, it was revealed that plain-clothes secret police had been involved in the events, intent on destabilizing the country in order to strengthen their position.

But for the time being, nothing could check the fury of revenge. Romanian villagers immediately descended upon the city and pitched battles occurred. The TV broadcast images of streets stained with blood; people on the ground were being clubbed with axes and pick handles. Hungarian malice has surfaced at last, it was said. The descendants of Attila are showing their true face.

Many of my relatives live in Tîrgu Mureş. On the phone, my relatives were crying, afraid for their lives. The unfortunates lying in the streets were not Romanians, they told me, but Hungarians. Each side was accusing the other.

The day after this news, the co-operative's workers were clamouring outside my office demanding buses. They wanted to go and kill Hungarians.

I refused, of course. I tried to talk sense into them. But they did not want to hear.

Where was that magic solidarity, that desire to start a new life, the invisible thread which had linked all of us in love and brotherhood at Christmas?

'You are a Hungarian, aren't you?' they shouted. '*Bozgor!*'

The ethnic fighting quietened down but from now on nothing could curb my workers' rancour.

They called me a capitalist and a 'royalist', knowing I was a member of the Liberal Monarchist Party. 'You should resign,' I was advised.

A few months earlier I had been a kind of symbol of moral integrity. Now I was a foreign spy. Rumours about my awful past started to get about, and I had a pretty good idea where they were coming from. Someone higher up did not like me again.

As the election day approached the Town Hall gave orders to each institution in the city: where the voting should take place, how the buildings should be arranged, who to be responsible for what. The only thing not explained was the method of voting, a new and complicated one that nobody understood, myself included. I asked the Mayor for advice.

'Your role is to make people vote and keep order, not to make them understand. There are others who deal with that,' he told me.

'What about my party?' I insisted. 'Where can we meet?'

Officially, the Town Hall was obliged to provide rooms for each opposition party, legitimate venues where new members could enrol.

'Who needs a monarchy in the twentieth century?' the Mayor asked.

I started recruiting members by phone, meeting them in my flat or on street corners where they whispered together, looking over their shoulders while talking to me.

'We will vote for your party, but don't put our names down.'

Four months after the revolution, the old fear had resurfaced. The feeling of strength and solidarity I had experienced in the streets of Bucharest was becoming part of a distant memory. Yet the need to hold on to it made me put my political activity before anything else, though I had never believed in the world of politicians before.

Our party's manifesto was muddled and confused. But one point at least was clear enough: we had to fight against Communism, by any means at our disposal. There weren't many 'monarchists' in the country at that time. In Bucharest, my party had a few hundred members, but in my city we were only five: me, my father, an old history teacher and two students. And we didn't have many resources available to us.

At that time, few opposition party newspapers ever reached our city, as the couriers – students mainly – were beaten up on the trains. Their copies of the newspapers were dumped.

A small gathering of the Liberal Party was violently broken up, apparently by gypsies. In a nearby village some people were beaten to death for joining the National Peasants' Party. Drunkards killing each other in a tavern brawl, the official reports said.

When I and the two students went to that village to discover the truth, we were booed. The villagers did not want to read our papers. They called us 'filthy capitalists' and threw stones at us. Iliescu had promised them land – what the hell did we think we were up to? To bring back that king, whose forefather had killed the peasants in the 1907 uprisings? Why didn't we like our new leaders? Weren't they so popular that France and England wanted to recruit them as heads of their countries? Iliescu couldn't accept, of course, because of his patriotism.

What chance did we have when the peasants genuinely believed such talk? We retreated.

The events in Bucharest, however, in the late spring of 1990 gave me hope. Real hope.

On 23 April, students from universities and colleges all over Bucharest gathered in the University Square. This was the same place where their fellow students had been killed during the revolution, the same place where, ten days earlier, a group of young people who demonstrated against the National Salvation Front had been dispersed by the police.

This time, the students cordon off the area with thick white tape, and put banners and placards at the margins. 'COMMUNIST-FREE ZONE' is written round the place, where they bunch up tightly. They then stage a sit-down, determined not to leave until . . . Until what?

At five the next morning, the police attack. They knock everybody about, and fill their vans with as many as they can snatch from the running crowd. Two hours later, as the students are returning to their protest, my phone rings.

'Come and join us! We need all those who were in the streets during the revolution.' It was the voice of Dumitru, the blond man I had recognized in Victoria Square.

I jump in the black car and rush to the office where I delegate myself to Bucharest – I was a president, don't forget. An hour later, my driver is speeding down the road. First stop – the Central Committee building.

'You go home, I'll take the train back!' I tell the driver. He nods.

That afternoon I am in the University Square. By now it is packed with demonstrators. I squeeze my way through to the middle of the square where it's easier to hear the words coming out of the loudspeakers. Representatives of 'the Students' League', 'the People's Alliance', 'the 16-21 December Association' are taking it in turns to address the crowd from the university balcony. People cheer, chant and applaud while teachers, writers, students and former dissidents come to the microphone one by one.

The speakers are not promising a brilliant future for the country. They are just giving their own personal testimony, simple truths. They ask for those arrested ten days before to be freed. The crowd responds, shouting and singing, 'Romanians awake!'

Hour by hour, minute by minute, more and more people are coming. By seven in the evening thousands are cramming the square and the numbers continue to grow. How many are we? Ten thousand? Twenty thousand? Men and women, young and old, some with children in tow; workers, doctors, engineers; relatives and parents of those detained and killed, people just freed from torture cells; they all melt with the students, becoming one, all united by one good cause. Justice must be done. The mockery of the new system must end.

My heart pumps like in the days of the revolution. I feel a resurrection in the air. I've already forgotten the compromised reality of my everyday life. The crowd gives me the strength I so much need. The voices around me echo the questions in my mind.

Why are the Communist activists still in power? Why are former dissidents still threatened? Why, after four months have only two people been found guilty for the thousands killed? What happened to all the help so desperately begged from the West? Food received from outside was rotting in the ports and railway stations. Into whose pockets was the money disappearing? What is this Romanian Intelligence Service if not the former Securitate apparatus, which now labels all opponents 'political stooges' and 'foreign agents'?

These questions pointed to one unavoidable truth. Innocent people had been shamefully exploited in a cynical *coup d'état*. From the university windows, the architecture students were unrolling huge posters of Iliescu shaking hands and playing chess with Ceauşescu. The crowds were responding with boos and chanted slogans. '*JOS ILI-ESCU!*' (Down with Iliescu).

'*JOS ILIESCU!*' I shout till my throat hurts, filled with hate. Ceauşescu ended his rule by perpetrating mass murder, while this man starts his reign with it. We all hate Iliescu in that square. Yet there are no violent scenes, and no one suggests any violence. We just boo and shout as loud as we can – getting the hate out of us.

Night falls over the city. Some people are leaving, intending to return next day. Most of us remain. The students carefully put back the tapes and banners round the Communist-free zone. They check us for alcoholic drinks. I sit on the pavement, near a small group with a tent. We exchange past experiences and recollect the time of the Golden

Epoch. The students are younger than me, but I'm seeing them at their most mature, much stronger in their convictions than most grown-ups I know. I feel love warming my heart again.

I was always close to the young, who strive to fathom life's true meaning, who rebel against the crashing wave of the world's indifference and its preconceptions – who still believe in beauty, purity and justice. But this time, I feel like taking each one of them in my arms. They all are my brothers and sisters. A guitar plays nearby; the singing is soft and tender. Sandwiches are brought into the square from the university canteen. Girls bring flowers and are met with cheers. A flower for each of us.

It's late, after midnight, and everyone has candles in their hands. We are singing 'Christ is resurrected' and mourning the dead when suddenly dark rumours spread among us. The Army and police are coming with motorized vehicles. They have orders to shoot. Incredibly, there's no panic. We huddle closer together, linking arms with one another. We won't leave, no matter what. I myself feel stronger as a person there than I ever felt as president of my co-operative. I don't feel like a useless puppet any more. Now I knew I had a meaning. Nobody could take it from me.

We are all in a huge circle. The braver ones sit at the edge to protect those in the middle. The critical hours are between two and five, we believe, but the night passes peacefully. Maybe the authorities have realized that they can no longer be seen to attack. Next to the square is the Intercontinental Hotel, from which the eyes of the international press are glued to their cameras.

Next day the numbers swell again. Intrigued by the news on the TV, other people come to join us. Those who left have come back with their friends. It's a warm sunny day and the square is so packed that there is hardly room to move. Heaps of sandwiches and drinks, brought from home for us, are left in the streets nearby. I don't dare leave, certain that I could not squeeze back in again. I stand, sit, stand and sit again, while new speakers appear on the balcony. This time they talk about what's happening in Timişoara, which seems to be seething again.

Timişoara, the city which became the heartfelt cry of the country four months before, is sick of the present mockery. Its people want to separate from Romania. They want autonomy, and the Proclamation of Timişoara is read. We applaud and agree with all its ten points. We don't consider the people of Timişoara to be spies and if the whole country wants to slip back into darkness, at least let them be free. I'm not surrounded by morons any more, morons who fervently believe that a state is more important than truth and love.

New placards appear on the University walls:

IN THE FIFTIES STALIN, THEN DEJ, THEN CEAUŞESCU,
NOW ILIESCU. WHEN WILL IT END?

JUSTICE, WEEPING EYES LOOK FOR YOU!
THE DEAD DON'T LET US LEAVE!

Then, the whole crowd unites and chants with one voice, again and again:

SINGURA SOLUTIE – ALTA REVOLUTIE!
(The only solution – another revolution!)

Nobody has anything in their hands except newspapers, placards and flowers, but my God, how strong we feel. We are ready for anything. Big Brother is changing his name. But we won't let it happen!

In the evening the loudspeakers broadcast a government statement. In a televised speech Iliescu has branded us '*golani*', hooligans. We look at each other and burst out laughing.

BETTER HOOLIGAN THAN PARTY ACTIVIST
BETTER DEAD THAN COMMUNIST!

In a matter of minutes everyone is writing on their chests, arms, foreheads, on notices round their necks the word HOOLIGAN. By late evening we are all carrying labels: 'Revolutionary man hooligan'; 'Mother of five children hooligan'; and 'Baby hooligan of my hooligan parents' is pinned to the jacket of a baby girl carried high on her father's shoulder. 'Architecture student hooligan', a young man with a broken leg has written on his plaster. A dog trotting among the crowds has 'Dog Hooligan' round its neck. I wear a card on my chest with 'President hooligan' written on it.

A second night finds me in the square and I don't want to leave, though I have started to feel exhaustion in my body. It's not the lack of sleep which has me shaking and dizzy but the tension of the last twenty-four hours. Nothing I experienced later, like the day in Prague when I joined a euphoric pro-Havel demonstration, can be compared with the passionate intensity of those hours in Bucharest.

The students attracted like a magnet those of us who still had hope in the bottom of their hearts. No one on the balcony or in the square had ambitions for power. We were not asking for a higher standard of living, as other demonstrators did, much later, in the same place. We only wanted the truth to be spoken. It was like a rose blossoming from the mire of opportunists and careerist politicians, in a garden where personal preoccupations were put aside.

After midnight, as on the previous night, there are rumours of approaching police. As before, we cling, huddle, bunch together. I sleep for several hours with my back propped against the back of another brother.

On the next day, 26 April, it starts raining. People shelter under large umbrellas and plastic sheeting. I leave the square for a few hours to ring my parents and tell them I'm OK. For a second it crosses my mind to call my secretary to tell her . . . To tell her what?

Back to the square. I decide to speak from the balcony. In front of the microphone, I stutter. There are more than ten thousand people down there and it is not so easy to talk about truth and things that hurt. People wait. Nobody pushes me aside. I finally find my words – they are different from those I mentally rehearsed minutes before. I talk about how the elections in my district are being rigged, about what I witnessed in the Town Hall back home. Then I stutter again as I try to talk about freedom.

'Dear brothers, I don't know what freedom means, that's the truth. But I know how my life was under Communism and I don't want to go through that again . . .' When I end – or did I end? – people applaud.

I join the crowds again. The government continues to ignore our requests to send a representative to talk with us. All these thousands of people are non-existent for them. Romanian TV is still not showing any images from the square, but Western journalists are taking interviews and shooting footage. Late that evening I ring Dudu.

'Come to be resurrected, my friend. Bring everybody you know with you.'

'Yes,' I hear his voice mocking. 'Radio Free Europe says that there are more than 20,000 of you there. That's good. Well, you might even start a real revolution, who knows? Be brave, but take care!'

Early the next morning, while candles are still alight, I leave the square to return to Bacău and get more people to join us. Now that the West is watching, there needs to be as many of us as possible.

Back at my office I convene a big meeting with my workers. I tell them about the events in Bucharest and who the so-called 'hooligans and fascists' are in the square. They don't believe me. I'm ready to provide buses at the co-operative's expense to take them all to Bucharest to see for themselves. They don't want to go. If I gave them buses to hunt down Hungarians they would happily fill them to bursting. What's going on in Bucharest is not their concern.

We have a full day of TV now; we can watch all the world's sporting events. Food is not rationed, we can use private cars all week, we can use as many light bulbs as we want – so what are the students after? We have two of the most cultured men in Romania at the top. Who do the students want to replace them with?

'The sun rises when Iliescu appears'; there were already paeans of praise being spread about by Iliescu's electoral campaigners. Instead of suffering from collective guilt about the madness of Ceauşescu's epoch, my workers saw the new smiling leaders as gods. Sickened, I dismissed the meeting. I never felt so much anger at my compatriots as on that day.

Soon after that meeting, I started to get the same old anonymous phone calls. What more did I want, I was asked, wasn't I content to be a president? So I was mad and a traitor again. The phone calls told me to watch my step. A human being doesn't live for ever, right?

In the middle of the crowd I had felt so strong and resolute. A few days back into my normal life and the great fear had caught my soul again.

A week later I returned to Bucharest, this time with my father. He wanted to see for himself what fired me with so much passion. And he wanted to see whether it was true that there was still hope for our people.

My father is a quiet, calm man, as I have said before. But, the few hours we spent together in the square, the miracle of that wonderful crowd, was enough to touch him to the quick. You should have seen the old fellow, normally so reserved. 'Down with Iliescu!' he cried, his eyes full of tears and his face burning with excitement. 'This is for real!' he started repeating to himself, so emotional that I feared he might collapse.

It was me who convinced him to leave. I thought I would come back later, alone. I did not know then that this was to be the last time I would ever see University Square. For it was soon to become a Romanian Tiananmen.

Returning home by train that evening we could not stop talking about what we had witnessed to those in the packed compartment. No, the students weren't demonstrating against poverty so much as a cruel, mean-minded, ugly system. It was the dishonesty they abhorred – we were going on like this when suddenly a man stood up and spat in my father's face.

'You fascist!' he shouted. I was momentarily too shocked to react. Then I saw the silent approval in the eyes of the other passengers. That made us keep our mouths shut until we reached Bacău and our provincial reality.

At home, we found my mum crying. She was terribly worried about us. She had just received a dirty phone call, but that was not the reason for her fear. While we were in Bucharest, she had gone to my flat to tidy it a bit as she used to do every Sunday. She saw something there that she didn't want to speak about.

'What?'

'Go and see. But don't go alone. Take your father with you. And ring Dudu. He should be there as well.'

And that's what we did. All three of us went to my flat, imagining all sorts of things on the way. It wasn't so disastrous. On my door, daubed in red paint:

YOU ROYALIST PIG! YOU'VE HAD IT!

My parents, Dudu and I spent that night in grim discussion of recent events. Major Doroș, I learned, had been made a full colonel in the local branch of the Romanian Intelligence Service. In the new Parliament, the city deputies were lying shamelessly about everything, while the newspapers started to sing their praises, just like in the old days . . . Others too had no illusions about the new Romania, and were leaving the country in their thousands every day. Aaron and Virgil were already in Germany, Austria, wherever.

Dudu was emphatic.

'Before, you were just a madman. You were of no importance in their eyes. Now you have an influential social position, you have taken a political stance, you have friends in the BBC – they can do without people like you just now. I'm not in your situation but I'd go too if I had the chance. I guess I'll be here till I die of sickness and disgust.'

That was the last time I saw Dudu.

I knew that the University Square protest would change nothing. The country was set firmly on its new course. How many would join the students' sit-in? Another thousand, a hundred thousand? The country had a population of more than twenty million. 'Stupid, but numerous, my Lord', as a boyar from an old Romanian play described a dangerous army.

I felt desperately guilt-stricken to be deserting my brothers, but I feared for my life. I didn't even know who it was I should fear most. Securitate, or ordinary citizens? In the chaos of that whirling time I felt that anything could happen to me. I wasn't cut out to be a martyr, as I've already told you. I was just an ordinary man who believed that life was the most precious thing you could have.

Two or three days later, the Securitate officer responsible for my co-operative before 'the revolution' approached me in the street.

'Let's have a beer,' he said. 'No ill feelings I hope?' he added ironically.

We sat in a bar. I had nothing against him as such. My real enemy was not the man himself, but the system which had created him.

'I hear you are going to England.'

I was staggered. Did they still have bugs in my parents' flat?

'Nice country . . . When I was a kid, I always wanted to see a football match at Old Trafford . . . But Securitate officers are not allowed such things, you know? By the way! I hope you are not carrying your hate against Iliescu in your luggage.'

I looked deep into his eyes.

'Are you threatening me?'

'No, no . . . I am your friend . . . *Noroc*! . . . But it would be a pity for a man like you to badmouth our beautiful free country. You might want to come back one day.'

I gazed at him open-mouthed.

'As for Iliescu . . . Don't worry about him, my friend,' he continued. 'Securitate changed Ceauşescu. It will change Iliescu too if he is not a good boy.' He started to laugh, as if he'd cracked a really good joke.

In Bucharest, the students went on with their vigil. My fellow-citizens in Bacău were preparing to vote for Iliescu; my mum, dad and I were packing in a hurry. My parents were going to travel with me for a while. I guess they wanted to make sure I wouldn't change my mind.

'*Securitate changed Ceauşescu. It will change Iliescu too if he is not a good boy.*' The officer's words followed me across Hungary, East Germany and Czechoslovakia. They are with me even now, as I write.

IX

Freedom at Last!

Budapest, Prague, Dresden ... They are all behind me. Wonderful cities, interesting people – but I still felt the greyness of home.

So here I was, in the cab of a truck next to the driver, a well-fed, unwrinkled red German face. My heart was beating like hell as we queued for customs at the border with the West.

We had met some hours earlier in Karlovy-Vary, a mountain pearl of Czechoslovakia, where I had just bid farewell to my parents. They had travelled with me for three days, and together we had shared the thrill of seeing foreign lands for the first time ever. When the moment came for us to part, our hearts felt unbearably heavy.

'Here's a gift for you. Three hundred dollars to make the best of things ... It's almost all our savings. Don't worry! We have our pension, we'll manage without it,' my parents said. We hugged, kissed and waved goodbye.

Would we ever see each other again? Their car disappeared as they headed back, and I ran into the first bar in front of me.

I sat at a table near the window, ordered a beer and looked around me. I was in a clean room, with people drinking from clean glasses. The waiters were smiling at me. I closed my eyes and leaned back. But no! No thoughts of the past. Not any more! The present and future were what counted. I had to be strong.

Of course, I was thinking, I would send the money back to my parents just as soon as I was rich. Rich? No. But I was rich already. I had never been so rich in my life. With $300 and a passport in my pocket what else could I need? I would see Paris and London, then travel round the world, free in movement and in thought. There would be no one to tell me, do this, don't do that, this is good and that's bad. I was on my own, at last!

When the truck driver sat down at my table, I really believed that $300 was a big deal. Trying to understand one another, we began with a bit of German, then a bit of English, and ended up in the universal language of hands and eyebrows. We threw in some proper names as well, to be clearer.

I started with Goethe. He continued with Schwarzenegger. I went on: Kant, Hegel, Rilke . . . It was his turn: Müller, Beckenbauer, Rummenigge . . . We understood each other pretty well, nodding and smiling. It was a perfect day, everything was OK . . . *Ja* . . . *Ja* . . . Perfect conversation.

Finally, to prove we were a little more profound, we shifted to politics.

'*Krieg ist nicht gut,*' we agreed, but that was too vague an idea.

'Me,' he pointed to his fat confident belly, 'Me . . . Kohl! Capitalism! You . . .' he said pointing to my tall, skinny, shadowy frame, 'You . . . Ceauşescu! Communism!' And he started to laugh. It seemed to be such an obvious idea that we continued our chat on politics in the gents', where he offered me a lift to Munich.

On the way to the border I had nothing to do but entertain him, talking about my life, my country, odd events from mysterious places. A bit of Dracula here and there. He was a strange man. No matter what I said, he laughed. He did not understand much, but he laughed.

As the truck drew up to the customs barrier, the driver leaned out to show his passport to the officer who, yawning, stamped it and handed it back. I could not believe it.

There was no checking of the truck. There were no soldiers searching the cab, looking between seat cushions, no dogs sniffing around, hunting for fresh human flesh hidden somewhere, no frowning faces making inquiries. In fact, the customs officer did not even look at the driver's face.

'Next!'

My turn now.

I gave him the passport through the window, my heart pounding. The officer almost stamped it when, suddenly, his eyes grew wider. He raised his head and stared at me. I felt like a beetle, like something that you want to get rid of as soon as possible.

'Romanian?' he asked, with no smile on his face. I had expected it.

Day by day, hundreds, thousands, tens of thousands of men and women, young and old, workers, tramps, teachers, students, were all leaving Romania. I'd read about it in the papers ... Romanians! Polluting the West. Infiltrating everywhere. Asking for asylum. Working illegally. Scabs. Crooks. Dirty gypsies ... A new kind of plague spreading across Europe. I saw it in the eyes of the customs officer, and not for the first time.

I had this feeling before in Bucharest, earlier that spring, outside the Austrian Embassy, where I had gone to apply for a transit visa. There had been a sea of people covering the pavement, the road, the walls, everywhere. After a week of standing in the queue – be sure to be there at first light, otherwise you lose your turn – I was getting nowhere. In the evening, when it was time for us to go home, officials collected names and put them on lists for the following day. The next morning at five, other officials would call other names from other lists, and it seemed that this hullabaloo would go on for ever. So I said to myself: to hell with Vienna, I'll see it when I'm old, and anyway I'm not that fond of Johann Strauss.

So I went to the German Embassy, at the other end of Bucharest, where things were different. There were no people around. Just a policeman standing in front of the gate, his bulldog face gazing at the sky. I was about to enter when he grabbed me by the arm.

'I'm travelling to the UK and I need a transit visa,' I explained, smiling.

'All right ... but first you have to enlist here,' he answered, turning his gaze on me, 'and then you must wait there,' he went on, pointing to the horizon somewhere.

There, in the distance, I beheld a park, and a few minutes later I saw another sea of people. They were like locusts, sitting, standing, lying under, in or between the trees, on the benches, bushes, flowers, everywhere on the grass, surrounding scores of tents from which a heavy smell of cooking wafted.

'How long do I have to wait?' I asked the bulldog-face later.

'According to this list, your turn is in two days,' came the answer.

Two days later, when I went to the gate again, I met another policeman.

'You have to enlist here and wait there,' he said showing me another piece of paper, and I realized what had to be done. I bought a tent, squeezed amongst the others and settled down to wait.

Two weeks later, inside the Embassy, at last:

'I need a transit visa . . .'

'Show me your train ticket!' the German employee demanded sternly, without looking at me. I had no train ticket.

'No train ticket, no transit visa,' he said with relief.

'Next!'

Go on boy, down to the railway booking office and wait. Another queue, more days, and finally some employee's voice which says to me:

'No transit visa, no train ticket. Sorry.'

Catch-22. Back to the Embassy! Another week, another employee, another story.

'Show me your train ticket!'

'I'm going by car!'

'Show me your international driving licence and your petrol money,' he said, countering my gambit with barely concealed delight. He won, but I did not give up.

Two months later, I had a 24-hour German visa stamped in my passport. That was just the beginning. I wanted to see other countries as well. That's how Romanians are. You give them a finger and they want the whole hand.

At the Swiss Embassy, things were much simpler.

'Romanian passport? Sorry, no transit visa for you!'

Simple as that.

What the hell was going on? Well, this was what was going on: after the revolution doors were open from the inside – 'You're free to go wherever you want, comrade' – but locked from outside – 'You're free to go anywhere you want, but not in our country.'

Once inside the French Embassy I had to beseech still other employees to let me visit their country. Why beseech? Because of my Romanian passport. It was like having the plague.

All in all, it took me three months to complete the formalities. As I prepared to leave, a bitter taste, the taste of being Romanian, lingered in my mouth.

And my heart ached again and again in Hungary, East Germany and Czechoslovakia where, with my parents, we looked for somewhere to stay. Every evening, the same story.

'Have you any rooms?' I would usually start the conversation with the hotel receptionist in good English.

'Of course,' came the reply. 'No problem.'

But when I showed them my passport the usual problem started up again. Bastards! What was wrong with us? Weren't we clean enough? We did not look like beggars. My poor parents! They smiled all the time, with eyes full of shame and fear, and gave small gifts to everybody we met. They gave gifts to receptionists, porters, cleaners, but it was not enough. For we had Romanian passports.

It all flooded back as I waited at the German border for the questions to start. When, where, why, for how long; there was no smile on the officer's face.

And then it happened. He stamped it. *My* passport. I felt like leaping into the air. But I did not. I was too scared. There was still a barrier in front of me. What if they sent me back, seeing my joy?

Some moments later, the barrier closed behind us. With a lump in my throat, I asked the driver to stop. I got out, with my trusty rucksack, all that I had from my past.

'*Das ist nicht München*', the driver said, a bit baffled.

He thought I was some kind of idiot. But I could not go any further with him. I wanted to be alone.

We waved, the truck drove off and I started walking down the road to the first village in the Western world. Free at last!

I was quite alone on that smooth tarmacadam road among the fields. Cars passed by at high speed. I guess nobody saw me crying.

I zig-zagged across Germany, wherever my lifts took me. From east to north, from north to south, from south back to north, and it was near the East German border that I realized I was travelling back to where I had started. Then a young man took me south again, at 200 kilometres an hour. He seemed extremely nervous, that man, continuously agitated by inner thoughts which I could know nothing of. All I could understand was that he had no time for East Germans.

'It'll take years and years for us to teach them all we know: competition, freedom, self-discipline, white bread and Coca-Cola,' he shouted at me.

He definitely didn't like the idea of a united Germany.

He left me on the highway, near a road sign for Munich, where I finally realized how far the cities were from the highways. I dropped the idea of seeing the Bavarian capital. According to my visa, I had only twenty-four hours on German soil. I hitched like a madman. It was still day when I found myself right in the middle of Germany somewhere.

Was it a city? A town? A village? I really don't know. I had a map of course – it's up on the wall here, where I write, but somehow I could not believe that I was covering such distances. Remember! At home it took me half a century to get from my flat to the school, which was just twenty miles away. What a struggle! What torments! Then I spent years cudgelling my brains to find a way to cross a stretch of just ten kilometres. Five to the Romanian border, five on the other side, where I could still be caught by the Yugoslavian guards. And now, I was swallowing the distances as if space did not exist in the West.

This German place I was in – my parents would've thought it was heaven on earth. The people were so self-assured, the streets so clean; there was so much quiet wealth. I felt scared.

I was hungry, but I did not have the courage to enter a supermarket or snack-bar. Eventually I dared. After all, nobody knew me, so I could pretend to be someone else. But the supermarket was so well-lit, so huge and luxurious; the endless shelving was crammed with so many goods that I felt frighteningly lost in all that abundance. I went out as quickly as I had entered. I decided to use the tins from home. At least I knew what was inside them.

I was eating on a bench, hidden between bushes, when a red Jaguar car drove past me and parked. It had a GB plate on the back and my heart started to pound. It always did that at home, when I saw a GB number plate.

They were a couple. The guy, a short, black-haired Italian, who wore dark glasses despite the time of night; the girl was a long-legged blonde English woman in a very short skirt. When they invited me to jump in, I knew a dream was about to come true. We drove for several hours talking bits and pieces about England and Italy. Towards midnight, they decided to rest and asked me whether I wanted to spend the night with them.

At first I thought they were going to invite me to a hotel, and I immediately began to worry about money. But the Italian was thinking of using his car as a bedroom.

We parked somewhere behind a petrol station.

'Are you unhappy?' the woman asked me while her man was in the toilet cleaning his teeth. I told her I was not.

'But your face looks so sad', she said gazing at me.

'In this world you have to be positive, otherwise you're lost,' she went on, stretching her bare legs out and smiling, to make me feel more positive.

The next morning, we were at the Belgian border. I did not have a transit visa for Belgium, but the couple assured me there'd be no problems. They'd help me go further. From there, in five hours we'd all be in England. I guess they got there, but the customs officer took my passport, put a cross on it and pointed me back the way I had come. No transit visa for Romanians. It seemed I still had a long way to go before my dream would be fulfilled.

I was back on the road, hitching again, alone.

There is no great loss without some small gain, my father used to say all the time. He was right. By midday I was in Cologne, on the steps of the cathedral.

It was cold and windy outside. I leaned against a column near the entrance, and for the first time I felt like writing in my pocket diary, about the mixture of feelings inside me.

When I am alone and discover something that moves me deeply, something created either by nature or man, I always feel confused. On the one hand there is the happiness of seeing the new and contemplating the beauty of it. On the other hand, there is the sadness of experiencing it all by myself, alone. Without someone near to share it with, the joy is always halved. This mixing of feelings went deeper as I gazed at the cathedral.

Just to look at the old towers took my breath away. But then, as I turned my head towards the city, the new buildings scratched my eyes.

For a moment I felt I had been born in the wrong century with all these people hustling and bustling about, unaware of anything but progress. Tourists or not, everyone was rushing. Most of them did not even notice this architectural masterpiece of the past.

Did they take it for granted? Maybe there was no time for contemplation here in the West . . . Go! Hurry! Run! . . . Eat fast! Gulp it down! Feel it hard! . . . Be happy! Cry! Laugh! Love! Hate! . . . all in one shot. That seemed to be the new story. Skyscrapers, monoliths of glass and steel, people trapped in their own creations. Was this the world that we Romanians had dreamed of? I felt scared again.

'Wherever you go, whatever you do, you will always be discontented. You have the character of a frustrated man,' my father told me once. I feared it was true.

What was happening to me? Since leaving Romania, I had seen things I had never dreamed of. And yet, I was not happy. Here, there was food in abundance everywhere. There were clean streets, parks, city squares, confident people everywhere. And yet, something told me I would find it hard to belong in this kind of world.

There was too much order everywhere. People seemed punctual, fair, precise and self-controlled, as if they were all living under rigid mathematical rules. You felt the discipline in the very air; too much perfection. 'A set of robots in a perfect society': Aaron's words echoed in my mind.

From Cologne I went south, hitching again. When evening came, it was still Germany. I had been going round in circles and I wondered if I would ever get out of it.

Eventually a car took me to France.

Two men sat in the front, one driving fast, the other constantly glancing in the side mirror as if they were being followed. There was no car behind, but he kept looking obsessively in the mirror. From time to time the men talked to each other in low voices, almost whispering. Looking at their shadowy, impassive faces I began to feel uncomfortable.

'Don't worry, *mon ami*,' the man on the right said, as if guessing my thoughts. '*Nous serons en France aujourd'hui.*'

Of course I hoped to be *en France* as soon as possible but I could not stop thinking that something weird was going on.

As we approached the border I saw a sign pointing to Saarbrücken. Suddenly we left the highway, turning right on to a narrow country road.

We drove slowly for a while, past a small grey building that resembled a pill-box from the war; two soldiers like statues nodded their heads slightly as we passed by. Then the car sped faster down the narrow winding road, until we finally reached the highway again.

Both men seemed more relaxed now. I even caught a glimpse of a smile on the face of the one in the passenger seat.

'*Nous sommes en France, mon ami,*' he said. I did not reply; I was silent as a tomb. In fact, I kept my mouth shut all the way. I was convinced I was in a car with two smugglers and had entered France illegally. There had been no customs barriers, no officers, no hold-ups, no stamps on the passport.

What an irony! I had waited twenty years for a passport, and now I was entering another Western country with nobody looking at it. Only I was too scared to see the funny side of this at the time.

There I was, it seemed, in a car with two bandits – like a stupid fly that drops into the hot milk, as the Romanians say. If the police stopped them, they would use my skinny body as a human shield. It always happened like that in the West. I had seen it in the gangster movies that I had translated for my fellow-citizens.

Then a more frightening thought occurred to me. Even if they let me go, how could I explain to the authorities that I had no entry stamp on my passport? And further, what would I say at the English border? Would they understand the possibility of leaving a country that you had not entered? They might stop me right there, and send me back to Romania. The thought so paralysed me that I hardly noticed the burst of neon lights as we approached Paris.

That's me. Instead of immersing myself in the joy of the new, I worry. On the way to Paris, I worried so much that I felt faint when the bandits left me near the Gare du Nord. I could hardly say '*Merci beaucoup!*'

Of course, I had panicked for no reason. When I left France, later on, once again nobody looked at my passport. As for 'the gangsters', they went out of their way to drop me near the railway station. They even gave me phone numbers, in case I needed somewhere to stay. Good fellows, bandits or not.

As soon as I de-flabbergasted myself, I decided to get rid of my rucksack and go for a stroll. When the old man at the Left Luggage told me I would have to pay 15F, I changed my mind. That money was three days' pay at home, as a president. I put the rucksack on my back and started walking at random down the cobbled streets. I preferred to be robbed by individuals than by a company.

I had not gone far when someone rushed out of a building I was just passing.

'*Une chambre, monsieur?*' a man asked, making me jump. I saw 'BELGE HOTEL' above the door, so I followed him into a narrow, dimly lit hall. A receptionist was waiting at its end.

'*150F la nuit.*'

That was a month's salary for me, but I felt dead beat. Why not spend a night like a king, for once in my life?

The room was definitely not for kings, though. It had a small bed, no table, no chair, dirty walls and was next to the creaking stairs. All my royal night long I heard couples climbing the steps – women giggling at men's whispers, the prelude to you know what – try to sleep if you can!

Early the next morning, I was in the streets, my hands free as a bird. Descending the Eiffel Tower, I started the tour that I had planned from home years before. Since I knew most of the place names by heart, I rarely needed to look at the map. I had made hundreds of tours by pencil on Paris street maps and had lingered in its alleyways in my dreams.

Paris! . . . Heine said that God looks at Parisian boulevards when He gets bored. I could believe it. Gazing at them from the sky wouldn't cost anything.

Late that evening, I drank *un petit café* on the terrace opposite the Moulin Rouge. What would Toulouse-Lautrec have felt if he had been there? Depressed? I'm sure of it. People like him or me can find signs of depression anytime, everywhere.

Good-looking men and beautiful women were walking past, but to me these opposite sexes didn't seem to talk to each other. They seemed completely blasé, as if they were used to a certain boredom in their lives.

I could not stop thinking of my mother. Her head down, washing by hand my father's underpants, all her life. She never walked down a street like these women. What would she think if she was there? What would she have thought about food for dogs and cats in the shops? Would she conclude that God had made a world for some people to live in like humans, while others spent their lives in a stable, with no way out? Or would she just be happy that her son was in Paris?

I was glad that nobody knew me. On the boulevard Clichy, glancing into sex shops . . . All those women waiting for you open-mouthed. But back in my little room at Hotel Belge I discovered the great truth about Paris: in just one day it had swallowed half my parents' life savings.

Just three days in the West and already I was thinking of money as never before in my life. I was counting pennies every step of the way.

The next morning, I was back at the Gare du Nord, to catch a train to Calais. My face turned pale when I discovered the price of the ticket. Close to the ticket office I noticed a teenager with a green rucksack on his back who looked as gloomy as me. I could see we were in the same boat. Good enough reason to become friends.

The hands of the station clock were pointing to nine when my new friend and I started walking north. At ten it began to rain, and we sheltered under a bridge. There I found out he was Australian, and had set out from Perth six months before. At four we were still under that bridge, holding our cardboard signs 'CALAIS, S.V.P!' Nobody cared for our *s'il vous plaît*. When the rain stopped we went on. You change the place, you change the luck, as we Romanians say.

It was getting dark. Paris was behind us and it seemed that we would have to walk all the way to Calais. Speeding through the puddles, cars drenched us as they passed. Those which slowed down were mostly driven by women, but they never stopped. A Renault, and a woman at the wheel, that was the very image of French style, and I now hated it as much as I had loved it the day before.

At last a van stopped for us; we felt like kissing the driver's hands. Later that night, he dropped us off in Amiens. We had no idea where Amiens was. It was close to the English Channel, the driver assured us.

Next day, I fell in love with that little town.

Paris is Paris, of course. But with so many foreign tourists, McDonalds, Sonys and BMWs and Michael Jackson posters, you quickly lose the feel of the place. It was in Amiens where I discovered the beauty of France that I had read about before.

We were eating lunch in a *petit café* when the owner, a fat old chap with a big red nose, invited us to share a bottle of red wine, on the house. He felt for us, he said.

We sat at a table in the window while he told us stories; of Jules Verne who had lived just opposite, about a Resistance shooting over there, by the church. I felt attracted to the cosy old chap, with his Cyrano de Bergerac nose, his gentle smile and his conviction that all was in its proper place in the world.

When he heard I was Romanian he brought another bottle.

'Well done, boy!' he said to me. 'First, you didn't let the Slavs spoil your language. That's good for a start. You were the bastion of the Latin language, a thorn in Russia's side . . . Then you killed that bastard and his bitch, which was even better. Today it's 21 May, isn't it? You've got the first free elections for forty-five years. You should be proud! Life is just beginning for you Romanians.'

I did not tell him what I knew about those who had killed the Ceauşescus, or about the 'free' elections that were taking place. I did not want to spoil the moment.

My friend was staggering when we left for Calais. I had not drunk as much as I would have liked. I was too worried. What if they smelled my breath at the border and turned me back? With no stamp on my passport, thanks to those friendly bandits – I was in the grip of dark thoughts. On the ferry-boat I was so tense that I thought I'd collapse.

Then, the great moment came. Nobody looked twice at my passport or asked me any questions.

When I took my first step on English soil at Dover, I knelt and crossed myself despite the bewildered looks of those around me. What did they know? And how many of them had ever had a dream come true?

X

Out of Romania

I spent my first weeks in England at a vicarage, a large Georgian villa with dark, grey brick walls and white-painted windows in a quiet street of North London. George had a room there and offered to share it with me, 'until you sort yourself out'.

It was great to find my old friend again. As soon as we met, the distance between us vanished in a second. And, of course, we talked and talked about everything and everybody. I was glad to discover that time and a different culture had not changed him much – or so I believed.

During our long talks we wandered through the rooms of the vicarage, which were all full of books. Bookshelves covered the walls of the sitting-room, living-room, bedrooms, hallway, bathroom, and even of the two toilets. There were books in cardboard boxes, under tables, on the stairs: old and new, bound in card, leather and vellum, thick tomes or flimsy pamphlets, you couldn't see for the written word.

Not that I spent much time reading them.

During the day, I was running. I was devouring London with my hungry eyes.

Crushed in the crowds of Covent Garden, crossing the river by every bridge I had read about, hurrying from Big Ben to the Tower and back to feed the pigeons near the lions of Trafalgar Square, leaning against the railings of Buckingham Palace and discovering the vivid green of London parks, then rushing back to have another glimpse of the city from the top of St Paul's . . . When evening came I was like a sponge squeezed dry.

Yet, once the lights were turned on, I abandoned myself in Piccadilly Circus, dazzled by the brilliant high windows of Regent Street. That was what my soul needed most of all. After so many years of darkness, the radiant streets and shops swallowed me.

Night after night I found myself in Leicester Square, jostling with the bustling crowds of young people and feeling I was in another world. What a spectacle! Especially when you think that Romanian students would get lifted from the streets for having long hair or a skirt a bit too short.

At the beginning, I was so elated by so much freedom everywhere that I took the people begging and sleeping in cardboard boxes as part of London's eccentricity, and I took the dirtiness of the streets as part of London's picturesqueness. Later on, my excitement waned as I began to find out how things really were behind the lights: the loneliness and crushing isolation of this anthill of people.

At the end of each exhausting day, I rested my eyes on the books in the vicarage. They sat peacefully on the shelves, side by side, while people were rushing about outside. Each day had its intensity of feelings. Sometimes I was happy, overwhelmed. Other times I was scared, confused and homesick. Surrounded by those books again I felt better. Discovering a familiar name on the spine, I felt more relaxed. They gave me a sense of security. A sense of significance. A feeling of belonging to the same world, no matter how different the cultures. Just looking at those books was enough to confirm that not everything in this world was made to be consumed at speed and thrown into the dustbin the next day.

In one room on the ground floor lived David, a quiet man who played classical piano. Since I never saw him do anything else but play the piano and drink beer, I asked him what he did for a living.

'Me, work?' he answered with the sweetest possible voice. 'Only stupid, greedy people work these days, and I don't consider myself to be either!'

David seemed happy enough with his life; in fact, he seemed happy most of the time, except when he fell in love, which happened quite often. I would see him staring moodily at the ceiling; I heard him sighing, and once I even saw him crying into his glass of beer.

I like men who do not hide their feelings. I always believed that the image of the tough male who never shows his feelings to a woman is a creation of the movies. I wanted to meet the person who made David sigh so much. And one evening, he promised, he would let me meet his love.

'Let me introduce you to Nigel,' he said while tenderly coiling an arm around his friend.

I thought it was a joke. But the way they looked at each other and the tenderness between them made me soon realize that indeed, Nigel was David's love. I felt uneasy. Later, I asked George for details.

'Forget your prejudices,' he said. 'You're in a civilized country now. What have you got to complain about?'

I had certainly brought my prejudices from Romania. And my instincts. I remember when I had a terrible toothache and I had to go to the dentist. George spent ages telling me to go there empty-handed. No Kent cigarettes for the doctor? Would she even look in my mouth without a tip? George did not convince me, so I at least took some flowers. You should have seen the dentist's face when I gave them to her. But what could I do? It was in my blood.

As for my prejudices . . .

Officially, homosexuality did not exist in Romania. Of course, there were rumours about men making love to other men, but they seemed always to be linked with two places: prison and the theatre. Homosexuality, it was said, starts either from frustration – where better than prison for that? – or from depravity and boredom – both attributed to actors, who were supposed to indulge in countless orgies. The doctors said homosexuality was a sign of mental disorder. The newspapers said nothing, and books never mentioned it.

But now I was in a new world. And George was right. I had nothing to complain about. David was a nice man; he was good company and was always ready to help. So, when he invited me on a day trip to Walsingham in Norfolk, I gladly accepted.

Early that morning we all met in the churchyard near the vicarage. I was part of two busloads of people, travelling to take part in a religious procession.

We were all in high spirits, talking loudly, smiling and laughing. The weather was unusually splendid, and I hardly noticed that everyone else in the bus was a man.

Once we arrived in Walsingham I had the same feeling I had experienced in Amiens. London is London, but here was the true England I had read about – in the villages and countryside.

The narrow streets and parks were packed with people waiting for the procession to start. Groups of men were drinking beer outside the pubs and arguing loudly with other religious groups – it seemed to me. I followed my friends, shaking hands, nodding all the time and accepting beers offered by men I had never seen before. Then, alongside David and the others, I joined the procession. Hundreds of tourists had gathered on the pavements to watch us pass, some shouting, others just curiously looking on. I was filled with the peace and piety you experience in a church or other sacred place as the procession wound slowly up the hill. I wished my father could have seen me there. He always wanted to be a priest.

Only later did I realize what was obvious to everyone except me. It was better that my dad had not been there, to see how proudly I pilgrimed among the gays.

Back at the vicarage I told George about my confusion. Instead of laughing, he started to lecture me. He opened a bottle of wine and began to accuse me of rudeness towards the people he had introduced me to. I asked personal questions, he said. He wondered if I had behaved badly at Walsingham. I assured him that I had not. But he was doubtful.

'Here, you can talk about the weather, gardening, cooking, anything. But don't ever ask how much people earn, what they really do in their business or what their life is like at home.' These were exactly the kind of questions I put to everyone.

'And never argue,' he went on. 'Never contradict them. They are English and are brought up to think they are the best in the world.'

'Is it so rude to disagree?'

'Yes, it is. You really must learn to be more polite.'

This was too much. My parents had taught me to respect others. I felt angry and hurt.

'Well,' he tried to explain, 'you might have been polite by Romanian standards. But that's not good enough for here. You still have the habit of looking deep into someone's eyes, and that is impolite. Your eyes must always be smiling, like your mouth. Don't try to penetrate the icy reserve of the person opposite. And, more than anything else: wherever you go, whoever you meet, whatever you do, just don't get personal! That's the first thing to learn about English culture.'

I wondered what had made George such a know-it-all. In Romania he never gave me lectures like this. And he still hadn't finished.

'Your way of letting your heart and soul participate in everything you say seems childish to them, even outlandish. Your way of jumping from one story to another, gesticulating crazily, and standing up while talking not only creates a bad impression, but could scare the quiet, calm Englishman. And another thing. I know you've had amazing experiences, but let me remind you that what Eastern Europe is experiencing now, the West has already been through. Revolutions, radical economic change, social disasters, wars; its history is full of them. Comparing East with West is like a child faced with his grandfather. They think they've seen it all before.'

What had happened to George after all these years in England? Had he really become cleverer, whilst I, on the other side of the Iron Curtain, had remained an undeveloped child?

We finished the bottle of wine, and another, while George talked about his new life. He was working for the BBC now; he had responsibilities. There were places where he had to be seen and others that he should avoid, in order not to lose credibility and respect. His grey suit had replaced his jeans. 'The days of the Hell's Angels are far behind me, forgotten,' he told me.

I had been wrong when I thought George had not changed. He had.

A few days later I was in the Albion, our local pub. I had just received news from back home. It was 15 June, and two days earlier the miners had stormed Bucharest.

The students' demonstration had continued in University Square even after the general elections at the end of May, which, amid accusations of vote-rigging, had put Iliescu and the National Salvation Front in power with an overwhelming majority. The voices of the young united now in a new cry: 'Parents, you sold us to Communism.' The students had continued to gather in Bucharest, expressing their anguish, demanding that those who had killed their brothers should be punished. The students posed no serious threat to Iliescu, of course. But still, this was not what the new President wanted to hear.

So, despite the presence of Western journalists, Iliescu called on the miners to crush 'these fascists who are mounting a *coup d'état*.' And the miners came, 20,000 of them. The new President was popular with the miners as he'd increased their salaries considerably. While in Romania, I'd heard Iliescu praise the importance of the miners for the country, saying how much his heart was with them. I did not realize then that he was creating a new army to back him up against 'the non-productive intellectuals'. The miners raged into the students and the seven-week sit-in came to an end.

Heads were broken, ribs cracked, teeth smashed in; batons were driven into faces. The miners laid about the students with all their fury. Thousands of people were injured. The dark, dirty faces – with scores of disguised secret police agents among them – attacked all the people in the square. Then they attacked all the people in the streets nearby, all those who were wearing blue jeans, all those who were under thirty. At the same time, the main opposition party headquarters and the homes of the main opposition leaders were devastated, their newspaper offices sacked and burned.

Cameras and videos were dashed against the walls. Romanian, French and German reporters were beaten with fists, sticks and stones. The students' leader, Marian Munteanu, was badly beaten, arrested and thrown into jail. Six more young people had to die before University Square was finally cleared.

At the end of the day, Iliescu warmly thanked the miners in a televised speech. Now, at last, the country was ready to become the new Switzerland of Europe.

The rose that had never bloomed had been crushed under the feet of the people. I felt unbearably saddened.

How could the children of Romania ever forgive their parents now? Most adults had stood cowering behind curtained windows during the dreadful events of Christmas 1989. And now they had let the very same young people who had risked their lives then be beaten to death in the square. I foresaw a dark future for my country.

When I left Romania, I had feared that the new government would take drastic measures against those who still rebelled. The powers that be, cynical and well-prepared, would never let the truth come out about these events. But still, deep in my heart, I had been waiting for a miracle to happen.

Now, my hope, small as it was, had been smashed. More than anything else, I felt terribly guilty. I felt I had betrayed my brothers in the University Square. Surely my place wasn't here drinking in the Albion. Shouldn't I be back home, among the victims of the revolution?

Earlier that evening, I'd called my parents. My mum's voice was shaking. She was well, but it was me she was worried about. She told me that someone had broken into my flat, smashed things up and daubed filth on the walls.

'Dan, you mustn't come back,' my dad said, trying his best to sound strong. I could imagine what he must have been feeling, telling his only child not to come home.

'And be careful who you speak to over there and what you say. Sometimes it's better to leave things behind . . . You understand!'

Was this paranoia? My parents were surrounded by the old whispers of Securitate people doing their work beyond the borders of the country. Or was this only rumour?

My brooding was interrupted by David as he came over and sat at my table. I must have looked terribly depressed, as he tried hard to lift my spirits.

'Dan. You are a free man now, in the land of opportunity. If you give way to depression, this world will crush you sooner than you think. Listen! You need someone to take you out of your dark thoughts. I think I know just the man, a millionaire . . . Don't laugh!'

Strange, this life of mine. Whenever I was down, something or someone always came along and helped me survive.

A few days later, David and I were standing on the steps of an elegant double-fronted house. A tall, distinguished, white-haired man opened the door, gave us a cold, polite smile, then ushered us into the entrance hall, where I trod cautiously on the Persian carpet, carefully avoiding the marble and golden statues and huge flower arrangements. The man led us into the drawing-room, where we were asked to wait.

'The master will be down shortly,' the man said. Only then did I realize that he was the butler of the house.

The room overlooked a quiet street at the front, and opened on to the garden at the rear. Two huge sofas, upholstered in rust and navy on beige, complemented the pale caramel glaze of the walls and the pale yellow tapestry of the carpet. A marble fireplace was guarded by statues: on the left, a skinny girl which I later learned was by Giacometti, on the right a Regency blackamoor, holding a Chinese lamp. It was the middle of the day but the light cast its lambent glow across the room. I remembered my father in Budapest, counting the twenty-seven light bulbs in a shop window, amazed at the extravagance.

I looked around at the antique vases, the statues, the Egyptian urns, the glass cabinet filled with crystal and the scores of paintings on the walls. A Matisse, a Cézanne, an El Greco over there.

Finally the master appeared. He wore a T-shirt that told me he was sixty years old. 'I'm 18 with 42 more years of experience,' the T-shirt declared.

We shook hands and smiled at each other. For a while we chatted about the weather, flowers and paintings, sipping Scotch from silver cups.

'You remind me of the good times I spent in Romania. Nice mountains you have there,' the master said after a bit.

'By the way,' he continued. 'Is it true that you're a real descendant of Dracula?'

So that was it! An eccentric millionaire wanted to see a descendant of Dracula in the flesh.

Ignoring George's advice to avoid personal things, I started talking about myself.

'Listen!' the man interrupted my monologue. 'I have some business interests with the East and you can tell me stories about it. Would you like to move in for a while?'

I looked at him, confused. Was he joking? Or, maybe, being a friend of David's, he had an ulterior motive.

'I'm honoured, sir,' I said blushing. 'But I'm not gay!' I blurted out. Undoubtedly, this was extremely rude. The master widened his eyes, looked at David and started to laugh.

'Do you ... Do you think I'd be interested in ... in your. BODY?' he said between little hiccups of laughter, pointing his fore-finger at me so disdainfully that I felt offended.

I thought of leaving, but the man was suddenly serious. We started talking about my skills, while David stared at me, ready to jump up and clap his hand to my mouth if he noticed a new pearl escaping. I'd been a manager, I knew four languages and had an international driving licence, I knew a lot about Eastern Europe ... and a little about garden-ing.

'Well,' the master said. 'If you will apply all of these skills for me during the day and tell me stories about Dracula before bedtime, to help me sleep, I'll give you in return some useful tips on Western business, and free accommodation in this lovely house. What do you think?'

What could I possibly think? It was like asking whether a horse liked oats.

'Don't worry', he concluded in a paternal voice. 'I may need your brains, if you have any. But not your body!' Then he laughed again.

Within three days I had moved my rucksack into an oak-panelled room on the second floor of the house where, centuries before, such luminaries as Francis Bacon and Oliver Goldsmith had lodged, I was told.

'God laid a hand on your head,' George told me, later. 'You know, I never met a man as lucky as you in all my life!'

I did indeed seem to be terribly lucky. But my heart sank when I heard that the house had been a CIA base in London before the master had moved in.

'From KGB to CIA,' George teased me. 'Better than under the surveillance of Securitate, anyway.'

That was how it started. The master's conviction that I was incurably dozy was how it ended. After a few months, it seemed that he did not like anything I did, though I tried hard enough to please him.

First, I cut my hair. The master did not like my wild looks, and he did not want to hear what my hair had meant to me in Romania.

Here I was in the free world, faced with my first real opportunity, and what did I have to do? Cut my hair – which I did, not to start the whole story over again.

Soon, the master asked me to shave off my moustache, too. He did not like the sad Hungarian look of my droopy plumage. So I cut that off as well, wondering what would come next. Maybe he would ask me to cut my legs, since I always thought they were a bit too long. He didn't. Instead, he asked me to walk his dog, first thing in the morning and last thing at night.

I did not mind this, since I have always liked dogs. But was this really the best way for me to become a successful businessman?

Apart from the master and the butler, two other men lived in the house. Sam, a handsome thirty-year-old literary agent, was in the room next to me, and a tall, striking American composer had a room across the hall. One glance at the sun-tanned bodies of these men, clad only in shorts in the morning, was enough to leave me feeling weak, pale and insignificant for the rest of the day. It was as though the vitality of the universe had found its expression in their Michelangelo-like bodies.

'Be positive, Daniel!' was the first thing the American said every morning, before slapping me on the back.

'Enjoy life! Don't torment yourself! . . . Is there a war in Iraq? Who cares?' Sam would chime in, trying to teach me the philosophy of survival in the West.

As far as I can remember, in the five months I lived there, this was all my housemates ever told me. I mean, everyone talked a lot, and their words were clearly spoken, their pronunciation was perfect, but I do not remember anything they said.

There were words coming out of their mouths, but nothing else. There were no substantial ideas, no emotions, no depth of feeling. Just flimsy, insignificant words: gossip and cleverness, cheap remarks always followed by cascading laughter. That was all I heard, all day long as I crept about my tasks.

I often eavesdropped on their private conversations. It was not very polite of me, but I was there to learn how to become a businessman, not a gentleman. So what did I overhear? Just more of the same meaningless conversations. It seemed to be an unwritten rule of the house: to talk volumes but to say nothing. Everyone submitted to this rule, the guests as well.

[213]

On cold days the guests lay draped on the sofas, sipping champagne in their designer clothes. On warm evenings they reclined in the garden. To me this was strange. Instead of singing after a glass of wine, they were yawning. Instead of dancing in the garden, they lay on the sofas. Instead of expressing the joy of life – if they, who were rich and famous, could not feel joyful, then who could? – they seemed completely apathetic.

Maybe I lacked the art of living in a sphere where nothing dramatic ever happens, where nobody has to fight for survival on the knife-edge between life and death. Or maybe I just was not able to decipher the rich man's world.

The master was not a bad man, and I grew to like him. One night, when he was drunk, he told me his life story, and we cried together, in his marbled kitchen. That night he showed me his human face. But why did he pretend to be so happy, all day long?

As for his guests, his friends . . . Cleaning their ashtrays as slowly as I could, I waited for something to give substance and meaning to that world.

'Come on Daniel! Speed it up!' the master frequently told me.

'You see . . . He's Romanian. A descendant of Dracula. I'm trying to teach him to be part of the civilized world.' He was at pains to explain to his guests.

I had dreamed that delicately scented girls would kiss me awake in the wonderful world of the West. But in the house of the millionaire, old ladies with rheumy eyes would touch my skin and stroke my cheek, cooing with pleasure to feel that Dracula's line was still extant. The descendant of Dracula was there, for real. This was all my life meant to them.

I preferred to spend my time with Charles, the dog. His eyes were full of joy and sorrow, suffering and understanding. Dear Charles! What a bizarre life he had. What an evolution was there, from Hector, the dog chained in the yard at Hagota, barking at bears, boars and wolves, to this pampered Charles in front of me, asleep on soft cushions or idly gnawing on plastic bones.

As for me, well, at the beginning it was exciting to send and receive letters on behalf of my boss. He knew the great and the infamous.

Once, Donald Trump mistakenly addressed a return letter to Dan Antal. I immediately sent a photocopy to my dad – 'one of my friends, Dad!' My dad's reply was fussy and anxious. 'I don't know who this Donald is, but I hope he's a good man and not a wastrel.'

I was living a life that few Romanians had ever experienced. How many of my people have ever been invited to a party given by a dog? For a whole month I did nothing but make lists, keep files, type invitations and deliver envelopes, all for Charles's eleventh birthday.

> I, Charles, his master's doggie,
> request your attendance . . . RSVP

was on the golden invitation card, with a picture of Rupert on one side, and a drawing of the house on the other. I had to deliver the cards to one hundred people, by hand. As if the honourable guests would be offended to receive an invitation from a dog through the Royal Mail.

At Charles's party, while Chinese waiters served plates of food and Russian dancers were performing in the garden, I was shaking hands with celebrities and important people, like the man with grey hair who had just returned from Romania. Along the way his wife had adopted a child, and he had tried a 'little business' as he called it, buying up two entire Romanian seaside resorts: hotels, restaurants, staff, streets, beach, part of the sea. He wanted everything 'on his terms'. He wanted only hard currency as legal tender in his resorts, which excluded most Romanians. This did not sound like good news to my ears.

After six months, the magic spell of wealth faded away before my eyes. I began to see the master's world with stark clarity. The meetings, the parties, the rich people traipsing across the hall, carrying only their names with them: this wasn't real life. There were no emotions. No spontaneity.

Tense, always worrying about making a mistake or saying the wrong thing, I began to feel stale. Was this the freedom I had looked for? Was this the world of perfection we dreamed of as teenagers? Was this the real West at all?

I began feeling homesick. I missed the purity of Hagota, the warmth of my parents, the long talks with Dudu, the passion of my own people in their few moments of joy.

Up until now, I had been like a bear in a cage. All my life had followed a clear path: to save myself and get out of Romania. Now, free at last, I felt useless.

'There's no redemption for us,' George told me. 'We came to the West too late. We spent too much time in Nero's world and, whether we like it or not, we are fated to be its disciples. May God not let Ceaușescu rest in peace!'

I refused to go along with this. And yet, how long would it take for the dark habits of a lifetime to give way to the light?

Eventually, my feelings became plain to see. The master grew less enthusiastic about my presence in his house.

'Daniel, cheer up! Why is your face so sad? You know I don't like it!'

'I'm sorry, sir. I do my best!'

'It isn't enough . . . And you're still so dozy.'

Of course I was dozy. December 1989, I am in the battle-torn streets of Bucharest. Six weeks later and I'm a big boss with a thousand people working for me. A month flies by and I'm walking in Ceaușescu's palace, my voice recorded by the BBC. Another month and I'm addressing the crowd from the balcony in University Square. Four weeks after, I'm tramping across Europe, finally to enter the land of my dreams. Eight weeks later and I'm driving a Bentley past Buckingham Palace. Just a short while after and I've made it to the heart of emptiness.

One evening, the master and I sat in front of a bottle of champagne.

'Daniel, I feel you need a change. Don't you?'

It was true. I needed a change. I did not belong to that world and it did not belong to me. I had started to feel close to my master, as often happens when you spend more time with a person. But I also craved the path of risk and uncertainty, the highs and lows of life. The next day, the master and I shook hands, and I left.

The time when I thought that life in the West was what I had seen in the house of the millionaire and in English magazines was now behind me. I finally realized that the word FREE written on a package or elsewhere means: It is free but . . . ! Only a little but, perhaps, but always with a price tag. And what could you pay with when you are living on the dole?

I started writing letters again. Hundreds of them. Not to the living or to the dead, but to 'Equal Opportunity' job offers advertised in the papers. I knocked on hundreds of doors, but always received the same kind of answer. No experience in the UK? Sorry!

Nobody wanted me as a teacher, nobody wanted me as anything. My first thought, that I could do almost any job in the West, soon vanished, and I began to fear that I was no good to anyone anywhere.

'Enthusiastic people needed to earn £500 a week. No experience needed,' an *Evening Standard* ad proclaimed.

Freshly shaved, in my new grey second-hand suit, I was early for my appointment. The employer was a sun-tanned, fast-talking, pony-tailed American. He started firing questions at me. What did I think about the job? Why did I want it? What were my strengths and weaknesses? How did I see myself as a human being? What did I want out of life?

Strange, I thought. He wants me to answer questions I've spent the last twenty years asking myself. I guessed he was not looking for philosophical answers, but for money-motivated people.

'Money,' I told him. I wanted only money out of life.

'Yes and what else?'

'A good car.'

'What car?'

'A red Lamborghini,' I answered jokingly.

'Good,' the American replied, with dead-pan seriousness. 'When?'

'When what?'

'When do you want to have the Lamborghini?'

I started thinking. The American looked grim.

'In a year or two? . . .' I pondered.

The conversation continued, and eventually he gave me his verdict. I was not good enough for the job. Why not? I was not determined, he said. Then he took time out to tell me about life.

'You want a Lamborghini in one or two years. Well, I need people who want one TOMORROW! Tomorrow is the answer I need to hear! You just don't have the determination I'm looking for.'

For other jobs I was too keen. Too soon. Too late. Too cool. Too hot. Too much a foreigner. All the verdicts were delivered with a smile.

There was not much to smile about on the streets of Peckham, where

I was now living. I met other refugees, people from all over with the same old stories of hardship and abuse back home. They all spoke of the loneliness of a life in exile, thousands of miles away from wives, children, parents and friends. Many of these refugees were university graduates, like the two Russians I met who were both engineers and spoke five languages fluently. Now they were stacking shelves in a corner of an off-licence, earning one pound an hour. I met compatriots of mine, and sometimes they made me feel ashamed. They pretended to be heroes of the revolution, though they had obviously never even been to Bucharest or Timişoara.

One night I encountered the criminal underworld, when I was approached while walking in Soho.

'You look like the kind of man who would like to earn some money,' said a man. He wanted me to deliver a dozen packets: that was all, and I'd earn £200 for an evening's work. I was desperate indeed. But I had no inclination to start a new life as a drug courier.

Wandering the streets, with no work, I had a crushing sense of nothingness. I'd felt empty before at various times in my life, but to be cut off from my roots heightened my anguish. It was Nick Rankin who reminded me that emptiness could be a prelude to something else.

Evenings spent with Nick and his wife gave me my only pleasure at this time. Above the door of their dining-room there hung a Romanian flag with a hole in the middle. It was the very same flag I had carried in the days of the revolution. For the short time it had been in my possession, it had been my greatest treasure. It was fitting that I had given it to the man who had opened the door to my new life. Whenever I visited Nick and his wife, Maggie Gee, I saw their curly-haired five-year-old daughter, Rosa. Once she greeted me, radiant of face, in an embroidered Romanian folk blouse. It broke my heart, I can tell you.

I promised to translate some Romanian fairy stories for Rosa.

'But not before writing about your experiences,' Nick broke in. 'Dan, you've got to write! You've got so many stories about Romania.'

Was he kidding? Write about Romania? Most people I met knew less about my country than about Antarctica. Some carts in a field, beggars in the streets queuing for bread, Nadia Comăneci, a president and his wife executed by fanatics who still believed in the death penalty, and those horrific state orphanages. If you look in the last page of most newspapers you can see the weather reports from all the capitals of the world. Bucharest still does not exist.

'Leave your paranoia at home,' Nick went on passionately, in the face of my Socialist inheritance of cynicism and distrust. 'You will find out that the English care! And you were part of history, right in the middle of the most exciting revolution of the end of this century. You have to write about it! Write about the truth of your life. Get it out of your system.'

Maybe there was something in what Nick said. But how was I to bring to life people and events that perhaps I wanted to forget, things that were part of my very body and spirit, lodged in a country that was elsewhere and otherwise – and all in a language that was not my own?

It was true that whenever I had felt uncertainty, grief or anger in the past, writing had helped me to get outside my emotion, to make sense of my experience and so to survive it. Rather than strike out, which would have had fatal consequences in those bad days, I wrote.

'Pour all your emptiness into a book,' Nick said. 'Then, if you are lucky, you'll find that it will fill you up.'

Nick's words became a call to my spirit. They pushed me to go to Whitby, where the sunset caught me gazing up at the stark ruined cloisters of the Abbey. Flittering bats were diving and swooping among its high arches and I asked myself why Bram Stoker chose Transylvania for the homeland of his monster. But then, why did I choose England as my first love?

How strange. Descended from an historical man, and, in another way, from a literary invention, I was in the same place where one hundred years ago Bram Stoker sought inspiration for his book. Why had I survived? Countless others, better men than me, heroes, truth-seekers, had had to pay the price of their Romanian heritage. Like the bats above me, I had dived and swooped among the nightmare structures of a sinister regime. Was it just random fate that I had survived?

Haunted by this question and by the image of that cruel ancestor of mine, I didn't find any answers in Whitby. But when I returned to London, I started to write.

*

Christmas 1992. Alone in an attic room near King's Cross, I am still working on this book. A small round table, a manual typewriter, an old chair and me, with plugs in my ears to keep out everything but the thoughts which are piling into and out of my head. No Christmas tree, no gifts on the floor, no greetings cards, no Handel. Just me, faced with a new language and all my memories. At this time of year they hurt more than anything else.

In one corner of the room there's a big pile of newspapers, their headlines warning of political and economic migration, a flood from Eastern Europe to the West. There is talk of a new Asylum Bill to stem the flow of immigrants.

Next to it, another pile, a more depressing one, stares up at me. There are press cuttings, pages from English and Romanian papers, letters I have received from home and from my friends.

Three years after the *coup d'état* still no one has been found responsible for the atrocities of Ceauşescu's era, except the dead couple, of course. Common graves have been found filled with naked corpses, their legs tied together with barbed wire. Were they victims of the 'revolution'? Or from before? Still more common graves, these filled with skeletons of people burned or buried alive – from the Golden Epoch? Or from the Stalinist era? They are part of our history which will never truly be known.

The 'terrorists' arrested during December 1989 were freed and still nobody knows who they really were. Most of the few high-ranking Party officials who were sent to jail were also soon free. The sentence of General Iulian Vlad, the former Head of Securitate, was reduced to three years. Nicu Ceauşescu, the dictator's son, was given twenty years. Then the court cut his sentence to sixteen. In the end his 'incurable' cirrhosis of the liver secured his freedom. I bet 1993 will see him tanned and healthy, driving his limousine in the company of beautiful girls.

The official investigations into the events of 1989, the ethnic fighting of Tîrgu Mureş in March 1990 and the student killings in June, all led to nothing.

A handful of gypsies and Hungarians were found guilty of provoking the fighting in Tîrgu Mureş, which left six people dead and hundreds injured. Yet, it was widely rumoured that former Securitate officers fuelled the hostilities to provide an excuse for creating a new secret police force.

The miners' arrival in Bucharest in June 1990 was portrayed as the spontaneous reaction of ordinary people. Later, the truth came out. Ion Iliescu called the miners, ordered former Securitate men to infiltrate them, and let them loose on the students and opposition party offices. By using civilians instead of the Army, Iliescu had thus avoided international condemnation.

The official death toll of December 1989 dropped from the 5,000 that had been announced a few days after Ceauşescu's execution, to a little over 1,000. Even so the perpetrators of these crimes sit as before in their sumptuous offices, or take their ease on pensions ten times as great as a factory worker's wage. Who's carrying the can? Nobody. Nobody at all.

To date, Romania remains the only country in Eastern Europe which has not disclosed its secret police files. Too many informers would be revealed – so-called dissidents and respected artists, people who spied on their friends, colleagues and family. It would break friendships and create hate. Romania doesn't need this in these transitional times, or so people are told.

It is undoubtedly true. There is too much explosive material there and too many self-seeking, careerist politicians would be exposed. But what about the people who refused to inform or struggled to keep their integrity? Nobody needs their stories, it seems.

And yet, secret files are used to discredit opponents of the new regime. Those who still fight for a new and free Romania are now portrayed as fascists, as is Marian Munteanu, the leader of the students' sit-in. The Amnesty International poster with his swollen face beaten by the miners hangs on the wall next to my typewriter.

Pastor Tökés is accused of anti-state and anti-national activities, of being a paid agent of the Hungarian Secret Service, a traitor. Doina Cornea and the poet Ana Blandiana, symbols of courage in Romania during Ceauşescu' time, are now denigrated and vilified. While in other countries of Eastern Europe former dissidents have become presidents, our heroes are dissidents again.

Outside Romania the Securitate's activities still cast a shadow. Dumitru Mazilu, a former Securitate chief, switched to the opposition in January 1990, threatening to tell the world 'embarrassing truths'. In March 1991 he was attacked in his Geneva hiding place by masked men wielding razors. The Romanian historian of religion and opponent of the Communist regime, Ioan Petru Culianu, was assassinated in Chicago in June 1991.

Inside Romania the old *nomenklatura* is regrouping itself in a new economic élite. Former Securitate officers have become businessmen, always the first with money to invest. Where does their money come from? Switzerland, perhaps, where Ceauşescu was said to have kept billions of dollars. Or maybe it came from secret arms dealings, known only to Ceauşescu and to a few Securitate men.

Many former Securitate officers have been promoted to the new Romanian secret police. Colonel Virgil Măgureanu, one of the prosecutors in the trial of the Ceauşescus, is now the head of the Romanian Intelligence Service. Others have become this year's angels, heading state orphanages, bankrolled by money flooding in from the West. What happened to all the money poured into the country by the EC? Nobody knows.

In September 1991 the miners marched on Bucharest again. This time they were protesting against the government which had failed to keep its promises of better living standards. Their calls for the resignation of the prime minister enjoyed popular support. Four people were reported killed in the violent clashes with police troops, and Petre Roman offered his resignation. All revolutions eat their own children, don't they? But then Petre Roman announced that he had changed his mind.

He was replaced the following month by a new prime minister with a not-so-new rhetoric: the national economy is a disaster ... stocks of food are lower than the previous year ... the legacy of Communism persists ... chaos threatens the country ... nobody works and there's no discipline in the family.

But who is responsible for transforming into apathy the spirit that was felt in the days of the uprising? Who's responsible for the perpetuation of the Lie?

With the same people holding office as before, the country still has no clear economic plan. The promised reforms are blocked or slowed to a snail's pace. Meanwhile, annual inflation has hit 200 per cent, the Romanian currency has tumbled in value, unemployment has increased. Romania faces the biggest economic crisis of the past fifty years.

After two years of turmoil and political tension, strikes, street demonstrations and economic chaos, the euphoria of the end of 1989 has become part of distant memory. Apathy and cynicism have reached new heights and people have again started to believe in a cursed fate. The spontaneous uprising has been hijacked. Everything was a Big Lie. Ceauşescu did not fall to the anger of ordinary people but to organized forces within the Communist Party élite, the Army and Securitate. Business as usual, you can't fight against it. Ion Iliescu and his government were elected again in September 1992.

Those who smiled while they killed or let others kill in the name of a party they all disavowed, are now shouting against Communism in the same way as they once shouted for it – and would shout for it again if Communism would shield their lack of love and their inhumanity to man. Those who lived well before live even better now.

Only the words have changed. 'Democracy' and 'free market economy' are bandied about by those who use such words to hide their greed; but the administrative structure is the same as in Ceauşescu's time. Though now Saatchi and Saatchi are negotiating to promote our new economy to foreign investors.

Like a man in a blizzard, I leaf through my press cuttings. All of them are different, yet all of them are the same.

> *'King Michael refused entry to Romania.'*

> *'Romania feels Big Brother's chill hand.'*

> *'Given complex situations in the Gulf, the Ministry of the Interior reminds all Romanian citizens that they are obliged to inform the local body of the Ministry about the arrival and departure of all foreigners*

within 24 hours.'

'During the Revolution and during the miners' second attack on Bucharest, chemical agents were used with later fatal effect.'

'Romania threatened by nationalism.'

'Romania to ration water supplies.'

'The gap between young and old was never so great.'

'A group of people march to lay flowers on Nicolae Ceauşescu's tomb.'

I read again and again the letters from my parents. My mother never writes more than a page. She's afraid of making spelling mistakes. I well know this fear that she has carried all her life: that others might think she's not cultured enough. Now, her son is a French teacher in London. Her dread of making a mistake tears at her son's heart. And he realizes at last that, in a state in which men are bitterly oppressed, diminished to nothing by an all-powerful élite, they pass on to their womenfolk the burden of their humiliations.

Darling Mum! How could I tell you that the light and love you took from *Hustinee!* and Hagota and passed on to your son, is now worth more to me than any words that man ever spoke or wrote?

My father's words don't make me feel better.

'Remember our friend Doroş?' he starts one letter. 'He's stopped coming to our philately circle. Now he is the General Commander of the Romanian Intelligence Service for our county.'

Then he tells me about recent changes in our city. Kiosks have appeared at bus stops, selling Kent and Marlboro cigarettes, whisky, Coca-Cola and peanuts. But in food shops, there are the same old queues. Though, he has to admit, chicken is easier to find. So are nice clothes and foreign cars, for those who have money. The new prices are so high that many people want Ceauşescu back . . . In his time, at least, everybody had a job. No, no, he's not complaining. And the money I sent him he doesn't need. He's put it in a bank and if things get tough I should give him a call and he'll send it back, return of post.

'I never believed I would ever witness such a deterioration of the human spirit,' my father writes. 'Ceauşescu is laughing at us from beyond the grave. In the scramble to get rich overnight, people have given up their lifelong convictions. Corruption is rife – prefects, mayors, judges, police. A new, uncontrolled freedom of the individual in a controlled chaos has led to anarchy everywhere.' The arrogance of the newly rich eclipses what solidarity and kindness he once knew. He doesn't recognize his friends any more.

Dudu writes that the government is issuing 'Revolutionary Certificates' for the living heroes of the revolution. These entitle the holder to benefits, such as free travel and exemption from taxes. Most former Securitate officers have them, it seems. Dudu could get one too, for a few dollars. But he's too embarrassed and disgusted. For others the whole feeling of disillusionment became unbearable.

One morning I opened *The Guardian* and was appalled to find the name of Dumitru Vlaic in a short news item. He could no longer bear the mockery and injustice in Romania and had killed himself, it was said. That day I cried again, full of shame and guilt for being one of those lucky enough to survive.

In the Romanian newspapers the government is complaining that too many young people and people with skills – doctors, teachers and engineers – are fleeing the country to live abroad. In reality the government is delighted to be rid of so many dissidents. The vacuum they leave behind is filled at once by a flood of bootlickers. The Romanian press label Romanians abroad as the dregs of the West. If they are not begging or sent back because of stealing, then they are eating and drinking too well, denigrating the mother country. I'm apparently one of these. And so are the other Hell's Angels. How happy are we really, here in the West?

'Emigration is a rehearsal for your own funeral,' George likes to say. Bacchus writes long, depressing letters from Israel. He's a fish out of water, he says. Aaron has been beaten up in one of the German hostels. He looks a bit too much like a gypsy, that's his mistake. Doctor Virgil – who waited twelve years to emigrate – went back to Romania from Germany when he got tired of cleaning toilets. A few months afterwards, his German car struck a tree at speed. He was killed outright.

As for me, I am still alive and I still have hope. I meet good and bad people, but none of them are informers. I pick up the phone and there's no tell-tale click on the line. Alone in a country which is not my own, I write my life story. My family, my friends and all who have kept my spirit alive are with me as I type each page.

And as for tomorrow . . . I'm meeting a woman whose advert I have answered. Her voice sounded tender and warm on the phone. It poured like honey into my loneliness.

'I want to experience the highs and lows of life,' she'd written in her advert.

I guess I have some ideas about that.